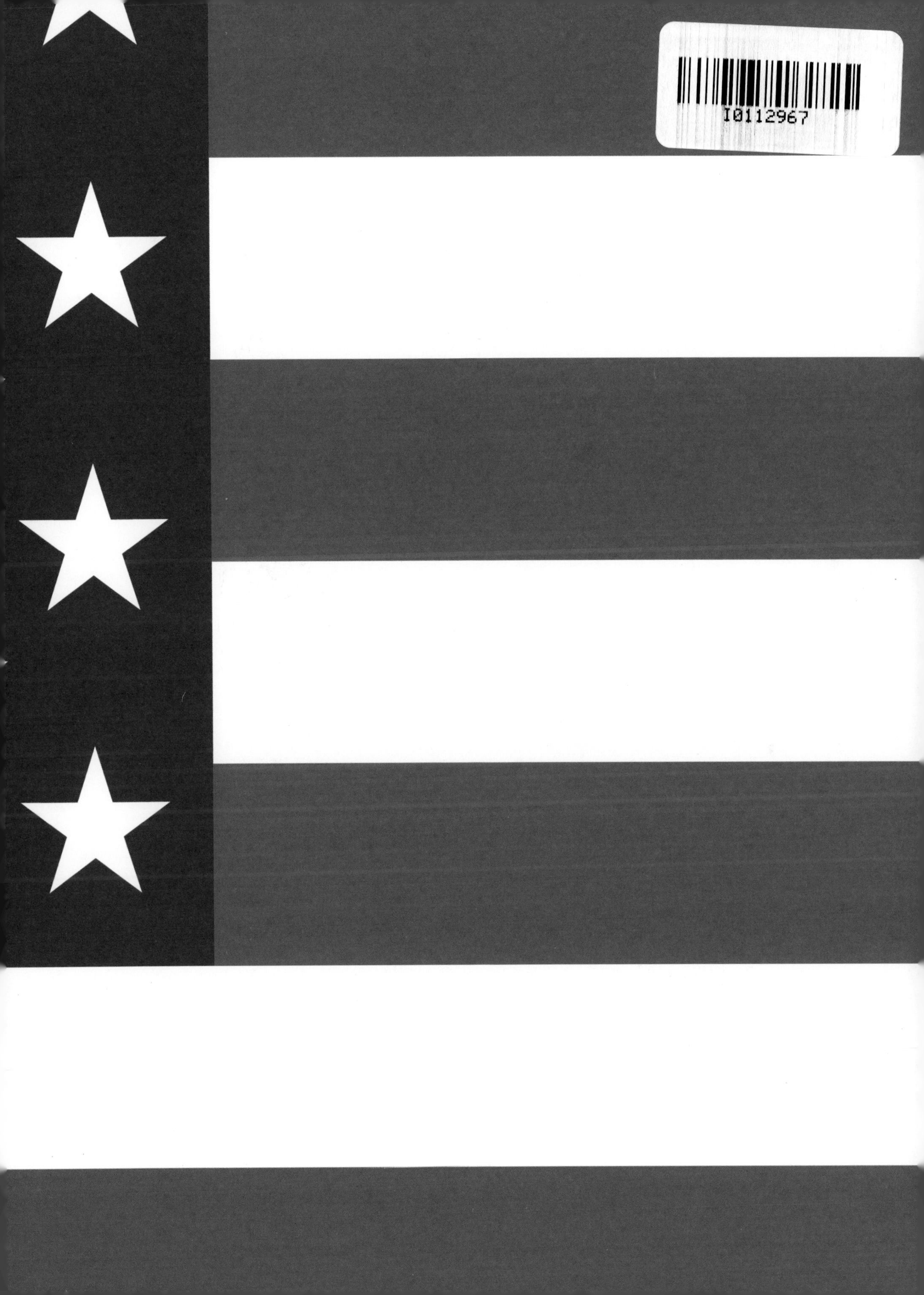

2W

Published in 2025
by Two Windmills Limited

Marine House, Tide Mill Way
Woodbridge, Suffolk, IP12 1AP
United Kingdom

www.twowindmills.com

Created by Frank Hopkinson
Design: Cara Rogers
Additional questions: Colin Salter

A CIP catalogue record for this book is available from the British Library.

ISBN 978-1-83555-387-9

Printed in Guangdong, China
10 9 8 7 6 5 4 3 2 1

FSC
www.fsc.org

MIX
Paper | Supporting
responsible forestry
FSC® C117745

THE GREAT AMERICAN QUIZ BOOK

Frank Hopkinson

2W

CONTENTS

INTRODUCTION

Welcome to *The Great American Quiz Book*. My mission has been to construct the most entertaining quiz book there is about the greatest country on Earth. No easy task. Compiled in these eight chapters are over 1,776 questions about the immense natural beauty of both the land and the creative, resourceful, pioneering people who live here.

This is not intended to be a quiz book to challenge the supernerds. The aim has been to put some amazing facts before you, pose a question, and give you the options to get it right, with an a), b) or c) answer. For some questions, where there's a very small chance of the reader knowing the answer already, for example – 'In which state would you find a corporate HQ in the shape of a seven-story picnic basket...?' – then it's a choice of two answers.

Sometimes, with a little bit of background knowledge, you might figure out the answer without making a total guess. The aim is to nudge the reader into making the right choice, not trick them into getting it wrong. Of course it's no fun if it's too easy, so there are few gimmes.

You will find chapters on Nature, Sport, Arts, Travel, Architecture, Transport, History and 15 questions on each state in the Union. You can find out what a 'yooper' is and which town in Iowa will be the future birthplace of *Star Trek*'s Captain James T.

Kirk. Creator Gene Roddenberry gave the Starship Enterprise's captain a background story that he was from a small town in Iowa and Riverside, IA, has claimed him as one of their future alumni. But when will he be born?

Plus there's a round on the quirky 'World Capitals' of America, such as the Loon Capital of the World in Wisconsin and the Cow Chip Tossing Capital of the World in Oklahoma.

There are short questions, medium questions and some longer questions to give you more of an insight to the subject at hand. If there is an accompanying photo with a question number posted in the corner, then that refers to one of the possible answers. It doesn't necessarily mean that's the *correct* answer...

I have had the privilege of editing the long-running *Then and Now* series from HarperCollins for the last twenty years, working on over 100 American titles, everything from *Albuquerque Then and Now* to *Washington D.C. Then and Now*, taking in *Route 66*, *Civil War Battlefields*, *Ballparks* and even extending to *San Juan* and *Puerto Rico*. Finally, I have got to use all this accumulated knowledge in a book of my own. I hope you enjoy reading it as much as I have enjoyed compiling it.

Frank Hopkinson

OPPOSITE: One World Trade Center rises above another American icon, the Brooklyn Bridge. How many feet to the top of the antenna? 1776, of course.

NATURE

FORESTS AND TREES

A state-by-state map of the forestry coverage of the country reveals an amazing percentage covered by trees. Maine and New Hampshire top the table of the most forested states. Try these questions on America's wealth of great forests and some of its remarkable trees.

1. Where is the only tropical forest within the U.S. National Forest System?
a) Hawaii
b) Florida
c) Puerto Rico

2. What name has been given to the oldest (non-clonal) tree in the world, growing in the White Mountains of California?
a) Methuselah
b) Noah
c) Silvanus

3. Who was the command module astronaut and former worker with the U.S. Forestry Service, who carried tree seeds to the Moon and back to Earth, where they were planted?
a) Stuart Roosa, on Apollo 14
b) Alfred Worden, on Apollo 15
c) Ken Mattingly, on Apollo 16

4. Which is the taller of the two giant sequoia trees in California named after U.S. military leaders?
a) General Grant
b) General Sherman

5. And which was christened 'the nation's Christmas tree' by President Coolidge?
a) General Grant
b) General Sherman

6. The oldest tree, the exact location of which is not publicized, is thought to be 4,856 years old. What kind of tree is it?
a) Giant sequoia
b) Bristlecone pine
c) Cypress

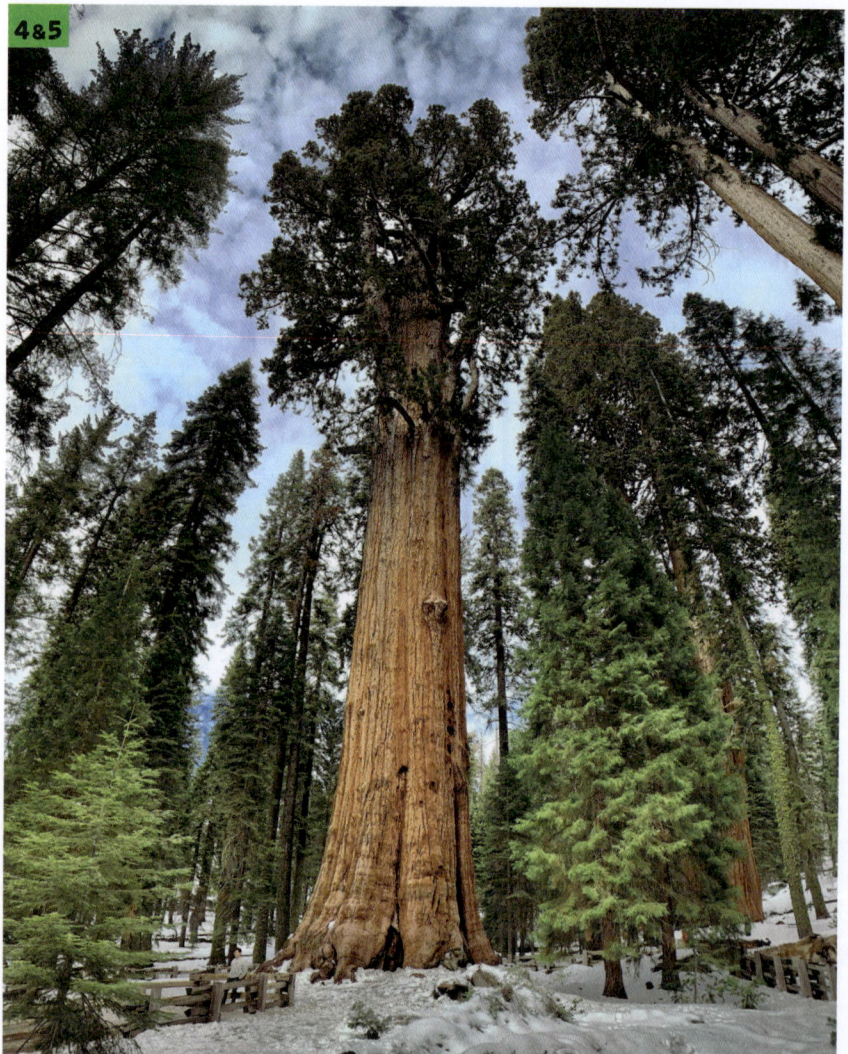

7. Shoshone National Forest was the nation's first, created in 1905 from which former national natural resource?
a) Wyoming Historic Mining Zone
b) Yellowstone Timberland Reserve

8. The Endicott Pear tree is the oldest living cultivated fruit tree in the U.S. Who was John Endicott after whom it is named?
a) A 17th-century governor of the Massachusetts Bay Colony
b) An 18th-century station master of the Danvers & Georgetown Railroad

9. Which trees are best at surviving hurricanes thanks to their strong, flexible wood?
a) Poplars
b) Loblolly pines
c) Live oaks

10. Discovered only in 2006, how tall is Hyperion, a redwood on California's Pacific coast?
a) 345 feet, the length of a soccer pitch
b) 360 feet, the length of a football pitch
c) 380 feet, the length of 63 bowling alleys

11. Some trees can survive the death of the trunk above ground by regenerating from the roots. One forest of 40,000 such clones all share the same root system, which is estimated to be up to 16,000 years old. Where is it?
a) The Shaking Aspens in Utah
b) The Quivering Pines in Nevada
c) The Swaying Sycamores in South Carolina

12. What happened beneath the branches of the Oak of the Golden Dream in California?

a) Franciscan missionary Junipero Serra dreamt of founding a state called California
b) Francisca Carillo and Mariano Vallejo, founder of Sonoma, were betrothed
c) Francisco Lopez, gathering wild onions, found gold in the earth around their roots

13. Who gave the first reading in the Southern states of President Lincoln's Emancipation Proclamation, beneath the branches of the Emancipation Oak in Virginia, in 1863?
a) President Lincoln himself, in a symbolic gesture of the new freedom
b) Mary Smith Peake, the first Black teacher of the American Missionary Association
c) Nat Turner, who led a slave revolt in Virginia in 1831

4&5

GENERAL SHERMAN

9

attacks on the Twin Towers. What happened to it?
a) Its wood was used to make tokens which were sold to raise funds for a memorial sculpture
b) It was nursed back to health by the NY Parks Dept and planted in the Memorial Plaza

20. The Sweetgum tree, native to the southeastern United States, is named for its amber resin. Which of the following are *not* among its common uses?
a) The manufacture of chewing gum
b) The treatment of diarrhea
c) The process of book-binding

21. The management and understanding of forests has long been an American concern. What was established in 1896 in the Biltmore Estate in North Carolina, which became the Pisgah National Forest?
a) The Biltmore Forest School, the first school of forestry in the United States
b) The Pisgah School, the first high school to have lessons in the forest

22. Tributaries of the Yellowstone, Missouri, Gallatin and Madison Rivers run through the Gallatin National Forest in Montana. What movie was shot there?
a) *Deliverance*, directed by John Boorman
b) *A River Runs Through It*, directed by Robert Redford

23. The Tongass National Forest in Alaska is America's largest and contains more designated wilderness areas than any other – 19. What regulations are unique

14. The National Park Service runs a program to protect ancient trees which have witnessed national historical events. What is it called?
a) Reading the Leaves of History
b) Counting America's Growth Rings
c) The Witness Tree Protection Program

15. The oldest palm tree in Los Angeles has been dug up and replanted many times in its 175 years. In which of these locations has it stood at one time or another?
a) San Pedro Street
b) Union Station
c) Exposition Park
d) All of them

16. The cherry trees which line the Tidal Basin of the Potomac River in Washington, D.C. were a gift from the city of Tokyo. When were they presented?
a) After the bombing of Hiroshima and Nagasaki in 1945
b) In 1912, before World War I
c) After the naval mission of Commodore Perry to Japan in 1853

17. The fossilized trees in the Petrified Forest National Park in Arizona are an amazing sight. Roughly how old are they?
a) 200,000 years
b) 4 million years
c) 225 million years

18. What is unusual about the Jackson Oak which grows in Athens, Georgia?
a) It owns itself, thanks to the will of its former owner Colonel William Henry Jackson
b) It was planted by President Andrew Jackson,
c) It was the favorite climbing tree of General Stonewall Jackson

19. A battered tree was pulled from the rubble of the 9/11

to Alaskan wilderness areas?
a) Bicycles and gold mining are allowed
b) Motorized vehicles and building construction are allowed
c) Horseback riding and camping are banned

24. Canopy walks allow visitors to experience forests from a bird's perspective, high up among the trees. At 1,400 feet, where is the longest canopy walk in the U.S.?
a) Myaka River State Park in Florida
b) Whiting Forest in Michigan
c) Atlanta Botanical Gardens in Georgia

25. Common in Florida and the U.S. Virgin Islands, why is the Gumbo Limbo tree commonly known as the Tourist Tree?
a) Its resin is used in a highly intoxicating cocktail
b) Twigs stuck in the ground readily take root, like tourists who overstay their welcome
c) Its bark is red and peeling, like the skin of sunburnt tourists

26. Driving a vehicle through a tunnel in a giant redwood tree remains a popular tourist attraction. The most recent tunnel was cut in the 1970s. When was the first such tunnel carved?
a) 1798
b) 1878
c) 1908

27. Probably the most famous tree in American history is the cherry tree which George Washington is said to have chopped down as a child and then made a confession to his father.

The story was a complete work of fiction. Who concocted it after Washington's death?
a) Mason Locke Weems, his biographer
b) Thomas Jefferson
c) Benjamin Franklin

28. The flowering dogwood tree, found on the coast from Maine to Mexico, has been used to make red dyes for printing and a quinine substitute to treat malaria. How did it get its name?
a) Its bark and roots were used to treat dogs with mange, a skin disease
b) Native Americans planted them to mark boundaries, like guard dogs
c) Its bark contains a resin that dogs love to chew

29. Not all trees are welcome. First introduced to the U.S. from

China in 1784, the Tree of Heaven is now considered a toxic weed. Why?
a) Its foul smell induces hallucinations in humans and animals
b) It emits chemicals which suppress the reproductive ability of other trees
c) It grows so vigorously that it strangles its competitors

30. The unofficially named Adak 'National Forest' in Alaska is very small. Exactly how many trees does it contain?
a) 33, planted to raise the spirits of troops posted there in World War II
b) 84, a legacy of the state's former Russian population who introduced them for firewood
c) 112, which seeded themselves after a packet of pine nuts was spilled

PLANTS

When voyagers from the Old World arrived on America's shores they were stunned by a whole new world of flora and fauna. How much do you know about American plants?

1. Tumbleweed blowing through a western town has been used as movie shorthand for 'not much going on' for many years. It's a non-native plant, so where did it actually originate?
a) Mexico
b) Russia
c) China

2. What do prickly pears have in common with hummingbirds and armadillos?

3. Seaweed is increasingly exploited for food, medicine and fertilizer. Alaska is a major producer, and which other state?
a) Oregon
b) California
c) Maine

4) Corn, beans and squashes were the three staple crops of Native American farmers. How are they known collectively?
a) The Three Sisters
b) The Three Dinners
c) The Three Gifts

5. Varieties of cotton grow all over the world, but the plant was a major economic asset to the Southern states in the early years of the nation. Which part of it is used to make thread?
a) The seed bolls
b) The flowers
c) The leaf tips

6. Cotton is not the only plant from which textile fibers can be produced. Dogbane, iris and cattail were all employed by Native Americans to make clothing. What else did they use?
a) The softened spines of the prickly pear
b) The fibrous stems of the nettle
c) The spun skin of gooseberries

7. Spotted water hemlock produces umbrellas of pretty, lacy, little white flowers. It is also America's most toxic plant when ingested and can cause vomiting, convulsions, cramps and death. Which of these alternative names is incorrect?
a) Beaver poison
b) Suicide root
c) The deadly bouquet

8. Hikers in the U.S. are routinely warned against poison ivy, which contains the chemical urushiol which is *highly* allergenic. In fact, get urushiol on your clothes and it can stay allergenic for how long?
a) Up to a year
b) Up to five years
c) Up to ten years

9. The Vandenberg Monkeyflower (*Diplacus vandenbergensis*) is one of the most localized plants in the nation. It has a tiny, bright, yellow wildflower and is found only inside California's Vandenberg Air Force Base. True or False?

10. How often do century plants (*Agave americana*) flower before they die?
a) Every year, for up to 100 years
b) Once
c) Every 100 days

11. Blueberries and cranberries are native to North America and were used by indigenous peoples long before European settlers arrived. Which one of

these is also a native fruit?
a) Blackcurrants
b) Raspberries
c) Concord grape

12. The Saguaro cactus grows in the Sonoran Desert. How much water can it absorb during a rainstorm?
a) Up to 10 gallons
b) Up to 100 gallons
c) Up to 200 gallons

13. Skunk Cabbage grows in snowy regions – how does it help melt the snow around it, allowing it to bloom in early spring?
a) It attracts animals that urinate on it (hence the name)
b) It can generate its own heat to melt snow

14. The Monarch butterfly is the most popular state butterfly in the U.S. but is mostly reliant on one plant to feed from. What is that major source?
a) Milkweed
b) Buddleja
c) Giant hogweed

15. Another species found in the Sonoran Desert, the fabulously named Boojum Tree (*Fouquieria columnaris*) can survive with almost no rain. What does it remind people of...?
a) An upside down carrot
b) A stubby umbrella
c) This is a fictional tree invented by Lewis Carroll

ANIMALS

With so much forest and so many wild open spaces, there is room for many indigenous species of animal to thrive. Try our questions on a whole variety of American species.

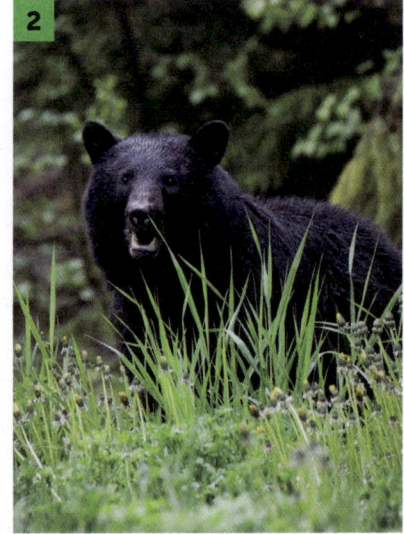

1. There are 36 species of rattlesnake, responsible for the majority of snakebite injuries in the U.S. What is the rattle made of?
a) Bone
b) Keratin

2. Apart from their color, what is the difference between the brown bear (*Ursus arctos*) and black bear (*Ursus americanus*)?
a) The black bear is larger than the brown bear
b) The black bear has a prominent hump
c) The brown bear has longer, curved claws

3. The jaguar, once widely distributed across the U.S., is now reduced to a handful of males in which state?

a) Arizona
b) Alaska
c) Alabama

4. The American alligator (*Alligator mississippiensis*) incubates its eggs at around 87°F. What happens if the temperature rises to 89°F?
a) It only produces female offspring
b) It's more likely to produce twins
c) It only produces male offspring

5. The hemlock woolly adelgid is an invasive species which could wipe out the hemlock tree in the eastern U.S. within ten years. What is it?
a) An insect
b) A spider
c) A worm

6. Of the three most venomous spiders in the U.S., which has only three pairs of eyes compared to the more usual four?
a) The black widow
b) The brown recluse

7. Armadillos can be found in many U.S. states, including Texas, Louisiana, Arkansas, Oklahoma, and Florida. Armadillos always give birth to four identical quadruplets. True or False?

8. Which mammal can dive 20 feet underwater to graze on aquatic plants?
a) Rocky mountain goats
b) Moose
c) Pocket gophers

9. Wild animals are learning to live in humankind's built environments. With an urban population of 1,500, which creatures are becoming a hazard in downtown Anchorage, Alaska?
a) Polar bears
b) Moose
c) Arctic foxes

10. What speed can grizzly bears run?
a) Up to 25mph
b) Up to 30mph
c) Up to 35mph

11. *Cryptops notandus* is a species of centipede found only in American Samoa and one other island. How many pairs of legs do centipedes have?
a) Between 98 and 102
b) Between 15 and 195

12. The Gila monster of Arizona is the only venomous lizard in the USA. What is the role of its relatively short, rounded tail?
a) It uses it to stun its prey before biting into it
b) It stores fat to sustain it after the plentiful food of spring
c) It allows the lizard to stand up on its back legs

13. They are often confused, but which is native to the U.S., the buffalo or the bison?
a) Bison
b) Buffalo

14. Despite its name, Death Valley is home to 90 species of land-based animals. How does the desert tortoise survive?
a) Its shell is detached from its body in places to allow cooling ventilation
b) It walks on its toes to minimize contact with the hot soil
c) It digs burrows and spends 95% of its life underground

15. The pronghorn, whose latin name is *Antilocapra americana*, i.e. the American antelope, is the fastest land mammal in the Western Hemisphere. Is it an antelope, and is it American?
a) It is not an antelope but it is native to central northern states of the U.S.
b) It is an antelope, but it was introduced to America from Africa
c) It is an antelope but it only migrates to the U.S. from Western Canada

16. The Colorado potato beetle began eating potatoes in Colorado in 1859 and spread rapidly eastward. But where was this agricultural pest first identified in 1811?
a) Minnesota, where it gorged on wild onions
b) The Rocky Mountains, where it fed on the buffalo bur
c) The Badlands of North Dakota, where it fed on chokecherry

17. Theodore 'Teddy' Roosevelt was an enthusiastic hunter, who gave his name to the teddy bear stuffed toy. How did this come about?
a) He shot a brown bear during a hunt in Mississippi
b) He refused to shoot a black bear when it was presented to him
c) He made a toy bear from a bear's fur as a child

18. Appalachian pillars breathe air, walk on muscular feet and live in damp woodland. What are they?
a) Salamanders
b) Caterpillars
c) Snails

19. According to a traditional Shawnee story, how did the bobcat get its spots?
a) It was singed by sparks from a campfire
b) It was splashed with tar from a tar pit
c) It was the child of a black panther and a mountain lion

20. Prairie dogs live sophisticated lives, living in family groups and 'towns', and sharing a highly developed system of vocal communication. What is the mating call of the male?
a) Standing on his hind legs with his head thrown back, emitting a long howl
b) A series of up to 25 barks, separated by a pause of up to 15 seconds
c) A cat-like meow and purr, accompanied by a fixed gaze toward the intended mate

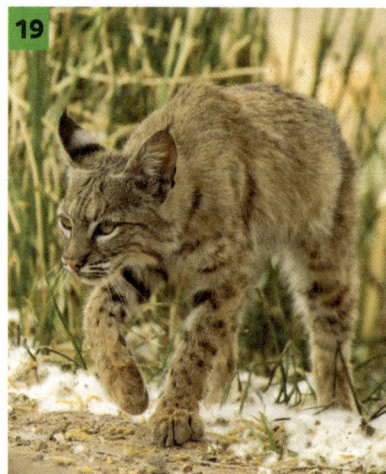

21. A disastrous collapse in the growth of seagrass in 2021 left the Florida manatee without its preferred food. How did the U.S. Fish and Wildlife Service help out?
a) It imported seagrass supplies from other regions around the world
b) It culled the manatee population so that survivors would have enough to eat
c) It distributed 3,000 lbs of lettuce every day to the manatees

22. States like to nominate their state bird. The most commonly nominated state bird is beloved by Illinois, Indiana, Kentucky, North Carolina, Ohio, Virginia and West Virginia. What is it?
a) American robin
b) Northern cardinal
c) Western meadowlark

23. The bald eagle first appeared on the Great Seal in 1784. Why is it called 'bald'?
a) It has no feathers on its head
b) The word used to mean 'white-headed'
c) It's an antique spelling of the word 'bold'

24. A new species, Rice's Whale, was discovered in the Gulf of Mexico in 2021. What was the estimate of its population at the time?
a) Slightly less than 100
b) Slightly less than 20
c) Less than 10

25. The starling was brought to the U.S. in the 1870s by various organizations dedicated to introducing European plants and wildlife to America. What is the word for their spectacular twilight swarms?
a) A congregation
b) A muttering
c) A murmuration

26. America is home to several species of salmon. What is the difference between Pacific salmon and Atlantic salmon?
a) Pacific salmon have paler flesh and a milder taste
b) Pacific salmon die after one spawning, while Atlantic salmon can reproduce again
c) Pacific salmon are larger than their Atlantic cousins

27. The Calliope hummingbird is the U.S.'s smallest native bird, weighing around a tenth of an ounce. In migration, however, it punches above its weight. How far do they fly between California and Mexico?
a) 3,400 miles
b) 5,600 miles

28. Death Valley, the hottest and driest place in the U.S., is home to the Death Valley Pupfish that can be found in the remaining salty creeks. How does it survive?
a) It can tolerate saline water that is four times that of the ocean
b) It has learned to take in water and spit out salt
c) It breathes air like a dolphin

29. The black-lined orange wings of the Monarch butterfly are a familiar sight along its migratory routes from north to south in the U.S. But what color are its caterpillars?
a) Black, white and yellow bands around the body
b) Green and white stripes along the body
c) Orange with black spots

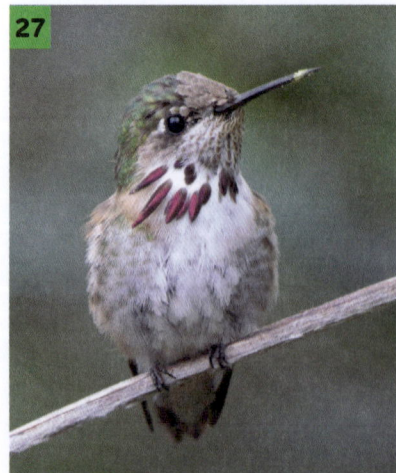

30. The white sturgeon is commonly found throughout the Columbia and Snake Rivers. They are bottom feeders and can grow up to seven feet in length and weigh 1,000 lbs (in fact almost like a small shark). How long do they live for?
a) Up to 30 years
b) Up to 60 years
c) Up to 100 years

31. The Alaskan wood frog has a special quality that helps it survive. What is it?
a) It can blend in with the bark of 14 different trees to fool predators
b) It can survive up to eight months frozen solid

32. The peregrine falcon is the fastest bird in North America. When it dives to attack prey it can reach speeds of...?
a) 120mph
b) 160mph
c) 200mph

33. Although it can fly, the Roadrunner bird prefers to outrun its predators. Even so, it's still not as fast a coyote, even Wile E. What is its top speed on the ground?
a) 20mph
b) 25mph
c) 30mph

34. Several limestone cave systems in Texas are home to pale, sightless cavefish. Two, the Toothless blindcat and the Widemouth blindcat, are sometimes drawn by artesian wells – from where?
a) Amistad National Recreation Area
b) The Caverns of Sonora
c) The San Antonio Pool of the Edward Aquifer

35. Machias Seal Island, whose ownership is disputed by the U.S. and Canada, is populated by harbor seals and gray seals. What, however, is its greatest attraction?
a) It boasts a rare population of the Purple Land Crab
b) It is home to the largest nesting colony of puffins south of the Gulf of St Lawrence

36. The Florida Horse Conch has the largest seashell to be found in U.S. waters, up to two feet in length. On the West Coast, the smaller Geoduck clam is impressive in which other way?
a) It can live for 180 years
b) It squirts a deep red ink when threatened
c) Females produce around fifty million eggs in a lifetime

37. Apart from moths and butterflies, the largest flying insect in the U.S. (five inches long) emerges from an aquatic larva called a hellgrammite. When winged, how is it known?
a) The Giant Robber Fly of the Plains
b) The Eastern Dobsonfly

38. In a huge conservation effort to save America's largest bird, the Californian Condor, the entire wild population was caught in 1974 for a captive breeding program. How many was that?
a) 22
b) 122
c) 222

39. What is the most commonly chosen state insect?
a) European honeybee
b) Seven-spot ladybug
c) Monarch butterfly

40. The American Woodcock thrives throughout central and eastern U.S. Which one of these is *not* a local name for the bird somewhere in America?
a) Bogsucker
b) Hokumpoke
c) Labrador twister
d) Mudbat
e) Night partridge
f) Timberdoodle
g) Wormguzzler

ISLANDS

There are more islands in America than you might think. There are distant islands, barrier islands, coral atolls, volcanic shields – and in a country blessed with so many rivers and lakes there are many river and lake islands, too. Try answering these questions on a whole pattern of islands.

1. The Niagara Falls are divided into three – the American Falls, the Bridal Veil Falls and the Horseshoe Falls – by Luna Island and Goat Island. Which country do the islands belong to?
a) Both to the USA
b) Both to Canada
c) One to each

2. How many islands are there in the Thousand Islands group in the St Lawrence River?
a) 794
b) 1,000
c) 1,864

3. ... and how many islands are there in Hawaii?
a) 8
b) 137
c) 1,017

4. Nantucket is an island in Massachusetts about 30 miles south of the Cape Cod peninsula. What was it famous for?
a) Home of the herring fleet
b) Home of the whaling fleet
c) The arrival point of the Atlantic telegraph cable

5. What territory borders on the U.S. Virgin Islands?
a) The French Virgin Islands
b) The Spanish Virgin Islands
c) The British Virgin Islands

6. Hilton Head Island in South Carolina, is a popular vacation spot known for its golf courses and what else?
a) Sea turtle nesting
b) Surf breaks
c) Pelican flocks

7. In 2016, the *Savannah Morning News* reported that councillors on Tybee Island in Georgia voted 4–1 to withhold news of what in case it affected tourist numbers?
a) The discovery of an accidentally dropped nuclear warhead in 1958
b) Shark attack numbers – unless the attacks were fatal

8. What is the present name of the island group known until 1911 as U.S. Naval Station Tutuila?
a) The Northern Mariana Islands
b) American Samoa
c) Midway Atoll

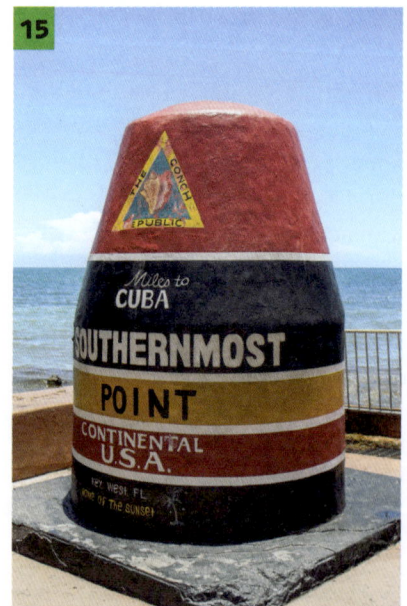

9. Machias Seal Island in the Bay of Fundy is disputed territory, with rival claims by the U.S., Canada and which third party?
a) The descendants of Tall Barny Beal, who ran boat trips to the island
b) Environmental campaigner Greenpeace, on behalf of the island's seal population

10. Mary Mallon, known as Typhoid Mary, brought the illness with her to the United States in 1884, but denied she had it because she was symptom free. She was eventually confined to which island in the East River?
a) Rikers Island
b) South Brother
c) North Brother

11. The Thimble Islands in Long Island Sound protect a precious deep-water harbor. Which notorious pirate is said to have buried his treasure on one of them?
a) William Kidd
b) Billy 'Bones' Thimble
c) Calico Jack

12. Robert Stroud, the Birdman of Alcatraz, was ironically not allowed to keep birds in that island prison. What is the translation of the island's name?
a) Cormorant
b) Gannet
c) Sea eagle

13. Which island, scene of the worst nuclear power accident in U.S. history, sits in the Susquehanna River?
a) Nine Mile Island
b) Seven Mile Island
c) Three Mile Island

14. Stockton Island, one of Wisconsin's Apostle Islands in Lake Superior, boasts one of the most concentrated populations of what?
a) Black bears
b) Albino raccoons
c) Lake otters

15. Key West in Florida, is the southernmost point of the continental U.S. How far is it from Cuba?
a) 311 miles
b) 176 miles
c) 90 miles

16. Palmyra Atoll, classed as a U.S. Minor Outlying Island, sits almost exactly at the center of the Pacific Ocean. Approximately how far is it from there to either New Zealand or the USA?
a) 3,300 miles
b) 5,500 miles

17. War broke out in 1859 between Britain and the U.S. over the shooting by an American of an Irishman's pig on San Juan Island, between Washington and Vancouver. What was it called?
a) The Storm in a Teacup
b) The Pig War
c) The Battle of the Bacon

18. Bedloe (now Liberty) and Black Tom (now part of Liberty State Park) were two of the three Oyster Islands in New York Bay. What is the third?
a) Ellis Island
b) Stuyvesant Island
c) Governor's Island

19. Catalina Island, off the coast of California, was once owned by which prominent American businessman?
a) William Wrigley
b) Benjamin Guggenheim
c) Henry Ford

20. The island of Catalina has one city, called Avalon – a name from Arthurian legend. What does Avalon mean?
a) Island of apples
b) Island of destiny

LAKES

America has an abundance of lakes – Alaska alone has over three million. Apart from the natural bodies of water, the U.S. has added to its stock with the Lake of the Ozarks, Lake Mead and Lake Powell – providing vital water resources and some great watersport opportunities. How much do you know about American lakes?

1. Four of the Great Lakes are bordered by both Canada and the USA. The fifth lies entirely within the U.S. – which one?
a) Michigan
b) Superior
c) Huron

2. What is unusual about Lake Windigo on Star Island in Minnesota?
a) It's in the shape of a perfect, six-pointed star
b) Star Island is in Cass Lake, so Windigo is in fact a lake within a lake

3. No water flows in or out of Crater Lake in Oregon. According to geologists, how long did it take for snow and rain to fill the crater after it was created by an eruption?
a) 17 years
b) 280 years
c) 740 years

4. The Industrial Canal in New Orleans, which was breached by Hurricane Katrina in 2005, connects the Mississippi to which lake?
a) Lake Maurepas
b) Lake Pontchartrain
c) Lake Cataouatche

5. The Great Salt Lake is shrinking through evaporation. According to a 2023 report, when will it dry out altogether?
a) 2028
b) 2038
c) 2048

6. Lake Superior is the largest of the Great Lakes. Which is the smallest?
a) Lake Ontario
b) Lake Erie
c) Lake Michigan

7. What did French explorers call Lake Superior?
a) Le lac Superieur
b) Le Lac Énorme
c) Le Lac Prodigieux

8. What links Iliamna Lake in Alaska with Lake Baikal in Siberia?
a) Both were named after Russian explorers
b) Both have rare populations of freshwater seals
c) Russian fur trader Grigor Shelikhov had homes on the shores of both

9. Eleven near-parallel glacial lakes in upstate New York are known as the Finger Lakes. They were the homelands of which powerful Native American tribe?
a) Iroquois
b) Chocktaw
c) Arapaho

10. To raise the water level of Lake Superior by one inch, how many gallons of freshwater would you need?
a) Five billion gallons
b) Fifty billion gallons
c) Five hundred billion gallons

11. There are three times as many moose as humans in the Moosehead region of Maine. Why is Moosehead Lake so called?
a) Moose were driven and cornered on its shores by early hunters
b) It's a misspelling of Moses' Head by the first settlers to cross the lake
c) The outline of the lake looks like a moose's head

12. What is the 'ice shove' which has been known to destroy houses on the shores of Lake Winnebago in Wisconsin?
a) The erosion by ice of the shore line on which the homes are built
b) Broken ice sheets piled up and driven onshore by strong winds in late winter
c) The build-up of frost on walls and roofs, which collapse under the weight

13. Lake of the Ozarks was the largest man-made lake in the United States when it was constructed in the 1930s. What river was dammed to provide the huge reservoir?
a) The Osage River
b) The White River
c) The North Fork River

14. Lake Tahoe is America's largest alpine lake and contains enough water to cover California in 14 inches of water. It was also the location for a Winter Olympics. When did that take place?
a) 1960
b) 1980
c) 2002

15. Which is America's deepest Lake – plunging to 1,949 feet?
a) Crater Lake in Oregon
b) Lake Tahoe in California/Nevada
c) Flathead Lake in Montana

16. Yellowstone Lake in Wyoming sits on top of a supervolcano and has hydrothermal vents beneath its surface, making parts of the lake bubble. As a result it has evolved a breed of tropical cichlid fish that only live within 100 feet from the vents. True or False?

17. Though smaller than the Caspian Sea (which is brackish), Lake Superior is the largest freshwater lake in the world by surface area. Which lake is runner-up?
a) Lake Victoria
b) Lake Huron
c) Lake Tanganyika

18. Lake Okeechobee in Florida is one of the largest freshwater lakes in the U.S. On average, how deep is it?
a) 41 feet
b) 22 feet
c) 9 feet

19. Can you identify this amazing reservoir lake – a mecca for watersports enthusiasts?
a) Lake Mead
b) Lake Powell
c) Big Bear Lake

20. Lake Wobegon was the setting for Garrison Keillor's famous radio program *A Prairie Home Companion* broadcast from Saint Paul, Minnesota. After the success of the program he said that constant visitors spoiled his home town and regretted putting it on the map. True or False?

RIVER DEEP

Rivers were key to the development of America, facilitating access to the vast interior and transporting goods to port before the arrival of the railroads. Today, they're more about hydro-electric power and nature conservation, leisure and amenity – how much do you know about America's rivers?

1. Which is the longest river in America?
a) The Missouri
b) The Yukon
c) The Mississippi

2. In which U.S. state does the Rio Grande have its source?
a) Texas
b) New Mexico
c) Colorado

3. ... and between which two states does it form a partial border?
a) Texas and New Mexico
b) New Mexico and Colorado
c) Colorado and Texas

4. When Annie Edson Taylor (at age 63) became the first person to go over the Niagara Falls in a barrel in 1901, what river was she going over the edge with?
a) The Welland
b) The Horseshoe
c) The Niagara

5. In the local Gwich'in language, the longest river in Alaska is called 'White Water River' after the milky glacial meltwater which flows into it. By which name is it better known?
a) The Mackenzie
b) The Yukon
c) The Blackwater

6. There are nine rivers named Blackwater in the U.S. How many of them rise in Alabama?
a) 0
b) 2
c) 4

7. Which two rivers meet in Montana to form the headwaters of the Missouri river?
a) The Monroe and the Adams
b) The Jackson and the Van Buren
c) The Jefferson and the Madison

8. Which river is interrupted by the Hoover dam, completed in 1936?
a) The Colorado
b) The Rio Grande
c) The Arkansas

9. ... and which Pennsylvania town was washed away in ten minutes after the failure of the South Fork Dam on the Little Conemaugh River in 1889?
a) Georgetown
b) Johnstown
c) Williamstown

10. Fifteen U.S. states are named after rivers that run through them. But where is the river after which Maine is named?
a) England
b) Sweden
c) France

11. ... and what is the modern name for the river formerly known as the Oregon?
a) Columbia River
b) Snake River
c) John Day River

12. The Yukon River in Alaska is the longest free-flowing river in the nation. Which is the longest undammed river in the contiguous U.S.?
a) The Yellowstone
b) The Chattahoochee

13. The Delaware River was originally called the South River by Dutch pioneers, and the Hudson was known as the North River. Where does the Hudson begin?
a) Henderson Lake
b) Hudson Bay
c) Lake Huron

14. At 28 miles in length, the Wailuku river is the longest on which island?
a) Puerto Rico
b) Hawaii
c) Tutuila in American Samoa

15. The Arkansas river flows through four states – Colorado, Kansas, Oklahoma and Arkansas. Where does its journey end?
a) Where it joins the Rio Grande in Colorado
b) Where it joins the Canadian river in Oklahoma
c) Where it joins the Mississippi river in Arkansas

16. Like many American rivers, the Minnesota river was key to the development of local industry. By what name is the Minnesota Valley Canning Company better known?
a) Libby's
b) Green Giant
c) Campbell's

17. Pittsburgh is known for its three rivers (and the old Three Rivers Stadium), two of which join to form the Ohio. Which two are they?
a) The Monongahela and Snake Rivers
b) The Snake and Allegheny Rivers
c) The Allegheny and Monongahela Rivers

18. At which significant Civil War location does the Shenandoah River meet the Potomac?
a) Harper's Ferry
b) Antietam
c) Gettysburg

19. The Mississippi is known as the 'Father of Waters' and 'Old Man River'. The Salmon River in Idaho is called the 'River of No Return' due to its strong currents. Which river is called 'The Big Muddy'?
a) Brazos
b) Missouri
c) Colorado

20. The Francis Scott Key Bridge in Maryland was partially destroyed when it was struck by a container ship in 2024. What river does it span?
a) The Chesapeake River
b) The Baltimore River
c) The Patapsco River

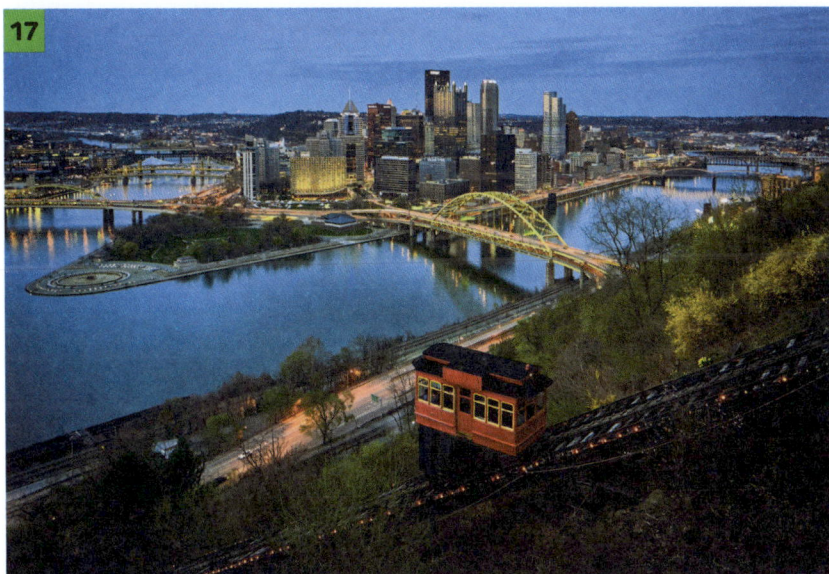

MOUNTAIN HIGH

Katharine Lee Bates was inspired to write *America the Beautiful* on a journey she made to the top of Pike's Peak in Colorado. The United States has a wealth of inspiring mountain ranges from the Sierra Nevada to the Appalachians. How much do you know about them?

1. The ten highest mountains in the USA are all in Alaska. What is the eleventh?
a) Mount Whitney in California's Sierra Nevada
b) Mount Elbert in the Sawatch range of central Colorado
c) Mount Rainier in the Cascades of Washington State

2. Alaska may claim the Top 10, but which state occupies 28 spots in the U.S. Mountain Top 50, as well as 52 in the Top 100?
a) Washington
b) California
c) Colorado

3. The Appalachian Trail is the world's longest hiking-only footpath. Between which two mountains does it run?
a) Springer Mountain in Georgia and Mount Katahdin in Maine
b) Brasstown Bald in Georgia and Bald Mountain in Maine
c) Screamer Mountain in Georgia and Kennebago Divide in Maine

4. Only 25% of those who attempt to thru-hike the Appalachian Trail (complete it in one journey) succeed. Just how long is it?
a) 1,800 miles
b) 2,000 miles
c) 2,200 miles

5. The oldest mountains in the U.S. were formed 1.8 billion years ago. Where are they?
a) The Blue Ridge Mountains, stretching from Pennsylvania to Georgia
b) The Black Hills in Wyoming and South Dakota

6. The faces of four notable U.S. presidents are carved into the side of Mount Rushmore: Washington, Jefferson, Lincoln and which other?
a) Theodore Roosevelt
b) Franklin D. Roosevelt
c) John Adams

7. Eight of the highest peaks of the Presidential Range are named after U.S. presidents. Where are they?
a) New Mexico
b) New York
c) New Hampshire

8. The eruption of Mount St Helens was the largest recorded in American history, and the ash cloud reached 80,000 feet in height. What was the effect on the mountain's height?
a) It gained 1,314 feet
b) None – what it lost during the eruption it gained in fresh lava
c) It lost 1,314 feet

9. In around 5700 BCE, the eruption of Mount Mazama produced 150 times more ash than that of Mount St Helens. Which lake in Oregon is all that remains of it?
a) Lake Mazama
b) Crater Lake
c) Volcano Lake

10. Explorers Lewis and Clark encountered many hazards in their famous expedition, but on which mountain did they almost die?
a) Bitteroot Mountain, Idaho
b) Grand Teton, Wyoming

11. The Sierra Nevada ranges in height up to 14,000 feet, creating a wide variety of different habitats for plants and animals. Which of these is the highest?
a) The sub-alpine zone, characterized by the whitebark pine
b) The upper montane forest,

18

characterized by the lodgepole pine

c) The pinyon pine woodland, characterized by juniper and pinyon pine

12. The Guadalupe Mountains in Texas are the remains of what?
a) An eroded volcanic shield
b) A fossilized coral reef

13. Which of the nation's great long-distance hiking paths connects Mount Whitney, Mount Rainier and Glacier Peak?
a) The Pacific Crest Trail
b) The Continental Divide

14. Many of the Collegiate Peaks in Colorado are named after major American universities, including Yale, Princeton and Harvard. Which summit is named after an English one?
a) Mount Oxford
b) Cambridge Mountain
c) London Peak

15. There are peaks called Bear Mountain in California, Washington, Montana and New York State. But where is the Bear Mountains range?
a) Minnesota
b) Kansas
c) New Mexico

16. Which of these island states has the highest mountain?
a) American Samoa (Lata Mountain)
b) Puerto Rico (Cerro de Punta)
c) Guam (Mount Lamlam)

17. The distinctive flat-topped Devil's Tower in Wyoming is sacred to many American Indians including the Kiowa, Lakota, Sioux and Cheyenne. How do they explain the mountain's grooved sides?
a) They are the stream beds from a now-dry sacred spring on the summit
b) Visitors from the sky made them as they fell to the ground

c) They were made by the claws of a bear trying to climb the mountain

18. If Mauna Kea on Hawaii was measured from the sea floor, it would be taller than Mount Everest. True or False?

19. Most mountains are grouped together in ranges, but some are a long way from the nearest mountain of comparable height. How far is Mount McKinley in the Denali National Park from a mountain of the same height?
a) 1,646 miles
b) 2,452 miles
c) 4,629 miles

20. At 345 feet, lowly Britton Hill is the highest point in its state. Which state is that?
a) Florida
b) Illinois
c) Louisiana

WEATHER

RAINY CITIES

Here's a list of some of the largest U.S. cities and their rainfall inches figures, with ten gaps. Your task is to put the correct ten cities against their average annual rainfall. The extra cities are for context (one of the 'supposedly rainy' cities was a surprise).

Miami, FL

Las Vegas, NV

Minneapolis, MN

New York, NY

New Orleans, LA

Washington, D.C.

Seattle, WA

Albuquerque, NM

Los Angeles, CA

San Francisco, CA

1.		4.2
	Phoenix, AZ	8.2
	El Paso, TX	9.7

2.		9.5
	Tucson, AZ	11.3
	Long Beach, CA	12.3
	San Diego, CA	10.3
	Denver, CO	14.3

3.		14.8
	San Jose, CA	15.8
	Colorado Springs, CO	17.4
	Sacramento, CA	19.9
	Oakland, CA	23.6

4.		23.6
	Omaha, NE	30.6

5.		30.6
	Wichita, KS	34.3
	San Antonio, TX	32.9
	Portland, OR	36.2
	Fort Worth, TX	36.7

6.		37.7
	Dallas, TX	37.1
	Kansas City, MO	39.1
	Chicago, IL	39.1

7.		39.7
	Columbus, OH	39.7
	Charlotte, NC	43.1
	Boston, MA	43.8
	Nashville, TN	47.3

8.		49.9
	Atlanta, GA	50.2
	Jacksonville, FL	52.4
	Memphis, TN	53.7

9.		61.9

10.		62.7

SUNNY CITIES

Here's a list of large U.S. cities, ordered from the sunniest to the cloudiest, based on their average annual sunshine hours. We have extracted five cities. Can you find their rightful place in the sun? Extra cities are added for context.

Pittsburgh, PA

Las Vegas, NV

Boston, MA

San Diego, CA

Dallas, TX

Phoenix, AZ	3,872
1.	3,825
Tucson, AZ	3,806
El Paso, TX	3,762
Fresno, CA	3,564
Sacramento, CA	3,607
Denver, CO	3,106

2.	3,054
San Francisco, CA	3,061
Los Angeles, CA	3,254
Honolulu, HI	3,035
Salt Lake City	3,029
Boise, ID	2,993
Tampa, FL	2,926
Jacksonville, FL	2,879
Oklahoma City, OK	3,089

3.	2,850
Richmond, VA	2,829
Charlotte, NC	2,821
Kansas City, MO	2,810
Virginia Beach, VA	2,695
Raleigh, NC	2,606
Austin, TX	2,644

4.	2,634
Washington, D.C.	2,528
Chicago, IL	2,508
Baltimore, MD	2,582
Houston, TX	2,578
Detroit, MI	2,436
Philadelphia, PA	2,498
St. Louis, MO	2,594
Cleveland, OH	2,280
Portland, OR	2,341
Seattle, WA	2,170

5.	2,021

HURRICANES

Florida is the true home of the hurricane in the U.S. Can you place these five missing hurricane states from data compiled between 1851 and 2018? We have added other states for context.

Alabama
Massachusetts
Mississippi
Texas
Louisiana

Florida:	120 hurricanes	
1.	64 hurricanes	
North Carolina:	55 hurricanes	
2.	54 hurricanes	
South Carolina:	30 hurricanes	

3.	24 hurricanes	New York:	15 hurricanes
Georgia:	22 hurricanes	5.	12 hurricanes
4.	19 hurricanes		

TORNADOES

About 1,200 tornadoes hit the U.S. each year. These are the figures for the number of tornadoes in 2023. Try and place the five states in the gaps (extra states for context).

Tennessee
Illinois
Iowa
Alabama
Texas

Colorado	89
3.	89
Mississippi	81
Nebraska	81
4.	73
Georgia	58
Ohio	56
5.	53

1.	136
2.	101

FOGGY DAYS

Some cities get it more than most, while San Francisco experiences two different kinds. See if you have the foggiest notion...

1. Point Reyes in California gets around 200 foggy days each year making it the foggiest place on the Pacific Coast. Bizarrely it is also categorized as what?
a) The windiest place on the Pacific Coast
b) The sunniest place on the Pacific Coast
c) The rainiest place on the Pacific Coast

2. Point Reyes is just up the coast from San Francisco, another legendary foggy spot. Fog is the reason many believe one of Europe's great navigators failed to spot the entrance to San Francisco Harbor on his survey of the California coast. Who missed the delights of SF?
a) Vasco da Gama
b) Sir Francis Drake
c) Ferdinand Magellan

3. Fog is a common occurrence in San Francisco and locals have developed a friendly name for it. What's it called?
a) Bart
b) Karl

4. Further up the Pacific Coast, in Washington state, there is a cape which sees (or doesn't see through) three and a half months of fog each year. It has a suitable downbeat name, what is it?
a) Cape Invisible
b) Cape Frustration
c) Cape Disappointment

5. Over on the Atlantic coast there is also fog to be found ... and lost in. Maine's Moose Peak Lighthouse can endure two months of fog in a year. Map-makers obviously had a bit of fun with this one, too. The lighthouse is located on which Maine island?
a) Mistake Island
b) Mermaid Island

6. San Francisco has two types of fog – advection fog in summer which pours down over the hills of Marin County. What type does it get in winter?
a) Convection fog
b) Reflection fog

7. Which great American poet wrote: 'The fog comes in on little cat's feet. It sits looking over harbor and city on silent haunches and then moves on.'
a) Walt Whitman
b) Carl Sandberg

ARTS

AMERICAN PHOTOGRAPHERS

Since the advent of photography in the 1840s, American photographers have been documenting the nation. Many are household names, some are not, but all of their work has had a profound effect on how we see the world. See if you can answer the questions inspired by their work and their careers.

1. The background is unmistakably Monument Valley, the Navajo tribal park in northern Arizona and southern Utah. It was taken by Carol M. Highsmith one of America's most prolific photographers who has spent over 40 years traveling the length and breadth of the country capturing landscape images that she donates to the Library of Congress. How many are there in her LOC collection?
a) 30,000
b) 50,000
c) 70,000

2. One of the world's leading portrait photographers, Annie Liebovitz poses in front of the famous Demi Moore photograph she captured for the front cover of *American Vogue*. In her career Liebovitz has created era-defining photos of major artists. She was also the last photographer to work with which iconic rock artist?
a) Jim Morrison
b) Kurt Kobain
c) John Lennon

3. During her groundbreaking career, this American photographer tackled many subjects but she is best known for documenting the suffering of migrant families during the Depression. In 2024 her work featured in an exhibition at Washington's National Art Gallery entitled 'Seeing People'. Her most famous image, taken in 1936, is of Florence Owens Thompson, known as Migrant Mother. Who was she?
a) Dorothea Lange
b) Imogen Cunningham
c) Marion Post Wolcott

4. Margaret Bourke-White was the first Western photographer allowed to enter the Soviet Union. In 1936, she was hired as this new publication's first female photojournalist. The accompanying photo shows her mounting her camera on New York's famous Chrysler Building. What was the publication?
a) *Forbes*
b) *Time*
c) *LIFE*

5. A 2016 Stanford University exhibition described his work as, 'among the most haunting photographs of children ever made.' Lewis Wickes Hine felt so strongly about the devastating effects of child labor that he quit working as a New York City school teacher and spent the next ten years traveling through New England, the South and the Midwest, photographing children at work in mills, coal mines and on street corners as 'newsies'. The resulting photographs proved to the authorities that child labor was thriving and helped tighten American labor laws. When was this photo of a mill girl in North Carolina taken?
a) 1888
b) 1898
c) 1908

6. Which photographer is best known for his large, breathtaking images of America's national parks. Indeed, the U.S. National Park Service commissioned him to create a photographic mural for the Department of the Interior Building in Washington, D.C. a project that was halted because of World War II and never resumed. This is his photo of the Old Faithful geyser in Yellowstone.
a) Edward Weston
b) Ansel Adams
c) William Henry Jackson

7. John Samuel Margolies was an architectural critic and photographer who loved capturing images of bizarre

roadside attractions on his travels. He built up a collection of novelty diners, kitsch motels and a whole host of other Americana. Typical of his 11,000-plus collection is this photo of the Big Fish Supper Club in Bena, Minnesota. Creating a building that imitates the shape of something else is known as what?
a) Mimetic architecture
b) Expressionist Architecture
c) Streamline Moderne Architecture

8. Hurled into action on D-Day, this war photographer landed in the thick of the action. He took 11 memorable photos as troops struggled ashore under constant gunfire, before returning to his boarding craft for the films to be rushed to London for processing. Though slightly blurred the images vividly capture the hell that was Omaha Beach that day. Who was it?
a) Robert Capa
b) Joe Rosenthal
c) Frank Capra

9. The Civil War was the first armed conflict to be comprehensively photographed, though the majority of photographers operated behind Union lines. One photographer with a studio in Washington, D.C. ventured out into the field accompanied by a processing wagon and various assistants. This allowed him to set up the frame and then sneak into the photo himself. Who was it?
a) Alexander Gardner
b) Timothy O'Sullivan
c) Mathew Brady

10. The long-running *Then and Now* book series from HarperCollins is the widest-read architectural series in America, selling in excess of 5.5 million copies. Regular Now photographer Karl Mondon took this dramatic photo for which edition?
a) *Toledo Then and Now*
b) *Dearborn Then and Now*
c) *Detroit Then and Now*

11. This photo by Jack Delano from 1943 shows one of the wipers at the Clinton, Iowa, roundhouse giving a giant 'H' class locomotive a bath of steam. Jack Delano was one of the many photographers who would become famous working under the Farm Security program (FSA) in the 1930s and 1940s documenting the working lives of Americans. Which of the following was not an FSA photographer...?
a) Arthur Rothstein
b) Marion Post Wolcott
c) Irving Penn

12. Controversial photographer Robert Mapplethorpe's early career was supported by his female partner, who worked in a bookstore to support them both before finding fame herself. Who was it?
a) Diane Keaton
b) Debbie Harry
c) Patti Smith

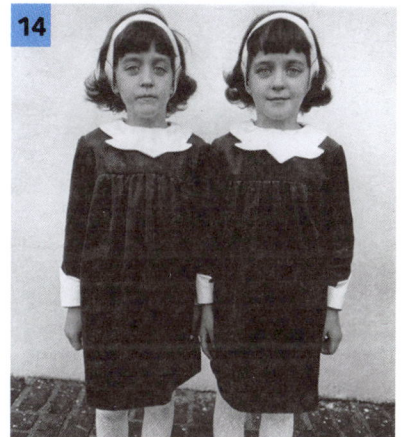

13. New York's leading aerial architectural photographer, Evan Joseph, mastered the art of image stabilization long before computer-aided camera-steadying became commonplace and has gone on to photograph the official book for which iconic New York structure?
a) Central Park Tower
b) Steinway Tower
c) One World Trade Center

14. Pioneering social photographer Diane Arbus's famous photo of twin girls inspired a scene in which Stanley Kubrick film?
a) *The Shining*
b) *Full Metal Jacket*
c) *A Clockwork Orange*

15. Lee Miller was the subject of the 2023 movie *Lee*, a fashion model in New York City in the 1920s before going to Paris, meeting Man Ray and becoming a fashion and fine-art photographer. During World War II, she became a war correspondent photographing through the London Blitz, the Allied invasion of France and the liberation of concentration camps at Buchenwald and Dachau. She teamed up with David E. Scherman, a *LIFE* magazine correspondent who took a notorious photo of her – where?
a) In Hitler's bathtub
b) In Goebbels' sauna
c) With Göring's model railway

SCREEN TEST

American towns and cities often feature in movie titles. We have assembled a whole festival of them – along with their brief description from the respected IMDb or Internet Movie Database. Your task is to read the movie description and match it to one of the 18 film titles we've lined up.

Escape From Los Angeles, 1996
Sleepless in Seattle, 1993
Atlantic City, 1980
San Francisco, 1936
Fargo, 1996
Things To Do In Denver When You're Dead, 1995
Brooklyn, 2015
Philadelphia, 1993
Beverly Hills Cop, 1984

Fear and Loathing in Las Vegas, 1998
Dodge City, 1939
The Manhattan Project, 1986
Bullets Over Broadway, 1994
The Cincinnati Kid, 1965
Gangs of New York, 2002
Carson City, 1952
Escape From New York, 1981
Paris, Texas, 1984

1. 'A Barbary Coast saloonkeeper and a Nob Hill impresario are rivals for the affections of a beautiful singer, both personally and professionally, in 1906 _____.'

2. 'Snake Plissken is once again called in by the United States government to recover a potential doomsday device from _____, now an autonomous island where undesirables are deported.'

3. 'When a man with HIV is fired by his law firm because of his condition, he hires a homophobic small-time lawyer as the only willing advocate for a wrongful dismissal suit.'

4. 'Minnesota car salesman Jerry Lundegaard's inept crime falls apart due to his and his henchmen's bungling, and the persistent police work of the quite pregnant Marge Gunderson.'

5. 'A high school prodigy builds an atomic bomb with stolen plutonium to win the 45th National Science Fair and expose a nuclear weapons lab posing as a nuclear medical research facility in Ithaca, NY.'

6. 'An oddball journalist and his psychopathic lawyer travel to _____ for a series of psychedelic escapades.'

7. 'A recently widowed man's son calls a radio talk-show in an attempt to find his father a partner.'

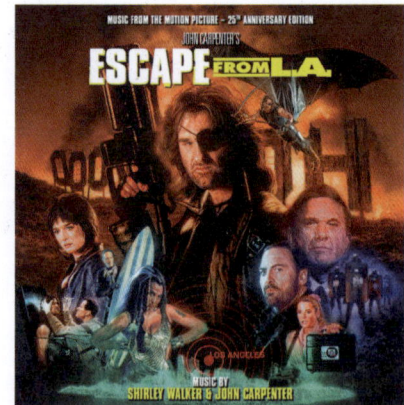

8 'A Texas cattle agent witnesses first hand, the brutal lawlessness of _____ and takes the job of sheriff to clean the town up.'

9. 'In 1997, when the U.S. president crashes into Manhattan, now a giant maximum security prison, a convicted bank robber is sent in to rescue him.'

10. 'When a banker finds his stagecoach shipments of gold from _____ are vulnerable to holdups, he commissions the building of a railroad through the mountains.'

11. 'A freewheeling Detroit cop pursuing a murder investigation finds himself dealing with the very different culture of _____.'

12. 'Travis Henderson, an aimless drifter who has been missing for four years, wanders out of the desert and must reconnect with society, himself, his life, and his family.'

13. 'In _____ in 1928, a struggling playwright is forced to cast a mobster's talentless girlfriend in his latest drama in order to get it produced.'

14. 'In a corrupt gambling city, a small-time gangster and the estranged wife of a pot dealer find themselves thrown together in an escapade of love, money, drugs and danger.'

15. 'An up-and-coming poker player tries to prove himself in a high-stakes match against a long-time master of the game.'

16. 'An Irish immigrant lands in 1950s _____, where she quickly falls into a romance with a local. When her past catches up with her, however, she must choose between two countries and the lives that exist within.'

17. 'Five different criminals face imminent death after botching a job quite badly.'

18. 'In 1862, Amsterdam Vallon returns to the Five Points area of _____ seeking revenge against Bill the Butcher; his father's killer.'

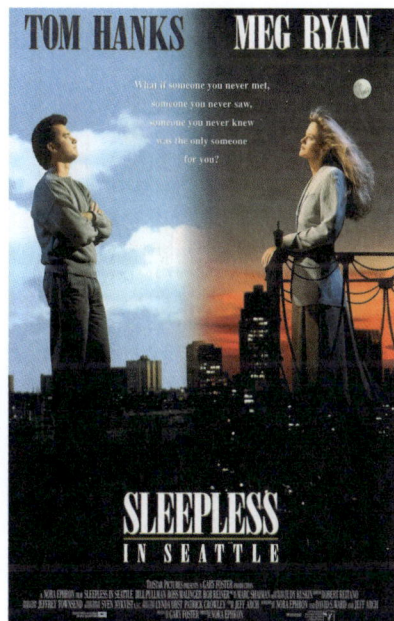

TOM HANKS   MEG RYAN

What if someone you never met, someone you never saw, someone you never knew was the only someone for you?

SLEEPLESS IN SEATTLE

PORTICO OVER PLYMOUTH ROCK, PLYMOUTH, MASS.

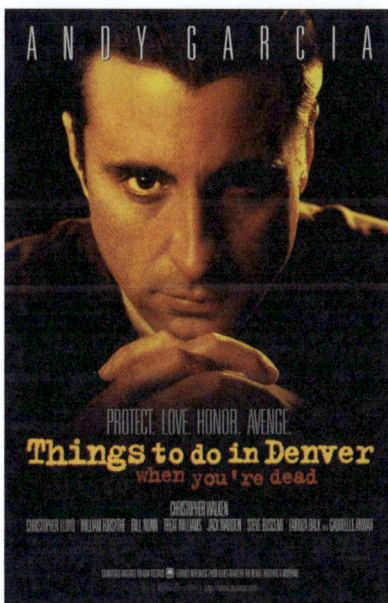

TWO COUNTRIES. TWO LOVES. ONE HEART.

BROOKLYN

ANDY GARCIA

PROTECT. LOVE. HONOR. AVENGE.

Things to do in Denver when you're dead

CHRISTOPHER WALKEN

JOHNNY DEPP   BENICIO DEL TORO

Fear and LOATHING in LAS VEGAS

The Coolest Soundtrack Of The Year - Featuring Classic Mind-Altering Music And Film Dialogue

WRITERS AND PLACES

In the 19th century, the American writing community was centered firmly in New England, exemplified by authors such as Henry David Thoreau (Concord) and Harriet Beecher-Stowe (Hartford). Today, of course, the distribution of American literary prowess is far more widespread. See if you can find the geographical connections to these great writers.

1. During his time at this French Colonial-style home, Ernest Hemingway wrote some of his best-received works, including the 1936 short stories *The Snows of Kilimanjaro* and the novel *To Have and Have Not* (1937). Where would you find it in America?
a) New Orleans
b) Florida Keys
c) Savannah

2. Like actor Harrison Ford, playwright Arthur Miller was a skilful carpenter and in 1948 built his own shed/studio in the backyard of his Roxbury, Connecticut, home. In splendid isolation he was able to complete one of the classics of world theater in six weeks. What was the play?
a) *The Crucible*
b) *Death of a Salesman*
c) *All My Sons*

3. Samuel Clemens, aka Mark Twain, created the classic boyhood novels *The Adventures of Tom Sawyer* and *Huckleberry Finn*, who in reality was the son of the town drunk. What was the town?
a) Boise, Idaho
b) Lancaster, Pennsylvania
c) Hannibal, Missouri

4. Nathaniel Hawthorne, author of *The Scarlet Letter*, wrote a Gothic novel with themes of guilt and retribution with hints of the supernatural and witchcraft. The title of the book was inspired by a house in Salem, Massachusetts, belonging to his cousin, Susanna Ingersoll. What was name of the house and the novel?
a) The House on the Hill
b) The House of Seven Gables
c) The House of Shadows

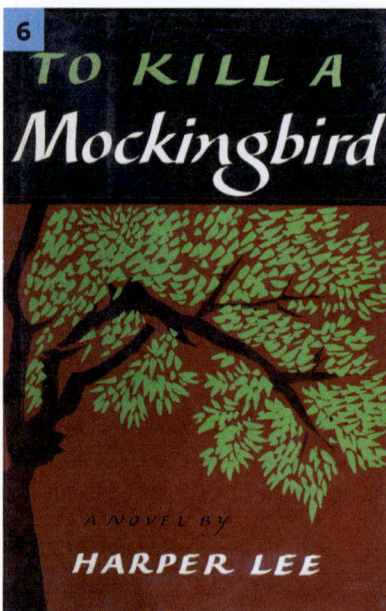

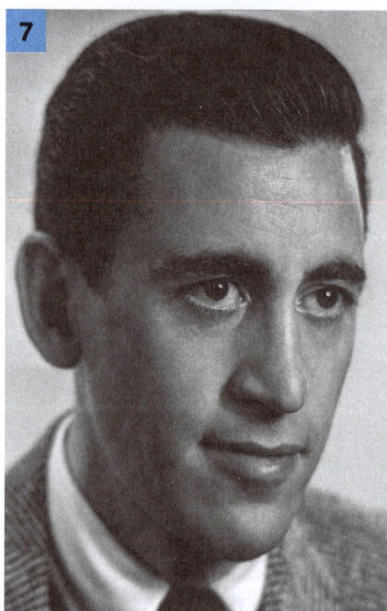

6. Harper Lee's book *To Kill a Mockingbird* was set in the small town in Alabama (Monroeville) where she grew up. Together with one of her childhood friends she would occasionally visit the local court where Harper's father was a lawyer. While Lee would win the Pulitzer Prize in 1961, her friend would be nominated in 1966 but fail to win. Who was it?
a) Tom Wolfe
b) Alice Walker
c) Truman Capote

7. *Catcher in the Rye* author J.D. Salinger had a fractious relationship with the media, fans and biographers. As the popularity of the book increased, along with its notoriety for bad language and anti-social behavior, so Salinger gradually retreated from view. Where did he move to escape interaction with a curious public?
a) Cornish, New Hampshire
b) Carmel, California
c) Carthage, Texas

8. Orchard House in Concord, Massachusetts was the childhood home of a beloved author who used it as the family home in which famous book...?
a) *Anne of Green Gables* by Lucy Maud Montgomery
b) *Charlotte's Webb* by E.B. White
c) *Little Women* by Louisa May Alcott

9. Toni Morrison worked as a teacher and a literary editor, before making a powerful impact as an author with novels such as the *Bluest Eye* and *Beloved.* She became the first Black woman to receive the Nobel Prize for

5. Herman Melville was a great friend of Nathaniel Hawthorne. In September 1850, Melville borrowed three thousand dollars from his father-in-law to buy a farm in Pittsfield, Massachusetts, close to Hawthorne. Melville named his new home Arrowhead because of the arrowheads that were dug up around the property. It was here that he wrote his classic novel, *Moby-Dick.* However, the original title was slightly different. What was it?
a) *Harpoon at a Venture*
b) *The Whale*
c) *On Stranger Tides*

Literature in 1993. *Beloved* was the first in a trilogy and was published in 1987. Where was it written?
a) A converted boathouse on the Hudson River in Nyack, New York
b) In her former childhood school building in Lorain, Ohio

10. The undisputed king of horror fiction Stephen King was born in Portland, USA – but which Portland?
a) Portland, Oregon
b) Portland, Maine
c) Portland, Arkansas
d) Portland, Georgia

11. In January 1845, Edgar Allen-Poe's poem, *The Raven*, appeared in the *Evening Mirror* and quickly made Poe a household name. In 1846 he moved into a cottage in the Bronx where his wife Virginia died from tuberculosis. Where would Poe end his days, found dead in the street in 1849?
a) Baltimore
b) Pittsburgh
c) Camden, New Jersey

12. John Berendt's sensational *New York Times* bestseller, *Midnight in the Garden of Good and Evil* included details of a real-life feud between two prominent preservationists and the death of Danny Hansford, one of their lovers. Where was it set?
a) Martha's Vineyard
b) Savannah
c) Charleston

FROM L.A. TO NEW YORK

American place names often pop up in hit songs. Here are 30, for which the answers are already supplied ... though not in the correct order. Try and match the artist to the song – they're set up in two sets of 15.

1. *Boulder to Birmingham*	**Bruce Springsteen**
2. *Going to California*	**Glen Campbell**
3. *Sweet Home Alabama*	**Elton John**
4. *New York, New York*	**Bob Seger**
5. *Walking in Memphis*	**Gladys Knight & The Pips**
6. *Midnight Train to Georgia*	**Olivia Newton John**
7. *The Lady Came from Baltimore*	**Emmylou Harris**
8. *Jackson*	**Patsy Gallant**
9. *Philadelphia*	**Phantom Planet**
10. *California*	**Frank Sinatra**
11. *From New York to L.A.*	**Lynyrd Skynyrd**
12. *Galveston*	**Tim Hardin**
13. *Banks of the Ohio*	**Marc Cohn**
14. *Philadelphia Freedom*	**Led Zeppelin**
15. *Hollywood Nights*	**Johnny Cash & June Carter**

16. *Get Out of Denver* — **James Taylor**

17. *24 Hours from Tulsa* — **Beach Boys**

18. *San Francisco* — **Glen Campbell**

19. *California Dreamin'* — **R. Dean Taylor**

20. *Rock Island Line* — **The Monkees**

21. *Kokomo* — **Crosby, Stills, Nash and Young**

22. *Wichita Lineman* — **Ray Charles**

23. *Indiana Wants Me* — **Bee Gees**

24. *Last Train to Clarksville* — **Joni Mitchell**

25. *Ohio* — **Bob Seger**

26. *Carolina in My Mind* — **David Bowie**

27. *Georgia on My Mind* — **Gene Pitney**

28. *Massachusetts* — **Scott McKenzie**

29. *Woodstock* — **The Mamas and the Papas**

30. *This is Not America* — **Johnny Cash**

A NIGHT AT THE... MUSICAL

Whether on stage or on film, musicals have provided many of the best songs for the Great American Songbook. Test your knowledge of these musicals which are linked by titles with U.S. streets or place names.

1. In *LaLaLand*, Seb and Mia go on a date to see a screening of *Rebel Without a Cause*. When the film breaks down through a projector malfunction, they spend the rest of the evening together with a romantic visit to a Hollywood landmark that plays a prominent part in James Dean's film. What is the landmark?

a) Angel's Flight elevator
b) The Griffith Observatory
c) The Hollywood sign

2. In *Blue Hawaii*, after being discharged from the U.S. Army, cool dude Chadwick Gates (Elvis Presley) returns home to Hawaii and wants nothing better than to hang loose and surf all day.

His family wants him to work for the family pineapple business. In an unlikely bit of casting his mother is played by...?
a) Angela Lansbury (*Murder, She Wrote*)
b) Lucille Ball (*I Love Lucy*)
c) Marlene Dietrich (*Blue Angel*)

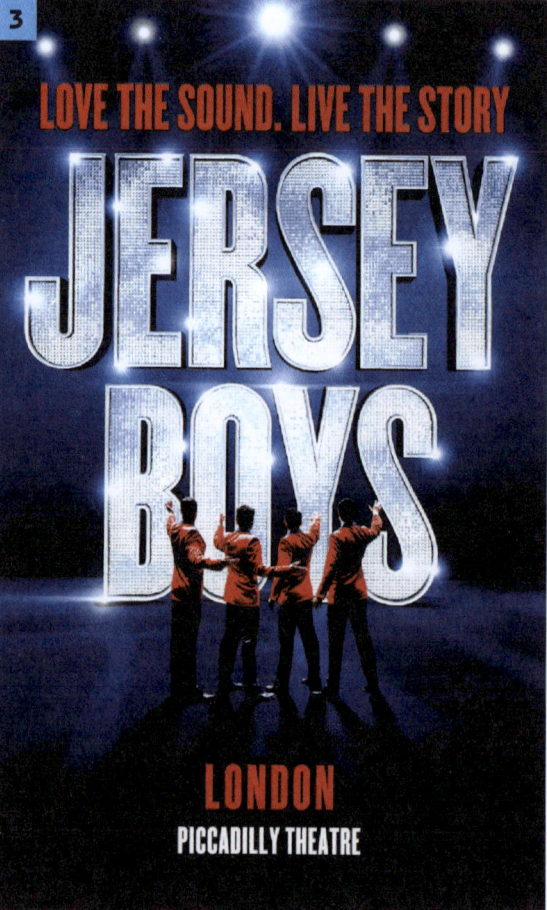

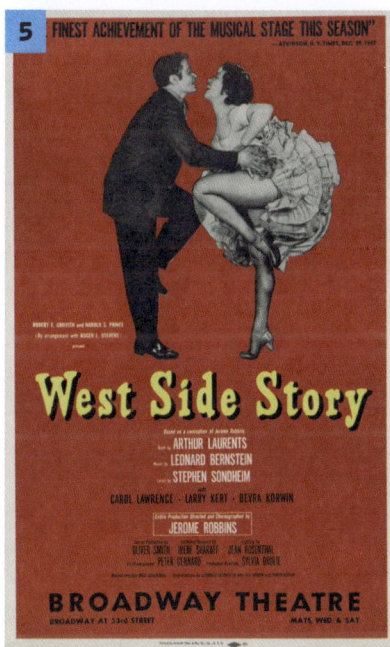

3. The story of *Jersey Boys* begins on a street corner in Belleville, New Jersey. It's a jukebox musical that features the hit records of which band?
a) Southside Johnny and the Asbury Dukes
b) Bruce Springsteen and the East Street band
c) Franki Valli and the Four Seasons

4. Set in 1933, *42nd Street* follows the story of Peggy, a small-town girl from Middle America and her dream to make it big in the heart of New York's theaterland, 42nd Street. The film was released in 1933. When did the stage musical take its first curtain call?
a) 1946
b) 1964
c) 1980

5. Another New York musical, *West Side Story*, featured music by Leonard Bernstein and lyrics by Stephen Sondheim. Set in the mid-1950s in the Upper West Side of Manhattan it explores the rivalry between two gangs the local 'Jet's and the 'Sharks', recent migrants from Puerto Rico. Which William Shakespeare play is it based on?

6. Perennial cowboy favorite, *Oklahoma!* was the first musical written by the duo of Rodgers and Hammerstein and set in farm country outside the town of Claremore, Indian Territory, in 1906. It tells the story of cowboy Curly McLain and his bid for the hand of Laurey Williams. In a sub-plot Will Parker is courting the flirtatious, Ado Annie. What word can't she say?
a) No
b) Yes
c) Oklahoma!

7. *Meet Me in St Louis* was a smash hit musical that became the second-highest-grossing film of 1944. What national event did it center around?
a) The 1904 St Louis Olympics
b) The 1903 St Louis World Fair
c) The 1902 St Louis to New Orleans riverboat Race

8. The Kander & Ebb musical *Chicago* made its debut in 1975 and featured many memorable songs from the 'merry murderesses' Velma and Roxy. Which song contains the lyric: 'Pop! Six! Squish! Uh-uh! Cicero! Lipschitz!'?
a) *All That Jazz*
b) *We Both Reached for the Gun*
c) *Cell Block Tango*

9. Another Kander & Ebb musical, *New York, New York* starred Liza Minnelli and Robert De Niro as a pair of musicians and lovers. Who directed the film?
a) Bob Fosse
b) Martin Scorsese
c) Stanley Kubrick

10. The 1964 film *Viva Las Vegas* follows Lucky Jackson (Elvis) who is in Sin City to compete in the first Las Vegas Grand Prix, but needs to pay for an engine to make the start. He falls in love with a hotel swimming instructor, Rusty Martin, played by which Swedish actress (to which the word 'bombshell' is normally added)?
a) Anita Ekberg
b) Ingrid Bergman
c) Ann-Margret

LIVE, ON STAGE!

Try answering questions about some of America's most storied music venues from grand ole Nashville to Red Rocks.

1. For many years the Ryman Auditorium in Nashville was the host venue of The Grand Ole Opry. It had many alternative names – spot the one that is *not* genuine in this list.
a) 'The Mother Church of Country Music'
b) 'The Dollywood Bowl'
c) 'The Birthplace of Bluegrass'
d) 'The Carnegie Hall of the South'

2. In 1970, a short residency at a Los Angeles club propelled Elton John towards a career of super stardom. Robert Hilburn of the *Los Angeles Times* wrote: 'Rejoice. Rock music, which has been going through a rather uneventful period recently, has a new star. He's Elton John, a 23-year-old Englishman, whose debut Tuesday night at the _____ was, in almost every way, magnificent ... He's going to be one of rock's biggest and most important stars.' What was the club?
a) The Whisky a Go Go
b) The Troubador

3. When Bob Geldof organized Live Aid in 1985, the UK gig was at Wembley Stadium. The U.S. half of the show included Black Sabbath in full *Spinal Tap* gear, Phil Collins, Tom Petty, Neil Young, Bryan Adams, The Beach Boys, Madonna and Led Zeppelin. Where was it held?
a) Shea Stadium, New York
b) JFK Stadium, Philadelphia
c) Memorial Stadium, Baltimore

4. The Greek amphitheater features in the 2018 adaptation of the film *A Star Is Born* starring Lady Gaga and Bradley Cooper. The Greek is located in which famous park?
a) Lincoln Park, Chicago
b) Central Park, New York
c) Griffith Park, Los Angeles

5. The Super Stage at Austin's Circuit of the Americas (now named the Germania Insurance Amphitheater) was the venue for this artiste's only live show in 2016, during the F1 grand prix. Manager of the race circuit Bobby Epstein believes her appearance helped stave off a financial crisis for the track. Who was it?
a) Beyonce
b) Madonna
c) Taylor Swift

6. The Apollo Theater in Harlem is famous for its Amateur Night with particularly fierce and discerning audiences. Soul legend Luther Vandross was booed off stage four times before he won, while James Brown's debut performance in 1952 did not go well. An official 'act remover' holding a broom, a chair or even weapon props would sweep Amateur Night performers from the stage if they were doing badly. What is this person called?
a) The Sweeper
b) The Executioner
c) Damocles of the Apollo

7. House of Blues is a chain of live music concert halls and restaurants across America. It was co-founded by which film actor?
a) Jack Black, star of *School of Rock*
b) Dan Aykroyd, star of *The Blues Brothers*
c) Rami Malek, star of *Bohemian Rhapsody*

8. In 2013, the management of Madison Square Garden announced a Billy Joel residency. The piano man would play one gig at the 19,500-seat venue every month for as long as demand held up. How many Gigs did Billy play?
a) 39
b) 87
c) 150

9. This venue supported the 1960s psychedelic scene in San Francisco, featuring acts like Jimi Hendrix, Pink Floyd and The Grateful Dead. What was it called?
a) The Castro Theatre
b) Starland Ballroom
c) The Fillmore

10. Red Rocks Amphitheatre in Colorado is one of the highest grossing venues anywhere in the world. Being located outdoors has its problems – apple-size hailstones fell on a Louis Tomlinson concert in 2023, hospitalizing some, and bad weather almost sank one act's appearance in 1983. The crowd shrank to 4,400 after many thought the show would be cancelled – it wasn't and they'd hired a whole movie crew to film it. What was the epic gig?

a) *U2 Live at Red Rocks: Under a Blood Red Sky*
b) *Fleetwood Mac: On the Rocks*
c) *Moody Blues: A Night at Red Rocks with the Colorado Symphony Orchestra*

ON LOCATION

Many hit television series are firmly embedded in their real-life locations. Try and uncover the truth behind these puzzling questions that need answers.

1. The HBO series *Deadwood* is set in the old Dakota Territory. Starring Timothy Olyphant and Ian McShane playing the real-life Deadwood residents Seth Bullock and Al Swearengen, its writer blended historical truths with fictional elements. Apart from Wild Bill Hickok and Wyatt Earp, which real-life character also appears?
a) Annie Oakley
b) Sitting Bull
c) Calamity Jane

2. In the UK, Ricky Gervaise's *The Office* was set in 'boring' Slough. In the U.S. where is Steve Carell's version of *The Office* set?
a) Toledo, Ohio
b) Scranton, Pennsylvania
c) Cedar Rapids, Iowa

3. The 'jacket-over-T-shirt' look became popular in the late 1980s thanks to actor Don Johnson in Miami Vice. What was the name of the Ferrari-driving undercover cop he played?
a) 'Sonny' Crockett
b) Ricardo Tubbs
c) Ricardo Crockett

4. Walter White was responsible for cooking up a whole lot of crystal meth in which New Mexico city in the hit series *Breaking Bad*?
a) Las Cruces
b) Santa Fe
c) Albuquerque

5. In the series *Ozark*, Marty Byrde, played by Jason Bateman, moves his family to the Lake of the Ozarks for what reason?
a) As part of a witness protection scheme, following a mafia murder
b) As part of a new money-laundering operation
c) As part of a supernatural investigation team

6. *It's Always Sunny in Philadelphia*, created by Rob McElhenney, is the longest-running American live-action sitcom by several seasons. What is the name of the fictional Irish pub where it all kicked off with 'The Gang'?
a) McGinty's Saloon
b) Top o' the Mornin' Bar
c) Paddy's Pub

7. Teen drama *The O.C.* ran for four seasons from 2003. O.C. is short for Orange County and there are eight Orange Counties in the U.S. Where was this one?
a) Florida
b) Texas
c) California

8. Widely regarded as one of the most influential television series of all time, *The Sopranos* was set in North Jersey and shot in New York studios and on location around the Garden State. Many sequences with Pussy Bonpensiero were shot at which east coast resort?
a) Coney Island
b) Atlantic City
c) Asbury Park

9. Another highly rated series *The Wire* starred Wendell Pierce, Dominic West, Aiden Gillen, Clarke Peters, Idris Elba and Michael Kenneth Williams as Omar. In which port city was it set?
a) Oakland
b) Baltimore
c) Philadelphia

10. The television series *Gotham* was based on the DC Comics' Batman characters and served as a prequel to his many adventures on screen. Is there a real-life Gotham in the United States?
a) No
b) Yes, Gotham, Wisconsin

SPORT

FRANCHISE-GO-ROUND

Sports teams can have immense bargaining power – especially when they want to build a new stadium or arena and the city doesn't want to finance it. In which case it can be, 'Arrivederci!' Try these question on teams from the NBA, MLB and the NFL which have swapped cities and even coasts, for a new life.

1. They were known as the Trolley Dodgers because of all the streetcars in Brooklyn where they played. In 1958 they donned their sunglasses and 'Dem Bums' shipped off to Los Angeles. What was the name of their last stadium (since demolished)?
a) Ebbets Field
b) Shibe Park
c) Polo Grounds

2. To boost baseball on the West Coast the New York Giants moved to San Francisco in the same season to continue their games with the Dodgers. Why did they leave?
a) They did not have the capital to build a new stadium
b) Fans' intense rivalry with the Yankees fans became too violent

3. The Atlanta Braves can trace their lineage back to the Boston Red Stocking team which became the Boston Braves in 1912. They moved out of Boston in 1953 for a new home city, before moving on to Atlanta in 1966. Where did they play before arriving in Georgia?
a) Kansas
b) Minnesota
c) Milwaukee

4. In 2005 the Washington Nationals took their place in the National League East. Which franchise did they take over?
a) The Quebec Pirates
b) The Montreal Expos
c) The Ontario Warriors

5. In 1970 the Seattle Pilots gave up their rain-soaked ballpark and moved to become…
a) The Milwaukee Brewers
b) The Houston Colts
c) The Miami Sharks

6. The Athletics or A's are a much traveled team. They moved from Oakland to Sacramento for 2025-2027 (but retained their name) and will be heading off to Las Vegas from 2028. They started life as the Philadelphia Athletics with legendary long-time manager Connie Mack. But in 1954 moved to which city before heading off to Oakland?
a) Pittsburgh
b) Minnesota
c) Kansas City

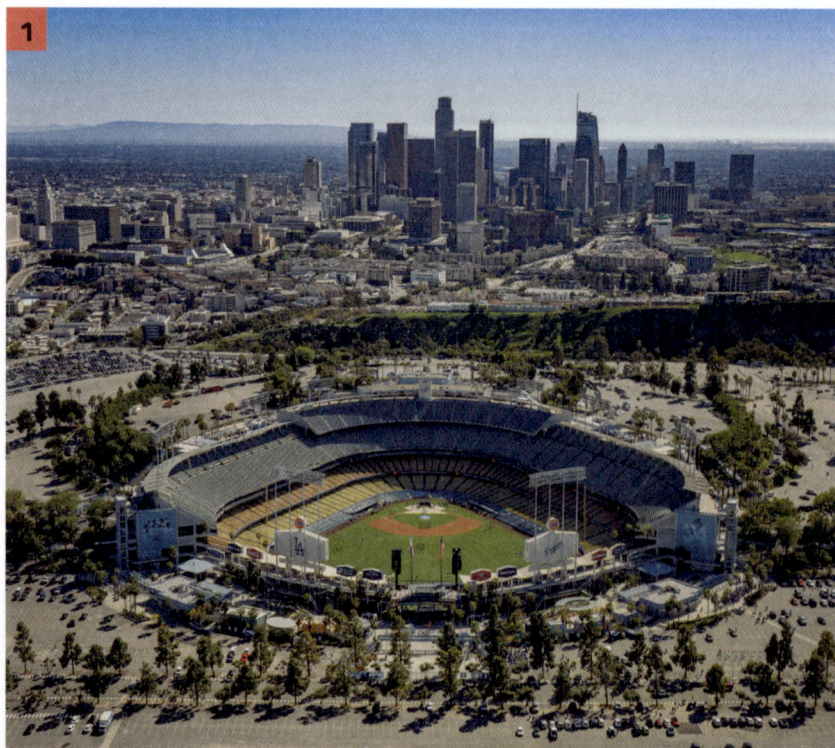

7. Utah is not particularly known for its love of jazz, so it's no surprise that NBA team the Utah Jazz started off in New Orleans. What year did they arrive in Salt Lake City from the 'Big Easy'?
a) 1963
b) 1979
c) 2001

8. The Los Angeles 'Lakers' inherited their name from an NBA team based in a state known as 'The Land of 10,000 Lakes.' Which state?

a) Florida
b) Minnesota
c) Wisconsin

9. Memphis and Tennessee do not have a grizzly bear population, so where did the Memphis Grizzlies find their franchise name? And 'the woods' is not an answer.
a) Vancouver
b) Denver

10. The Detroit Pistons eyed a far bigger market for their

sporting skills and changed cities in 1957. Where did they move from?
a) Des Moines
b) Fort Wayne

11. The NBA Atlanta Hawks have played under various names before 1968. Which of the following is *not* one of their incarnations?
a) St. Louis Hawks
b) Milwaukee Hawks
c) Buffalo Falcons

12. The Kings relocated to Sacramento in 1985 and since the move they have not done so well. But when they do win, a cry goes round: 'Light the Beam!' The arena they play in, the Golden 1 Center, emits a purple laser beam, hence they've been nicknamed the 'Beam Team'. Which city did they move from?
a) Charlotte
b) Knoxville
c) Kansas City

13. The New Orleans Pelicans can trace their origins to a team from 1988. Which team?
a) Charlotte Hornets
b) Charleston Hornets
c) Nashville Hornets

14. Like its fellow Oakland baseball team, the Athletics, the Oakland Raiders have been on a journey. Oakland was home to the Raiders from 1960 till 1981 before they moved to Los Angeles and became the Los Angeles Raiders. They returned home in 1995, but have since left for Las Vegas. When did the Las Vegas Raiders start playing at the Allegiant Stadium in Paradise, Nevada?
a) 2017
b) 2020
c) 2023

15. The Baltimore Colts franchise was sold to Indianapolis after a row with the city about Memorial Stadium, and from 1984 they were the Indianapolis Colts. What was

particularly unusual about the move?
a) Only a quarter of the playing roster was retained
b) It was done overnight with no prior announcement

16. The Rams have been another pinball team. They started off as the Cleveland Rams (1936–1945), then became the Los Angeles Rams in 1946 all the way through to 1994. Then they charged off to St Louis for 20 years before returning to Los Angeles in 2016. Where do they play their games?
a) SoFi Stadium
b) Los Angeles Memorial Coliseum
c) Rose Bowl

17. Fans of the Cleveland Browns were furious when their team got sold. The fury resulted in the NFL creating a new franchise in 1999 for the city, renamed the Cleveland Browns to keep the fans happy. What team did the old Browns become?
a) Tampa Bay Buccaneers
b) Jacksonville Jaguars
c) Baltimore Ravens

18. Whatever happened to the Houston Oilers?
a) They became the Houston Texans
b) They became the Tennessee Titans

19. The growth of Phoenix and its surrounding cities made it an ideal destination for an under-supported team. Where did they find the team that would become Arizona Cardinals?
a) St Louis
b) Baltimore

20. The all-conquering Kansas City Chiefs were created as a major city's second team. When attendances didn't live up to expectations the franchise was sold to the Missouri-based Kansas City in 1963. Which city couldn't sustain a second team and 'gave up their team for adoption'?
a) Chicago
b) Dallas
c) Detroit

PAR, BIRDIE, EAGLE

Golf is one of the few sports where amateurs can compare their performance to the pros – though without the nerve-shredding anxiety of playing the 17th hole at TPC Sawgrass. Less anxiety inducing is our round of 20 questions on the *auld* game.

1. The original Augusta National designer, Alister MacKenzie, was a prolific golf course architect, born in Yorkshire of Scottish parents, who went on to design some of the world's greatest courses. Which classic West Coast course did he also contribute to?
a) Cypress Point
b) Spyglass Hill
c) Bandon Dunes

2. Bobby Jones and Clifford Roberts created the course at Augusta with the aim of hosting the U.S. Open, but the U.S. golf governing body rejected it as a venue. What was the reasoning?
a) Poor rail connections to Augusta
b) There were not enough quality hotels nearby
c) It would be too hot in Georgia at the time of the U.S. Open

3. What famous Augusta tradition started in 1949?
a) The award of the green jacket to the winner
b) The pre-tournament par-3 competition

4. Gary Player was the first non-U.S. golfer to win the Masters, who was the next?
a) Seve Ballesteros
b) Nick Faldo

5. After the attack on Pearl Harbor, the United States entered World War II in December 1941, which meant the cancellation of the 1942 Masters. True or False?

6. Which three holes on the course make up the much-feared 'Amen Corner' where Rae's Creek is always a factor?
a) 5th, 6th, 7th
b) 11th, 12th, 13th
c) 16th, 17th, 18th

7. Spectators – known as patrons – at the Masters are both knowledgeable and respectful. What is expressly banned at Augusta, but allowed in other competitions?
a) Visible tattoos
b) Cell phones

8. Former European tour player-turned-journalist-and-broadcaster David Feherty has never been shy about sharing his opinions. Who is he describing here? 'Watching _____ play golf is like watching a drunk chasing a balloon near the edge of a cliff.'
a) Phil Mickelson
b) Bryson DeChambeau
c) Rickie Fowler

9. The 16th hole at TPC Scottsdale has gained a reputation as the rowdiest in golf. The reason? It is a par-3 entirely surrounded by grandstands filled to the brim with partying golf fans. This raucous behavior has gained it what nickname?
a) Bear Pit
b) The Ballpark
c) The Colosseum

10. Nelly and Jessica Korda had a big impact on women's golf. Nelly has been the No.1 woman's golfer and won a gold medal at the Tokyo Olympics. Jessica retired in 2023 with back problems, but Nelly continues and helped the U.S. win the Solheim Cup in 2024. What is their age difference?
a) They are identical twins
b) Six years

1

11. In an act of great sportsmanship – for which he was criticized by his own team – which American player conceded a short birdie putt to halve a hole and a match against Tony Jacklin, saying to the British player: 'I don't think you would have missed it, but I wasn't going to give you the chance either.'
a) Jack Nicklaus
b) Johnny Miller

12. After a meeting between Jack Nicklaus and the Earl of Derby it was decided that something should be done to make the Ryder Cup more of a contest in the post-War period, which saw unprecedented dominance by the U.S. team. When were European players first involved?
a) 1979
b) 1985
c) 1989

13. The temperature at Wolf Creek golf course in Mesquite, Nevada, averages out at 91F during July and August. However further south, in Death Valley, golfers at Furnace Creek can experience temperatures of 120F! What do members jokingly call their annual competition?
a) The Heatstroke Open
b) This-is-Not-Ireland Open

14. Black bears often wander onto golf courses. They normally will shy away from contact with humans. On some courses golfers are recommended to carry what in their golf bags?
a) A low-velocity BB handgun
b) A personal attack alarm
c) Pepper spray

15. The second U.S. Open was held at a course that is still used for the tournament today. Which venue played host?
a) Shinnecock Hills, New York
b) Kiawah Island, South Carolina
c) Pebble Beach, California

16. Which regular U.S. Open venue is cut in half by a four-lane highway? Players and spectators must cross above it.
a) Pinehurst, North Carolina
b) Brookline Country Club, Massachusetts
c) Oakmont, Pennsylvania

17. The first floating par-3 hole was introduced on an American course. It gave greenskeepers the ability to vary the distance from tee to green depending on the wind strength. Where will you find it?
a) Bandon Dunes, Oregon
b) Chambers Bay, Washington
c) Coeur d'Alene, Idaho

18. In the high-tension Ryder Cup of 1999 at Brookline, which American golfer hit the 45-foot putt that saw the American team, including wives, celebrating on the green?
a) Tiger Woods
b) Jim Furyk
c) Justin Leonard

19. English businessman and golf fan Samuel Ryder sponsored the first event in 1927. How did Ryder make his money?
a) Selling penny packets of seeds by mail order
b) Renting Model-T Fords
c) Importing the rubber used in the core of golf balls

20. The Streamsong golf resort in Florida boasts three top courses. Before it was developed for golf what had it been used as?
a) A military assault course
b) A phosphorous strip mine
c) The failed Gatorland theme park

GRIDIRON GREATS

Welcome to the house of pain. A career in football is not for the faint-hearted and requires speed, agility and nerve – and those are just the offensive linemen... How much do you know about these stars of the NFL?

1. Quarterback Tom Brady, four-time Super Bowl winner with the New England Patriots and the Tampa Bay Buccaneers was drafted in 2000. But which round was he drafted in?
a) First, 3rd overall pick
b) Sixth, 199th overall pick

2. The draft system first came into effect in 1936 in a bid to even up the talent pool across the teams. This first draft was held at Philadelphia's Ritz-Carlton Hotel. As their No.1 pick the Eagles chose Heisman Trophy winner Jay Berwanger from the University of Chicago. What happened next?
a) He signed to play baseball for the Chicago White Sox instead
b) He signed as the Eagles' starting halfback
c) He opted for a career as a foam rubber salesman

3. Aaron Rodgers was hotly predicted to be the No.1 draft pick in 2005 and was expected to be picked up by the San Francisco 49ers. Instead he was only the 24th selection by the Green Bay packers (since voted as one of the Top 10 Draft Day Moments). Who did the 49ers go for instead?
a) Drew Brees
b) Eli Manning
c) Alex Smith

4. Brock Purdy was the last pick – No.262 – of the 2022 NFL draft. Yet he became the starting quarterback for the San Francisco 49ers after injuries to Trey Lance and Jimmy Garoppolo. The last pick is known as what?
a) Tail-end Charlie
b) Mr. Irrelevant
c) The caboose

5. The much-missed John Madden, so long the voice of the NFL, was a coach who never had a losing season. Madden holds the highest winning percentage among NFL head coaches who coached at least 100 games. Who did he coach to their first Super Bowl?
a) New York Jets
b) New York Giants
c) Oakland Raiders

6. On the subject of NFL legends, the inimitable Tom Landry was the Dallas Cowboys head coach for 29 seasons. Coaches need a strong nerve and Landry had been a B-17 Flying Fortress co-pilot in WWII, flying 26 missions. What was his trademark look?
a) A constant stogie (not lit) clamped between his teeth
b) A short-brimmed gray fedora hat
c) A Dallas Cowboys cap with a 493d Bombardment Group badge added (for luck)

7. Who was voted the Most Valuable Player (MVP) of the NFL in 2024?
a) Lamar Jackson
b) Saquon Barkley
c) Josh Allen

8. There are many brothers who have played in the NFL – Eli and Peyton Manning, Jason and Travis Kelce, JJ and TJ Watt and the Bosa brothers Nick and Joey.

Both Bosa brothers have been voted 'Rookie of the Year' for their position. Joey's a linebacker, what position does Nick play?
a) Nose tackle
b) Defensive end
c) Defensive tackle

9. At the south end of Soldier Field, near Gate O, you will find a 12-foot statue of a Chicago Bears legend. Who is it?

a) William 'The Refrigerator' Perry
b) Bears' Super Bowl XX-winning coach Mike Ditka
c) All-time rushing leader Walter Payton

10. Who was the No.1 draft pick in the 2024 draft – selected by the Chicago Bears?
a) Caleb Williams
b) Bryce Young
c) Travon Walker

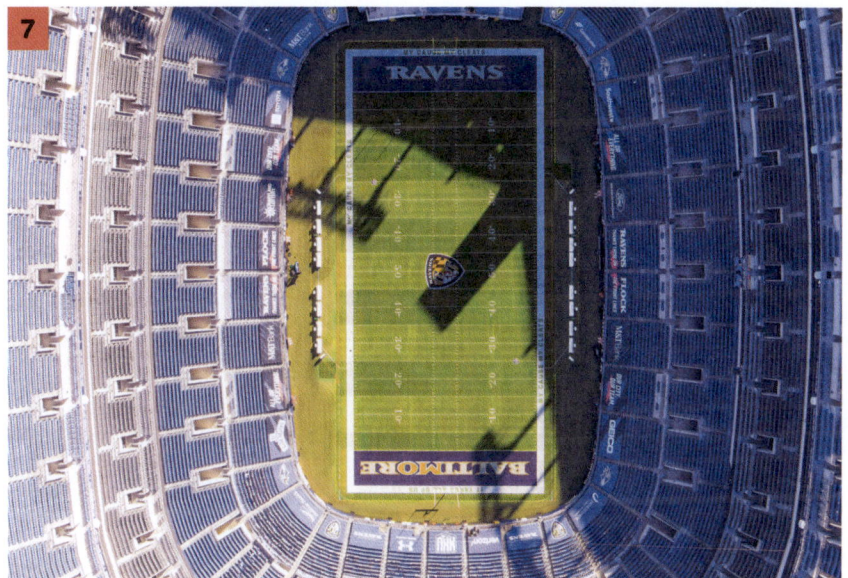

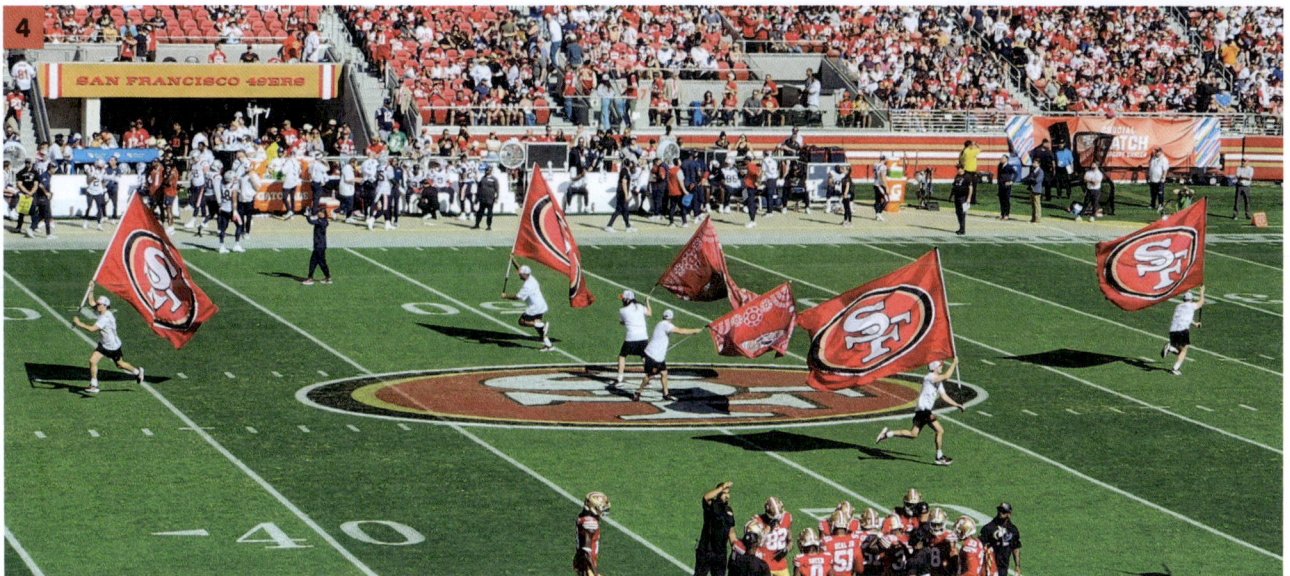

WE ARE THE CHAMPIONS

These American champions have spent years at the top of their respective games – some are contenders to be GOATs. How much do you know about them?

1. Serena Williams is rightly acknowledged as a tennis legend. She was ranked as the World No. 1 in women's singles by the Women's Tennis Association for 319 weeks. She won 73 WTA top tier singles titles, including 23 major women's singles titles. But ironically, she never won the tennis Olympic gold medal. True or False?

2. John McEnroe was a charismatic U.S. Open and Wimbledon tennis grand slam champion and also the scourge of umpires across the tennis world – especially at Wimbledon. Which one of these phrases did he use as the title of his autobiography?
a) 'I saw chalk dust!'
b) 'You cannot be serious!'
c) 'This is the pits of the world!'

3. Cyclist Greg LeMond was the first American to claim Tour de France victory. He won the elite race three times and were it not for an ill-fated hunting accident in 1987 he may well have won five. At his comeback in 1989 he beat Frenchman Laurent Fignon in a dramatic time trial on the Champs Elysée to win the two-week race by what margin?
a) 56 seconds
b) 38 seconds
c) 8 seconds

4. Muhammad Ali was not the favorite to take the world heavyweight boxing title when he stepped into the ring on February 25, 1964, in Miami Beach. The champion he was intending to dethrone was an intimidating personality, an aggressive fighter with ties to the mob. Then known as Cassius Clay he taunted his opponent dubbing him 'the big ugly bear' and saying 'I'm gonna give him to the local zoo after I whup him.' Ali won with a technical knockout. Who was the opponent?
a) Joe Frasier
b) Floyd Patterson
c) Sonny Liston

5. If there were a Godfather of U.S. motorsport it would be Mario Andretti. He has won almost everything – the Indianapolis 500, Daytona 24 Hours, 12 Hours of Sebring and in 1978 he became F1 World Champion. Who was he driving for in F1?
a) Lotus
b) McLaren
c) Brabham

6. There are great Olympic champions, and then there is the U.S. basketball Dream Team Olympic champions of 1992. In the first year that professional

basketball stars could compete, the United States selected what has often been described as the greatest sports team ever assembled. The team defeated its opponents by an average of 44 points per game en route to the gold medal. The first ten included: Scottie Pippen of the Chicago Bulls, John Stockton and Karl Malone of the Utah Jazz, Magic Johnson of the L.A. Lakers, Larry Bird of the Boston Celtics, Patrick Ewing of the Knicks, Chris Mullin of the Golden State Warriors, David Robinson of the San Antonio Spurs, and Charles Barkley of the Philadelphia 76ers. Which major figure have we deliberately left out?

7. Derek Jeter spent his entire 20-year MLB career with the New York Yankees. A five-time World Series winner with the Yankees, he owns all the statistics: hits (3,465), doubles (544), games played (2,747), stolen bases (358), times on base (4,716), plate appearances (12,602) and at bats (11,195). What was his number, which the Yankees retired?
a) 2
b) 4
c) 7

8. Widely regarded as the greatest professional surfer of all time, 'the GOAT on a board' Kelly Slater has been crowned World Surf League Champion a record 11 times. He has won the Laureus World Action Sportsperson of the Year four times, but is probably best known for his appearances on which television series as 'Jimmy Slade'?
a) *Hawaii Five-0* (2010 series)
b) *Baywatch*
c) *Surviving Summer* (Netflix)

9. Tiger Woods has created golf records that will probably never be beaten. He was the official World No.1 for 281 consecutive weeks between 12 June 2005 and 30 October 2010. He has reached No.1 11 times. If all these weeks were added together it would amount to how much time?
a) 8 years
b) 11 years
c) 13 years

10. The term 'legend' is overused in sport, but it applies to Richard Petty, who many believe to be the greatest stock car driver. Competing from 1958 to 1992 (34 years and survived!) most notably driving the No. 43 Plymouth/Pontiac for Petty Enterprises. He won a record 200 races during his career. What was his nickname?
a) Richard the Lionheart
b) Tricky Ricky
c) The King

OLYMPIC LEGENDS

They have re-written sporting history and provided inspiration for countless generations of athletes. But how many of their exploits do you remember?

1. Bode Miller is the most successful U.S. athlete at this discipline at the Winter Olympics, picking up six medals: one Gold, three Silver and two Bronze in the five games he competed at from 1998 to 2014. What is his event?
a) Bobsleigh driving
b) Alpine skiing
c) Ski jumping

2. Lindsey Vonn won gold in the 2010 Winter Olympics and is one of the all-time greats of her sport. What events does she compete in?
a) Alpine skiing
b) Speed skating
c) Curling

3. The unmistakeable Florence Griffith Joyner or 'FloJo' – won three sprint gold medals in the Seoul Olympics of 1988. Sadly she died of an epileptic seizure in 1998 at just 38 years old. However, which of her world records stood till the 2024 Olympics in Paris?
a) 100m
b) 200m
c) Both 100m and 200m

4. If you had to name the two greatest sprint legends of modern times, they would be Usain Bolt of Jamaica and Carl Lewis of the United States. However, whereas Bolt was an out-and-out sprinter, Carl Lewis also competed in which other event?
a) 110m hurdles
b) High jump
c) Long jump

5. Arguably the greatest athlete of the pre-war era, James Cleveland 'Jesse' Owens won four gold medals at the 1936 Olympics in Munich. During a Manhattan ticker-tape parade along Broadway's Canyon of Heroes, someone handed Jesse a paper bag. Owens paid it little attention until afterwards. When he opened it up, he found the bag contained $10,000 in cash. After the parade, Owens was not allowed to enter through the main doors of the Waldorf Astoria New York and was instead forced to travel up to the reception honoring him in a freight elevator. Which of these stories is true?
a) Just the cash in a bag
b) Just the front door ban
c) Both

6. Michael Johnson is a gold-medal-winning track and field athlete with four golds across the Barcelona (1992), Atlanta (1996) and Sydney (2000) games. What was his most successful Olympic distance?
a) 100m
b) 200m
c) 400m

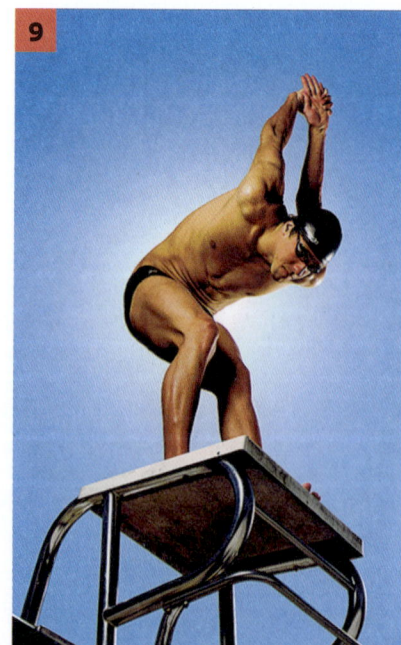

7. One of America's greatest divers, Greg Louganis, won four golds across his Olympic career. However he is probably best remembered for an incident at the Seoul Olympics. What happened?
a) He hit his head on the diving board and was concussed in the preliminaries
b) He suffered an embarrassing 'wardrobe malfunction' as he entered the water

8. In an era when there were less Olympic swimming events, Mark

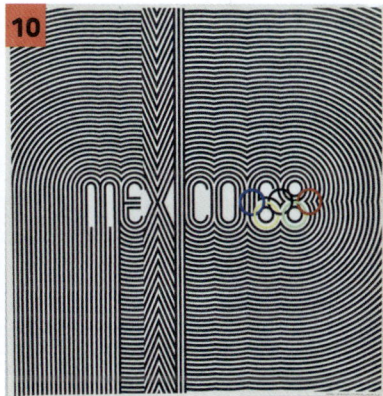

Spitz took the headlines in 1972 winning a then-record number of gold medals at one games. How many?
a) Five
b) Six
c) Seven

9. He was succeeded by the greatest Olympian, who took the medal-winning record book and simply threw it out of the window. Michael Fred Phelps II has been a serial records holder including: Most World Records set for Swimming (male), Most Individual Swimming Olympic gold medals and Most medals won at the FINA Swimming World Championships. Of his 28 Olympic swimming medals, how many are gold?
a) 16
b) 19
c) 23

10. At the 1968 Olympics in Mexico City Bob Beamon set an extraordinary world record for the long jump with a first jump of 8.90m (just over 29 feet), beating the existing record by 55cm. When the announcer called out the distance, Beamon – unfamiliar with metric measurements – did not realize what he had done. When his teammate and coach, Ralph Boston, told him that he had broken the world record by nearly two feet, his legs gave way. How long did his Olympic record last?
a) 25 years
b) 45 years
c) It still exists today

11. Simone Biles is the most successful American artistic gymnast of all time with 11

Olympic medals and 30 World Championship medals across floor, vault, beam and asymmetric bars. After a return from injury she won three gold medals in Paris and is open to competing at the 2028 games in Los Angeles. How tall is she?
a) 4'8"
b) 5'
c) 5'2"

12. The United States has already hosted the Winter Olympics four times: in 1932, 1960, 1980, and 2002. That figure will notch up to five in 2034 when the Winter Olympics will be held where?
a) Sun Valley, Idaho
b) Lake Placid, New York
c) Salt Lake City, Utah

MAXIMUM REVS

America has a long association with motorsport, indeed Gordon Bennett organized international motor racing before the first European grand prix. See how much you know about U.S. race tracks and drivers.

1. Formula 1 cars raced down the Las Vegas strip for the first time in 2023, but the sport had already visited in 1981, with a race laid out in a casino car park. Which casino?
a) Circus Circus
b) Sands
c) Caesars Palace

2. Who was the first American F1 World Champion?
a) Phil Hill, Ferrari
b) Dan Gurney, Eagle
c) Mario Andretti, Lotus

3. Michael Andretti, son of the great Mario, got his chance to drive in F1 in 1993 with the Marlboro McLaren team. Unfortunately he was teamed up with one of the sport's all-time legends. Who was it?
a) Alain Prost
b) Ayrton Senna
c) Nigel Mansell

4. Who was the last driver to win both the Indianapolis 500 and a Formula 1 race?
a) Jacques Villeneuve
b) Takuma Sato
c) Juan Pablo Montoya

5. The Circuit of the Americas was opened in 2012 and quickly became a favorite among F1 drivers, especially as it copied some of the best corners from

other famous circuits. Which of the following tracks is *not* represented in the layout?
a) Hockenheim
b) Silverstone
c) Monaco

6. The Laguna Seca track in California has a famous, fast, twisty corner that plunges downhill and makes great television viewing whether its sportscars or Indycars. What is the corner called?
a) Whirlpool
b) Corkscrew
c) Helter skelter

7. The Indianapolis 500 is traditionally held in which month?

8. At the turn of the century James Gordon Bennett Jr., millionaire owner of the *New York Herald*, devised a motor racing contest which would be raced for by national teams from countries such as the USA, France, Germany and eventually Italy. Each country would have their own racing color. The idea of national colors caught on so well that in Formula 1 they lasted through till the end of the 1960s. In the first cup, France was blue, Germany was white, Belgium was yellow, so what was America?
a) Green
b) Silver
c) Red

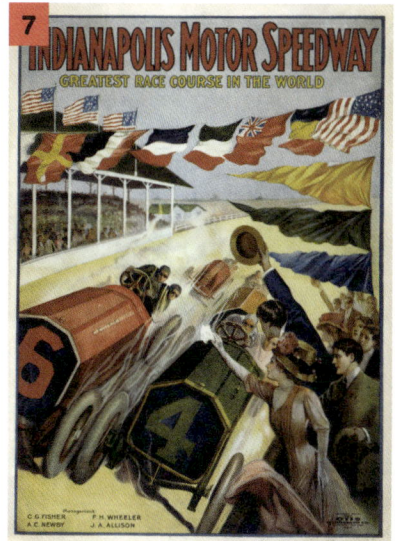

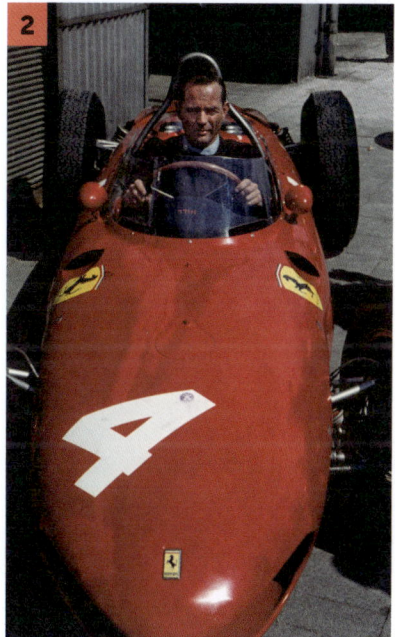

9. The Miami Grand Prix became Formula 1's second U.S. race in 2022. It takes place at the Miami International Autodrome around the Dolphins' Hard Rock Stadium. To make it more exotic the race promoters added what?

a) 50 Cheerleaders (F1 has placed a ban on grid girls)

b) Fake boats in a fake marina

c) A trackside dolphinarium

10. Which American-owned F1 team, and its charismatic team boss Guenther Steiner, featured heavily in the first Netflix series of *Drive to Survive*?

a) Cadillac

b) Haas

c) Williams

COLLEGE FOOTBALL

College football holds a unique place in American sports culture. In some respects it rivals or even surpasses the NFL in terms of passion and attendance. The largest stadiums in the country are college football venues, with places like Michigan Stadium ('The Big House') seating over 107,000 fans. Schools such as Penn State, Ohio State, Louisiana State and Alabama regularly sell out stadiums with over 90,000 fans. In contrast, the average NFL stadium holds between 60,000 and 80,000 spectators. So it's no poor relation, plus you get a marching band. Try and match the colleges below with their team name.

1. Ohio State	11. Brigham Young (BYU)	**Mustangs**
2. Notre Dame	12. Southern Methodist (SMU)	**Tigers**
3. Oregon	13. Clemson	**Wolverines**
4. Texas	14. Michigan	**Cougars**
5. Georgia	15. Iowa State	**Bulldogs**
6. Arizona State	16. Alabama	**Longhorns**
7. Boise State	17. Florida State	**Ducks**
8. Tennessee	18. Utah	**Broncos**
9. Indiana	19. Oklahoma	**Gamecocks**
10. Mississippi	20. South Carolina	**Cyclones**
		Crimson Tide
		Seminoles
		Utes
		Sooners
		Buckeyes
		Fighting Irish
		Sun Devils
		Volunteers
		Hoosiers
		Rebels

MAJOR LEAGUE SOCCER

Some of the Major League Soccer teams have very straightforward names, such as FC Cincinnati, Austin FC or FC Dallas. Others have opted for English names to fit in with the founders of the game, such as Atlanta United, or D.C. United, or Spanish with the vaguely humorous Real Salt Lake. Can you match up the following club names with their correct city?

1. Chicago	**Revolution**
2. Columbus	**Dynamo**
3. Inter	**Galaxy**
4. New England	**Timbers**
5. Philadelphia	**Earthquakes**
6. Colorado	**Sounders**
7. Houston	**Sporting**
8. LA	**Fire**
9. Portland	**Crew**
10. San Jose	**Inter**
11. Seattle	**Union**
12. Kansas City	**Rapids**

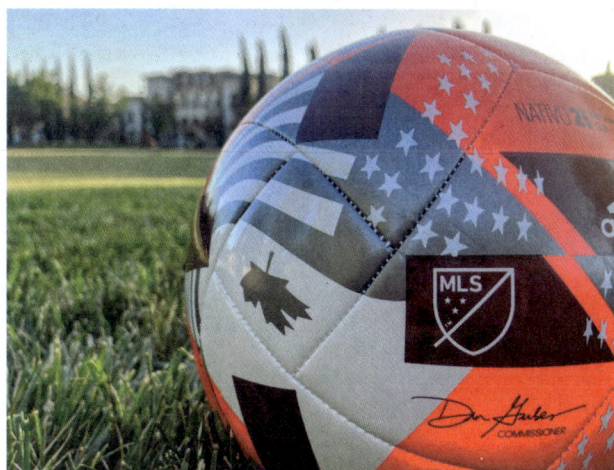

TRAVEL

TRAVELING ABROAD ... AT HOME

With a whole continent to fill with place names, it's no surprise that settlers from the Old World imported a few of their own. In America you can travel the world without anyone stamping your passport.

1. Which is the larger city – Athens, Georgia or Athens, Alabama?

2. There are 26 Berlins in the U.S. – some hardly more than ghost towns. Berlin, Connecticut, had a population of 20,175 at the 2020 census. It's described as having two hamlets. One is called East Berlin, what is the other called?
a) West Berlin
b) Kensington

3. By contrast there are only two Copenhagens in America. One is in Louisiana and the other is in which state?
a) New York
b) Utah
c) Minnesota

4. Pekin is a city in Tazewell County, Illinois. It took its name from Peking in China. The Chinese capital was known as both Peking and Pékin (France still refers to the city as Pékin). When Peking officially changed its name to Beijing, the city of Pekin, USA, lost a vote to change its name to Beijin. True or False?

5. Scottish tourists sometimes take on the challenge of visiting the 21 places in the States named Glasgow. Which is the smallest Glasgow of this trio?
a) Glasgow, Fallen Timber County, Pennsylvania
b) Glasgow Kentucky
c) Glasgow, Valley County, Montana

6. Lisbon, the seat of Ransom County, North Dakota, is home to The Scenic movie theater, which was established in 1911 and claims to be the oldest, continuously running movie theater in the United States. Which city was it named after?
a) Lisbon, Portugal
b) Lisbon, New York

7. The famous line from *Casablanca*: 'We'll always have Paris' could not be more true in the United States. There are seven listed cities, from Paris, Arkansas to Paris, Texas, and many more towns and communities with that address. But in which state would you find Paris Mountain State Park?
a) Maine
b) New Mexico
c) South Carolina

8. Irina Vasiliev, a professor of geography at the State University of New York, investigated the reasons communities had named themselves Moscow. In her research she found that Napoleon's siege of Moscow and his expulsion by the Russians in 1812 played a large part. The people of Northfield, Maine, renamed their city after the events of 1812 – for which reason?
a) The heroic Russian stand against the mighty French empire
b) A large forest fire nearby that reminded people of the Russian capital burning in 1812

9. After the opening of the Sac and Fox Reservation in Oklahoma with a land run on September 22, 1891, Czech immigrants settled and founded which town?
a) Brno
b) Pilsen
c) Prague

Greetings From BERLIN Connecticut

Greetings from PEKIN ILLINOIS

MOSCOW

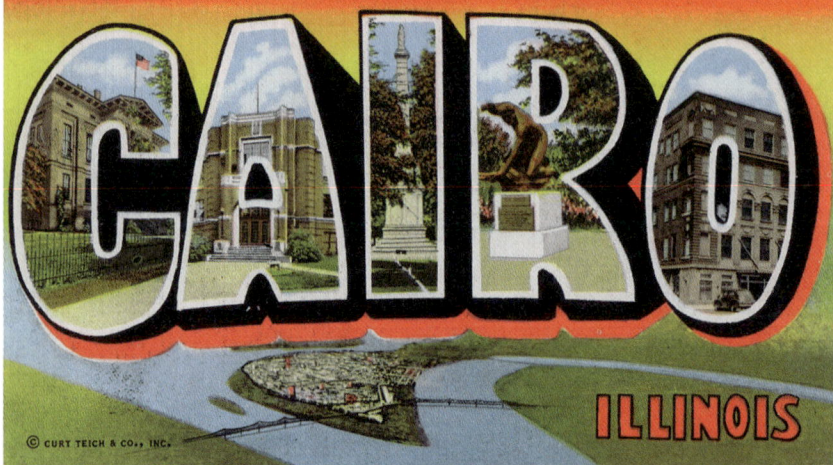

Greetings FROM CAIRO ILLINOIS

12. Cairo, Illinois, was a familiar stop for Mark Twain when learning the troublesome shoals of the Mississippi river. It was named after the Egyptian capital for what reason?
a) Its location where the Ohio meets the Mississippi was reminiscent of the Nile Delta
b) The first settler was a French/Egyptian explorer who named it after his native city

13. There are 19 settlements named Jericho in the U.S. Which is the oldest (1648) to take its name from the city in the biblical Promised Land?
a) Jericho, New York
b) Jericho, Vermont
c) Jericho, North Carolina

14. Damascus, Virginia, has long been known for its convergence of major trails. It is sometimes known as 'Trail Town USA' due to the intersection of five scenic trails in the town. They include the well-known Appalachian Trail, the U.S. Bicycle Route 76 and The Iron Mountain Trail. Damascus also lies on the route of the Daniel Boone Heritage Trail and the Crooked Road Music Heritage Trail. Which is why its annual festival is known as 'The Road to Damascus'. True or False?

15. Delhi in Louisiana has a much smaller population than Delhi, India. By how much?
a) 14,567,736
b) 21,583,378

10. 'See Naples and die' is an Italian saying. It means that after seeing the coastal city of Naples (Napoli) you will never see anything more beautiful. Citizens of Naples in Florida have miles of beautiful white 'sugar' sand, but not an active volcano. The place name is an evolution of the Greek word 'neapolis' which means...?
a) Neat city
b) New city
c) New plan

11. Bethlehem is a city in the West Bank of Palestine. Bethlehem is also a city in eastern Pennsylvania. Jesus Christ was born in the former, while Michael Andretti, son of Mario, was born in the latter. Which has the greater population today?
a) Bethlehem, PA
b) Bethlehem, Palestine

16. In the 1970s, Tripoli, Iowa, which was named after the Libyan capital, was visited by a curious Colonel Gaddafi, who expected it to be bigger. True or False?

17. Unsurprisingly with so many Polish immigrants coming to America there are a host of Polish names, and you can visit 17 different Warsaws. How close are Warsaw, Pennsylvania and Warsaw, New York?
a) 7 miles
b) 144 miles
c) 284 miles

18. In Australia, Sydney and Melbourne are in different states. In the USA they are in the same one. Which one?
a) California
b) Florida
c) Kentucky

19. We know New England has a lot of English place names – hence the title – but they have an incredible five Manchesters squeezed into the six states. Which state hasn't got one?

a) Vermont
b) Maine
c) Rhode Island

20. And finally, the ancient city of Carthage, once home to an empire, has inspired settlers to take up the name as far afield as Illinois, Indiana, Maine, Mississippi, Missouri, New York, North Carolina, Ohio, South Dakota, Tennessee and Texas. If they wanted to visit the original Carthage – what would they find?
a) A bustling port city of 12,700
b) A small fishing village of 550
c) An archaeology site

PREMIER ATTRACTIONS

America has some of the biggest and best attractions for international visitors and home tourists alike. Many are based on adrenalin-filled thrill rides while others are steeped in history. So how much do you know about them…?

1. Though both Disney theme parks are untouchable in terms of attendance figures – each around the 17 million mark – the California Six Flags Magic Mountain park is top when it comes to a specific ride. It holds the world record for the number of what…?
a) Log flumes
b) Roller coasters
c) Train rides

2. The Disney organization provide the top destinations in Florida and California, locking out the top two places with the Magic Kingdom Theme Park and the Disneyland Park. Which park comes in at No.3 though…?*
a) Epcot at Walt Disney World, Florida
b) Universal's Island of Adventure, Orlando
c) Disney's Hollywood Studios, Florida

3. Griffith Observatory looking out over Los Angeles contains what is billed as the 'most viewed telescope' in the world. It has offered free admission since its opening in 1935. Griffith Park and the Observatory were gifts from which benefactor?
a) Hollywood film mogul D.W. Griffith
b) Mine owner Griffith Jenkin Griffith

4. The original Hollywood sign was illuminated with 4,000 lightbulbs and flashed in three segments: 'HOLLY', 'WOOD' and 'LAND'. The 'LAND' has long disappeared and by the 1970s the sign was dilapidated and needed replacing. The Hollywood Chamber of Commerce raised $250,000 for a replacement – donors included Hugh Hefner, Andy Williams and which heavy metal star?
a) Ozzy Osbourne
b) Lars Ulrich
c) Alice Cooper

5. Dolly Parton has always been seen as a shrewd businesswoman and given the popularity of the Great Smoky Mountain National Park, what better place to have your own home grown theme park. Which of the following is not an attraction at Dollywood?
a) Calico Falls Schoolhouse
b) Big Bear Mountain
c) Dolly's Tennessee Mountain Home
d) 'I Will Always Love You' Lurve Train

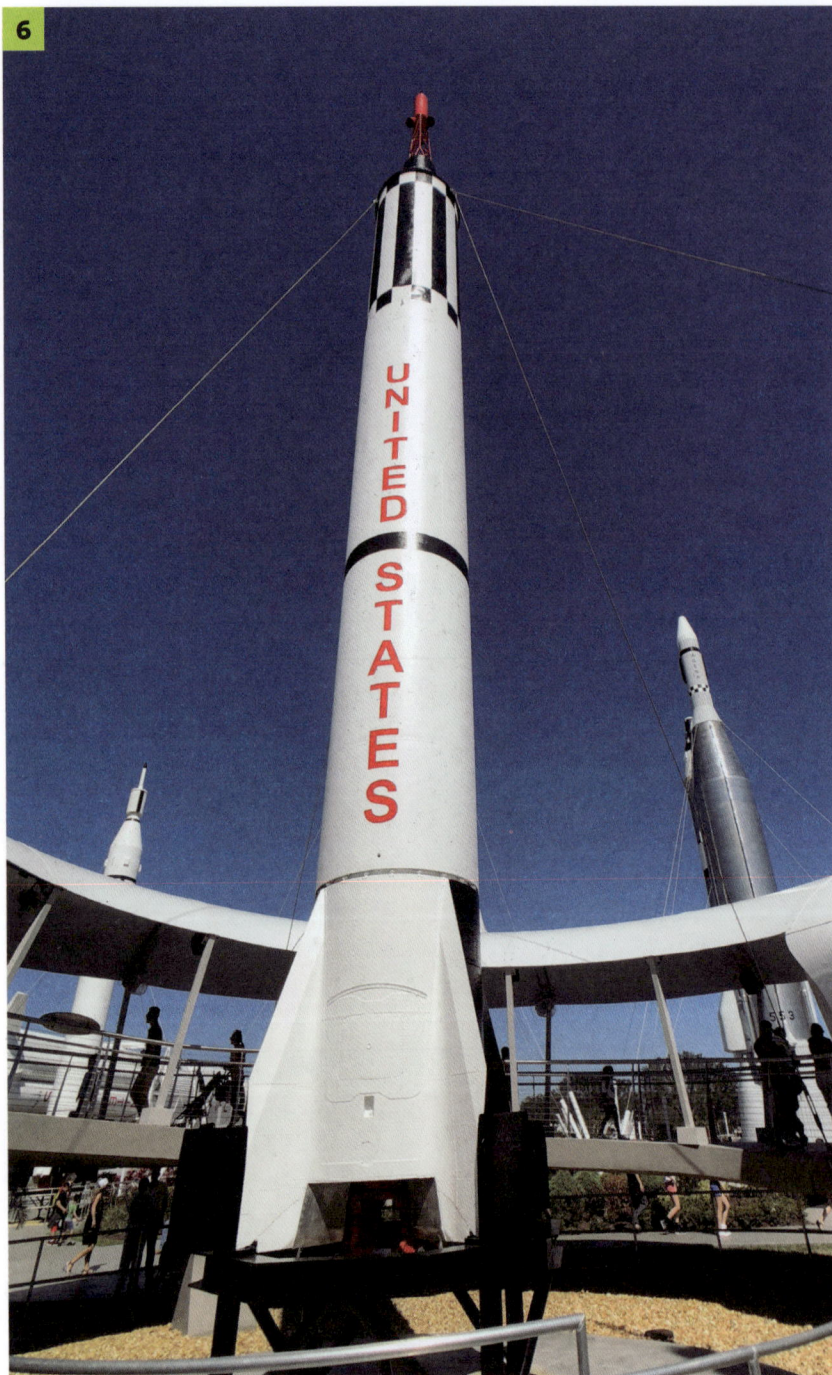

6. The John F. Kennedy Space Center (KSC) displays the Mercury-Redstone 3 rocket which propelled Alan Shepard into space for the first U.S. human space flight. It is one of a collection of rockets from the space program that can be viewed. What does KSC call its collection of historic rockets?
a) The Rocket Garden
b) The Rocket Range
c) The Rocket Stand

7. Long before the development of The Strip in Las Vegas, Fremont Street was the heart of all the gambling activity. Now covered by an arched LED display the street is anchored at one end by the Plaza casino resort. What used to sit in the place now occupied by the Plaza?
a) Las Vegas railroad station
b) Nevada State Jailhouse
c) Madame Bouverie's House of Infinite Pleasure

8. The Smithsonian Castle in Washington, D.C. is the oldest of the Smithsonian museum buildings. The institute was founded with a large donation from British scientist James Smithson, who died in 1829 without a surviving heir. In his will he specifically asked for an institution to be set up in Washington, 'for the increase and diffusion of knowledge among men.' However, he had never visited the United States. True or False?

9. The Mount Rushmore National Memorial is a colossal sculpture by Gutzon Borglum and his son Lincoln Borglum. It features four presidents. The idea for a monumental sculpture was the idea of South Dakota historian Doane Robinson, who thought it would make a great tourist attraction. However his idea for the carved figures was not former presidents – who did he propose?
a) Lewis & Clark, Buffalo Bill and Chief Crazy Horse
b) John C. Fremont and George Armstrong Custer
c) Ulysses Grant, William T. Sherman, Philip Sheridan and Admiral David D. Porter

10. Walter and Cordelia Knott first settled in Buena Park, California, in 1920 and ran a roadside berry stand. They added a chicken diner to Knott's Berry Farm that became so popular that attractions were needed to keep diners occupied while they waited for a table. What was the first major attraction of what would become a nationally known theme park?
a) Woodchuck Chip's Junior Carousel
b) Old MacDonald's Petting farm
c) The Ghost Town

*figures from 2023

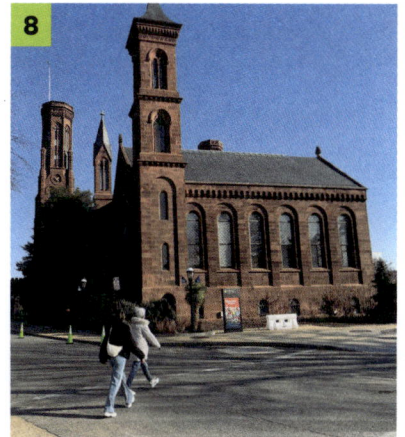

NEW YORK, NEW YORK

By far the biggest tourist destination in the United States, New York has so many different attractions, but how much do you know about 'the city that never sleeps'?

1. The Statue of Liberty was conceived by French historian and abolitionist Édouard de Laboulaye in 1865, after the Union victory. France would pay for the statue if America built the plinth on Bedloe Island. Who was Liberty's sculptor?
a) Auguste Rodin
b) Frédéric Auguste Bartholdi
c) Daniel Chester-French

2. The 843 acres of Central Park in Manhattan is easily the most popular urban park in the U.S. with 42 million visitors. It was designed by landscape architects Frederick Law Olmsted and Calvert Vaux who won a design competition for the park with their 'Greensward Plan'. The central reservoir is dedicated to which former first lady?
a) Eleanor Roosevelt
b) Jacqueline Kennedy Onassis
c) Lady Bird Johnson

3. The Brooklyn Bridge has been free to pedestrians since 1891. When it opened in 1883 it would have cost a penny to cross. How much would you have needed to pay to take a cow with you? (Cows, sheep and hogs were all priced).
a) Two cents
b) Five cents
c) Ten cents

4. The Staten Island ferry has been a familiar sight in New York Harbor since 1817. How many ferries are there in the fleet?
a) 3
b) 5
c) 10

5. Times Square is on every New York tourist's bucket list making it the busiest pedestrian area in the city. It is where Broadway, Seventh Avenue, and 42nd Street meet and between 330,000 and 460,000 pass through every day – giving it the nickname...?
a) Grand Tourist Central
b) The Crossroads of the World
c) Backpack Corner

6. When the New York Central Railroad's West Side Line through the Meatpacking District became defunct city planners drew on Paris for inspiration. They created the High Line a linear park inspired by the 2.9-mile-long *Coulée verte* (tree-lined walkway), an elevated park in Paris completed in 1993. Opened in 2009, how many people take the High Line each year?
a) 2.7million
b) 5 million
c) 8 million

7. Vessel is a unique structure designed by Thomas Heatherwick. It was built as a visitor attraction for which major real estate development in Manhattan?
a) Sunset Pier Studios
b) Chelsea Piers
c) Hudson Yards

8. The Metropolitan Museum of Art is the most visited museum in the United States and the fifth-most visited art museum in the world. The main building can be

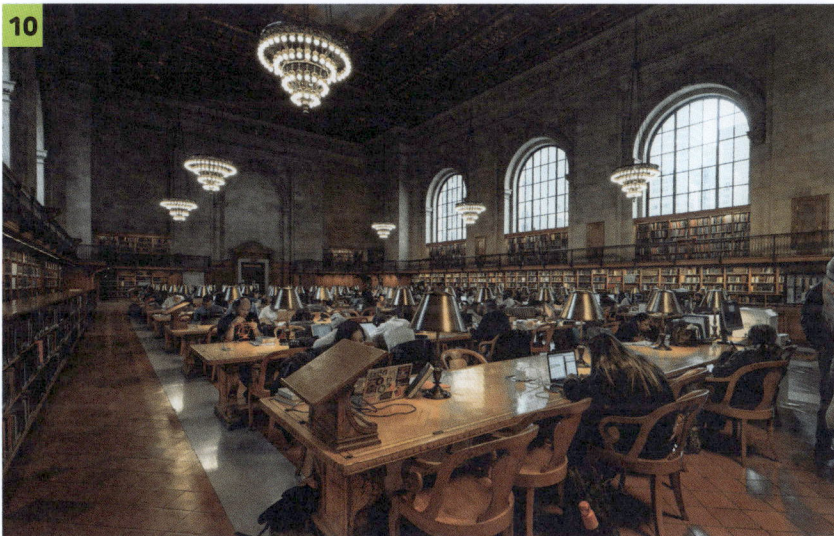

10. New York Public Library is a giant amongst public libraries. The main entrance steps are on Fifth Avenue and four stories of the magnificent Beaux-Arts building are open to the public. During World War II, American soldiers managed to decode a Japanese cipher based on a Mexican phone directory and the last remaining copy among Allied nations existed at the Main Branch. What is the name of the main reading room?
a) The Rose Main Reading Room
b) The Carnegie Room
c) The Walt Whitman Room

found at 1000 Fifth Avenue, along the Museum Mile by Central Park. The museum's substantial fundraiser is the Met Gala, organized by *Vogue* magazine and dubbed as 'fashion's biggest night'. Anyone who is anyone in the fashion world simply must attend. How much did a ticket cost in 2024?
a) $30,000
b) $50,000
c) $75,000

9. In the world of New York theater, the cachet of having a successful 'Broadway production' is very important. 'Off Broadway' shows are in the small theaters. How big does a venue in Manhattan's Theater District have to be to count itself as the full 'Broadway'?
a) 200 seats
b) 350 seats
c) 500 seats

ROAD AMERICA

The United States possesses some of the most stunning scenery through which to go touring. Picking 'the road trip of a lifetime' is a tough call, there are so many to choose from: lush, forested mountains or winding coastal roads. Try these questions on Scenic Byways and All American Roads – road trips that exemplify the very best of escapes.

1. Route 66 from Chicago to Santa Monica was less a scenic byway and more an economic necessity when share-croppers in the dustbowl headed west to find agricultural jobs in California. The agonies of farming families uprooting themselves was vividly portrayed in John Steinbeck's novel, *Grapes of Wrath*. Historic Route 66 heads through eight states: Illinois, Missouri, Kansas, Oklahoma, Texas, New Mexico, Arizona and California. Which state has the shortest section?
a) Kansas
b) Missouri
c) Oklahoma

2. At one time, Route 66 was known as the Will Rogers Memorial Highway, after the much-loved cowboy-philosopher-film star. The road passes through his hometown, where there is a museum dedicated to his work. Where's that?
a) Claremore, Oklahoma
b) Tulsa, Oklahoma
c) Oklahoma City

3. Bob Waldmire was one of the prime movers in the rebirth of Route 66. A hippy cartographer, he would spend his winters in the Arizona mountains and his summers traveling in a converted Chevrolet school bus. In the animated movie *Cars* he is the Fillmore character. In 1992 he re-opened the abandoned Northside Grocery and Conoco station in Arizona and turned it into one of the must-stop places on Route 66. What is it called today?
a) Hackberry General Store
b) Bob's

4. Another Route 66 veteran, Angel Delgadillo, formed the Route 66 Association of Arizona after Interstate 40 bypassed his town. It was also the site of a famous *LIFE* magazine photo showing a hitcher at the side of the road. What's the name of the town?
a) Two Guns
b) Kingman
c) Seligman

5. The Eagles famous song, *Take it Easy* has the lyric: 'I'm standing on a corner in Winslow Arizona, such a fine sight to see.' Today the corner bears a statue of its writer Jackson Brown, and the corner is part of Route 66. True or False?

6. For many, the great highlight of the Pacific Coast Highway is the section around Big Sur, especially the stretch that involves the Bixby Bridge about 120 miles south of San Francisco. Before the opening of the bridge, residents of Big Sur were often isolated during winter due to blockages on the often impassable Old Coast Road. Mud slides and rock falls are still a hazard on the PCH. When was the Bixby Bridge built?
a) 1922
b) 1932
c) 1942

7. Another celebrated driving route is the Blue Ridge Parkway in Virginia and North Carolina, that runs mostly along the spine of the Blue Ridge, part of the Appalachian Mountains. It's an All-American Road and also the longest linear park in the U.S. What is the length?
a) 246 miles
b) 352 miles
c) 469 miles

8. One of the highlights of the Blue Ridge Parkway can be found at Milepost 304.4 – the elegant Linn Cove Viaduct. Which mountain does the viaduct snake round?
a) Snake Mountain
b) Grandfather Mountain
c) Grandmother Mountain

9. The Great River Road, devised in 1938, follows the Mississippi River from Minnesota down to Louisiana with dedicated route marking all the way. It is 2,340 miles long and links up a lot of state roads, nearly all of which are National Scenic Byways. How many states does it pass through?
a) 6
b) 8
c) 10

10. Because of its remote location and lack of traffic, Highway 50 in Nevada is known as what?
a) The Desolation Highway
b) The Loneliest Road in America
c) The Road to Nowhere

11. Which celebrated route starts its journey north from in front of Monroe County Courthouse in downtown Key West?
a) The Overseas Highway
b) Florida Keys Parkway

12. The Beartooth Highway is an All-American Road forming a section of U.S. Route 212 in Montana and Wyoming. It crests at Beartooth Pass in Wyoming at close on 11,000 feet, and is known for its spectacular scenery. On average, how many months of the year is it open?
a) 5 months
b) 7.5 months
c) It is kept open all year

13. Similar to the Pacific Coast Highway, the Oregon Coast Highway hugs the Pacific coast from Astoria down to Brookings, taking in lighthouses and Cannon Beach along the way. What is its

highway designation?
a) State Route 1
b) U.S. Route 101
c) U.S. Route 111

14. If you're not done with driving by the time you get to the end of the Blue Ridge Parkway, you can continue along the Skyline Drive in Virginia which delivers the beauty of which national park?
a) Brandywine National Park
b) Shenandoah National Park

15. The Natchez Trace Parkway follows along traditional routes used by American Indians, traders, early settlers and troops during the Civil War. It starts in Natchez, Mississippi and ends where, 444 miles later?
a) Nashville
b) Chattanooga

16. State Route 12 in Utah sometimes goes by the name of Scenic Byway 12. And if you want scenic, you have certainly got it on this 123-mile-long state highway. It crosses part of Dixie National Forest and Bryce Canyon National Park, taking in a part of Grand Staircase–Escalante National Monument. Drivers

with a fear of heights should be mindful of 'The Hogback', a narrow ridge with no guardrails and steep drop-offs very much like Pike's Peak. What is the route also known as?
a) Journey Through Time Scenic Byway
b) The Rollercoaster Scenic Byway
c) The Four Parks Highway

17. Going-to-the-Sun Road is a scenic mountain road in Montana's Glacier National Park, created in the early 1930s. For brevity's sake the National Park Service shortens it to the 'Sun Road' in documents. What important geographical feature does it cross?
a) The Canadian border
b) The Continental Divide

18. For those who find joy in circling Great Lakes there are many official designated circular tour routes: Lake Michigan, Lake Erie, Lake Huron and the Lake Superior Circle Tour which made its debut in 1988. The 1,280-mile Lake Superior route follows state and provincial highways that loop around the entirety of the lake through Michigan, Wisconsin, Minnesota, and which Canadian state?
a) Ontario
b) Alberta
c) Quebec

19. 'The Million Dollar Highway' in Colorado has another name: the Highway of Hell. It is one of the most exhilarating stretches of road in the 50 states, just 25 miles in length with outstanding views but with s-bends that need to be taken at 10mph and steep drops off a barrier-less road. It is not for the faint-hearted. How many people have had their sightseeing fatally interrupted since 1992?
a) 200
b) 400
c) 800

20. Another Colorado highlight is the Pikes Peak Highway, a road that takes motorists from the valley floor right the way up to the summit at 14,115 feet. It's a 19-mile journey to the clouds, some of it unguarded, and provides the course for an international hillclimb. Romain Dumas didn't stop to take photos when he broke the hill record in 2018. What was his average speed?
a) 62.3mph
b) 78.7mph
c) 90.5mph

NATIONAL PARKS

There is simply nothing to match the stunning variety of natural landscapes that can be found in the United States and the U.S. National Parks Service showcase them at their very best. We have compiled 20 of the most visited parks across the country, split into two sets. Try and match the national park to their host state(s).

1. Great Smoky Mountains National Park
2. Grand Canyon National Park
3. Zion National Park
4. Yellowstone National Park
5. Rocky Mountain National Park
6. Acadia National Park
7. Grand Teton National Park
8. Joshua Tree National Park
9. Olympic National Park
10. Glacier National Park

California
Colorado
Maine
Washington
Utah
Montana
Tennessee & North Carolina
Wyoming
Arizona
Wyoming, Montana & Idaho

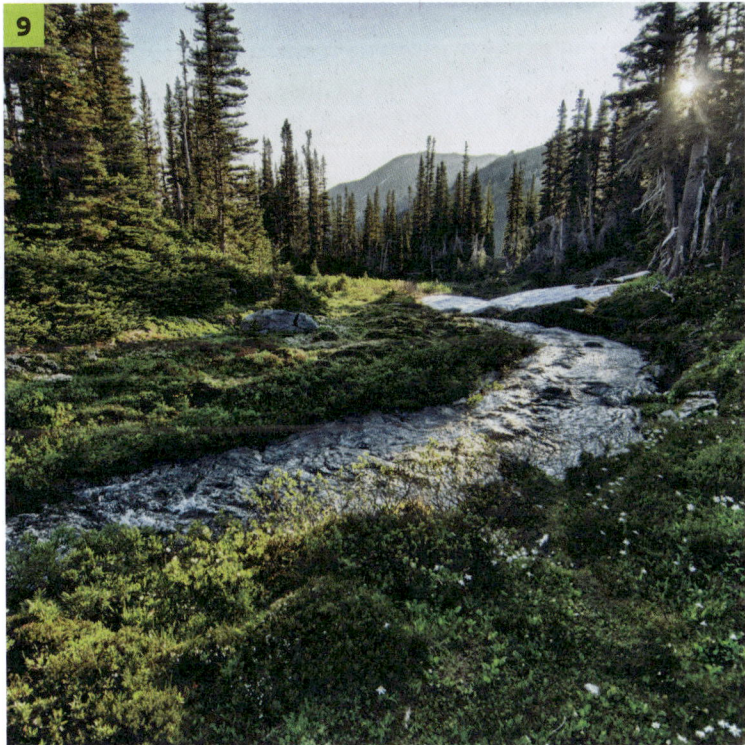

11. Cuyahoga Valley National Park
12. Hot Springs National Park
13. Gateway Arch National Park
14. New River Gorge National Park
15. Shenandoah National Park
16. Death Valley National Park
17. Badlands National Park
18. Gates of the Arctic National Park
19. Crater Lake National Park
20. Carlsbad Caverns National Park

Virginia
Oregon
Ohio
Arkansas
South Dakota
Alaska
New Mexico
California & Nevada
Missouri
West Virginia

HOTELS, MOTELS, HOLIDAY INNS...

A round focused on accommodation through the nation – with questions on hotels and motels to suit every pocket – from Motel 6 to the Waldorf Astoria.

1. William and Mary Menger opened the Menger hotel in 1859 close to The Alamo in San Antonio, Texas. Over the years it has welcomed countless U.S. presidents including Ulysses S. Grant, Theodore Roosevelt, Woodrow Wilson, William H. Taft, Harry S. Truman, Richard Nixon, Ronald Reagan, Lyndon B. Johnson, George H.W. Bush, and Bill Clinton. One of its famous literary guests was *not* critical of his hotel room's wallpaper. Who was it?
a) Dylan Thomas
b) Charles Dickens
c) Oscar Wilde

2. The Peabody Hotel in Memphis has a unique animal feature, especially for a historic luxury hotel. Guests come from far and wide to see...?
a) The Peabody Ducks
b) The Peabody Hogs
c) The Peabody Cats

3. Close to Pershing Square in downtown Los Angeles, the Biltmore Hotel takes its place in the history of the Oscars. The Academy of Motion Picture Arts and Sciences was founded at a lunch meeting there in May 1927, when industry moguls such as Louis B. Mayer met to propose the annual awards. What did MGM art director Cedric Gibbons supposedly draw on a Biltmore napkin?

4. The Beverly Wilshire Hotel in Hollywood was the long-time residence of Elvis Presley and Warren Beatty and which member of the Beatles?
a) Ringo Starr
b) George Harrison
c) John Lennon

5. Another long-time residence for a more downbeat creative clientele was the Chelsea Hotel in New York. Arthur C. Clarke wrote *2001: A Space Odyssey* while staying at the Chelsea, it was also home to the beat poets including William S. Burroughs, Welsh poet Dylan Thomas, and singer Joni Mitchell who wrote *Chelsea Morning* about her time at the Chelsea Hotel. Another Canadian

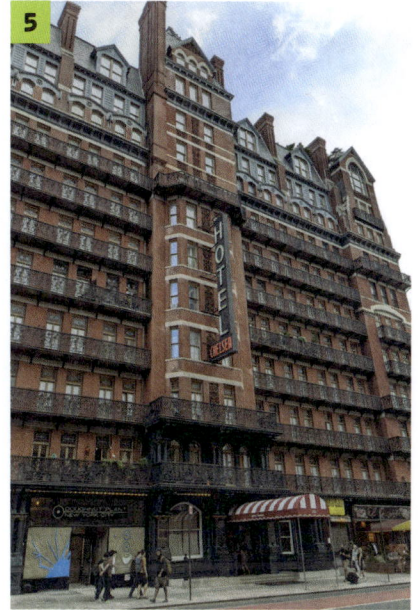

poet and singer, Leonard Cohen, wrote *Chelsea Hotel #2* about which 1960s star?
a) Joan Baez
b) Melanie
c) Janis Joplin

6. The Algonquin Hotel at 59 West 44th Street in Midtown Manhattan is famous for hosting literary and theatrical set the Algonquin Round Table club, known for their scathing wit and critical barbs. Which was its most famous female member?
a) Tallulah Bankhead
b) Blyth Daly
c) Dorothy Parker

7. The imposing Mount Washington Hotel in Bretton Woods, New Hampshire, was the location for a 1944 meeting that set up which important global institution?
a) UNESCO
b) The International Monetary Fund (IMF)
c) The World Wildlife Fund (WWF)

8. In the 1860s, which author wrote that the Willard Hotel in Washington, D.C., 'more justly could be called the center of Washington than either the Capitol or the White House or the State Department.'
a) Nathaniel Hawthorne
b) Mark Twain
c) Walt Whitman

9. Former U.S. president Dwight D. Eisenhower maintained a residence at which upmarket New York hotel until his death in 1969?
a) The Plaza
b) The Sherry-Netherland
c) The Waldorf Astoria

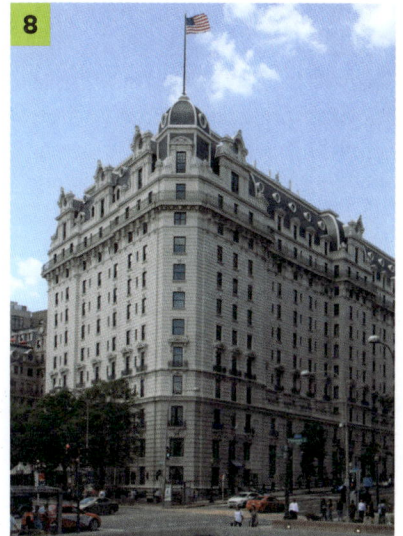

10. The Historic Hotels of America is a group set up to identify U.S. hotels that have maintained an authentic feel and architectural integrity. To be included in the program, a hotel must be designated as a National Historic Landmark or eligible as having historic significance. So, very few in Vegas. How many in the group?
a) 178
b) 288

11. A charter member of Historic Hotels of America, the Mayflower Hotel or 'The Grand Dame' of Washington has a tradition of hosting presidential balls. Which president stayed there while the White House was being redecorated?
a) Franklin D. Roosevelt
b) Harry S. Truman
c) Dwight D. Eisenhower

12. Universal Studios Orlando created a replica of the Bates Motel from the Alfred Hitchcock horror movie, *Psycho* in 1988 (in 2005 the site was replaced with 'A Day in the Park with Barney'). A replica of the Bates Motel can still be found in Winnemucca, Nevada. Built by Joe Robinett in 2010 to celebrate the film's 50th anniversary, its façade painstakingly copies the original. Guests can choose to stay in one of the lodges or up on the hill ... in 'Ma's room'. True or False?

13. The Stanley Hotel is a large Colonial Revival hotel in Estes Park, in the mountains of Colorado, that dates to 1909. It was the hotel that inspired one of the greatest horror/thriller movies. Which one?
a) *Friday 13th*
b) *The Shining*
c) *Misery*

14. Billy Wilder co-wrote and directed one of the great screen comedies, *Some Like it Hot*, as two jazz musicians (Jack Lemon and Tony Curtis) go under cover as female musicians with 'Sweet Sue and her Society Syncopators', an all-female band headed by train to Miami. Which hotel provided the backdrop to the memorable beach scenes?
a) The Don CeSar Hotel, St. Pete Beach, Florida
b) The National Hotel, Miami Beach, Florida

c) Hotel del Coronado, San Diego, California

15. The Bellagio resort hotel on the Las Vegas Strip is famous for its fountain shows (providing Lake Mead has enough water). Which hotel-casino did it replace?
a) The Dunes
b) The Sands
c) The Sahara

16. The largest hotel complex in America – and in terms of room numbers, the second largest in

the world – is also present on the Las Vegas Strip. It has an astonishing 7,115 rooms. Which is the resort?
a) Fontainebleau, Las Vegas
b) The Venetian
c) Wynn & Encore

17. The mega-resort casinos in Las Vegas share the guests out between different buildings – so which hotel has the biggest capacity in just one building, a total of 5,124 rooms?
a) MGM Grand
b) Caesars Palace
c) Mandalay Bay

18. The Wyndham Hotel Group is the largest in the USA. It has amassed a number of hotel chains over the years. Which of the following is not a 'by Wyndham' hotel or motel?
a) Days Inn
b) La Quinta
c) Ramada
d) Super 8
e) DoubleTree

19. The Days Inn chain was founded in 1970 by Cecil B. Day. Where was the first one located?
a) Tybee Island, Georgia
b) Kissimmee, Florida
c) Hershey, Pennsylvania

20. One of the Eagles' greatest hits was the single and album *Hotel California*. The hotel in question appears on the cover. What is the hotel?
a) The Hollywood Roosevelt
b) The Beverly Hills Hotel
c) Chateau Marmont

ARCHITECTURE

AMERICAN ARCHITECTS

With the huge wealth created by the American economy in the 19th and 20th centuries, architects had the budget to create some epic buildings. This round explores the most influential American architects who have helped reshape the skyline and created some iconic buildings along the way.

1. The man who designed the U.S. Capitol was a real polymath – an American physician, inventor, painter and architect. He also served as the first Superintendent of the United States Patent Office. Who was it?
a) Thomas Jefferson
b) Benjamin Franklin
c) William Thornton

2. Frederick Law Olmsted was a prolific landscape architect who designed Prospect Park in Brooklyn, the main park ground for the 1893 World's Columbian Exposition in Chicago and the grounds of the Capitol Extension in Washington, D.C. But what is he most famous for?

3. Daniel Burnham designed many regular buildings in his career, but he is often best remembered for which New York structure?
a) The Woolworth Tower
b) The Roosevelt Island tramway
c) The Flatiron Building

4. Built from 1884 to 1885, the ten-story Home Insurance Building in Chicago is considered the first skyscraper. The building was the first fully steel-framed structure and literally changed the landscape of cities, particularly Chicago. Who designed this pioneer of multi-story?
a) William LeBaron Jenney
b) Dankmar Adler

5. Despite not having designed the Home Insurance Building, another Chicago-based architect, Louis Sullivan, would pick up the unofficial title 'Father of the Skyscraper'. What is Sullivan's most celebrated building?
a) Carson Pirie Scott store
b) The Field Museum
c) Marshall Field store

6. The aesthetically more eccentric Frank Lloyd Wright worked for Sullivan before starting out on his own. He designed the innovative Fallingwater (page 98) and at the end of his career the Guggenheim Museum in New York. Hilla von Rebay was the director of the Guggenheim's collection of avant-garde art and wanted a building that reflected an unconventional museum approach. However, Wright almost didn't get the commission. What was the reason?
a) He was far too expensive
b) He wanted the site to be in California where he could supervise it
c) Rebay thought the 76-year-old Wright was dead

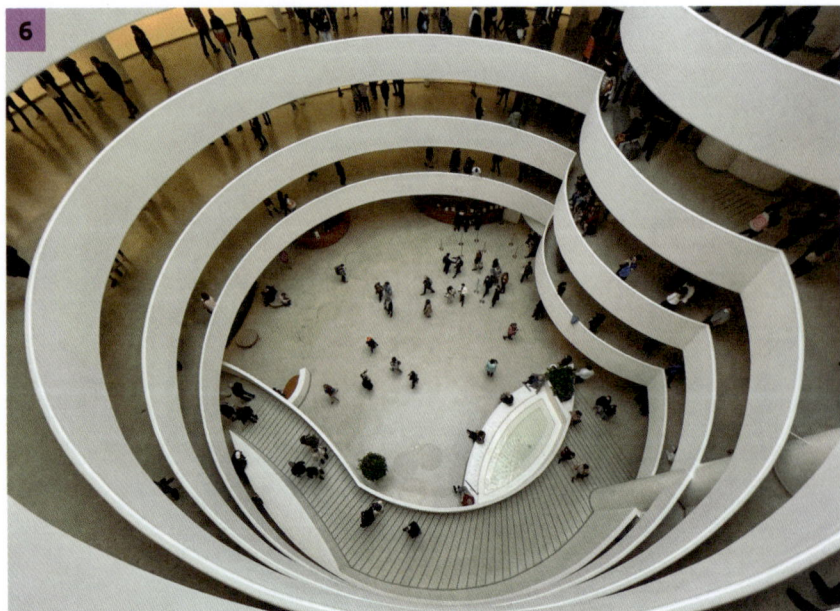

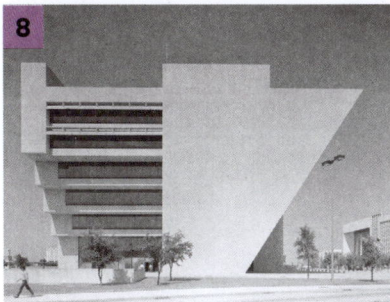

9. When Lillian Disney commissioned Frank Gehry to design the breathtaking Walt Disney Concert Hall in Los Angeles it was not going to be a dazzling metal structure. But Gehry claimed that after the commissioning team saw the Guggenheim Museum in Bilbao which he had designed, 'they had to have metal'. What was the architect's original choice for the façade?
a) Stone
b) Ceramic tiles
c) Glass

10. Designed by Adrian Smith and Gordon Gill Architecture, Central Park Tower is a gravity-defying skyscraper at 225 West 57th Street, along Billionaires' Row, in Midtown Manhattan. It rises 1,550 feet which equates to 98 stories. How does it compare to the Empire State Building?
a) 100 feet taller than the Empire State spire
b) 100 feet taller than the Empire State observation deck
c) 100 feet lower than the Empire State observation deck

7. Eero Saarinen designed the mighty Gateway Arch in St. Louis and also the TWA Terminal at JFK Airport (now a hotel). The photo shows another of his airport terminal designs – which one?
a) Dallas Fort Worth
b) Dulles, Washington, D.C.
c) Seattle-Tacoma

8. The 1963 assassination of President John F. Kennedy was very bad news for the city of

Dallas which became known as the 'City of Hate'. Dallas Mayor Erik Jonsson wanted to reinvent the city's image, and a long overdue new city hall was commissioned as part of the plan. Which well-known architect designed it?
a) I.M. Pei
b) Eero Saarinen
c) Buckminster Fuller

AMERICAN HOUSES

Building styles of American homes became more and more elaborate as the centuries passed culminating in the opulence (for some) in the Gilded Age. See how much you know about the evolution of house building.

1. An example of early Native American house building can be found in Grand Canyon Village on the South Rim. Today it houses a gift shop. Which Indigenous group is this building style particularly associated with?
a) Paiute
b) Hopi
c) Navajo Nation

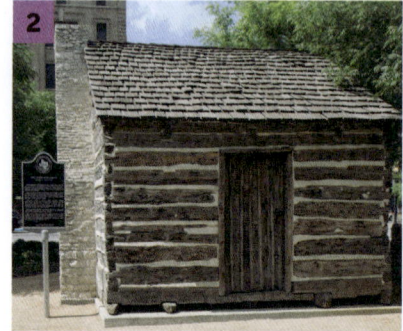

2. The John Neely Bryan Cabin is a one-room replica of the home of this city's founder. It's typical of a log cabin frontier house. In which city will you find it?
a) Houston
b) Dallas
c) Austin

3. The single most important building material in Spanish Colonial America can be found on ancient buildings across Texas, New Mexico, Arizona and California. What is it called? As a clue, it's the same name as the leading graphic arts software company.

4. Colonial houses and colonial-building style reflected the building skills of the incoming English colonists and the materials they had to hand when they arrived in the 17th century. They are simple, symmetrical, at least two stories tall with a steeply pitched roof. Some had an extended rear section with the roof sloping down to one story at the back, named after a kitchen item. What were they called?
a) Tea chest houses
b) Salt box houses
c) Cheese wedge houses

5. As settlers pushed west in the early- to mid-19th century, land was made available by various government initiatives, including the Homesteaders' Act of 1862. But in the treeless prairie there was little that could be used to build a house other than sods. These 'sod houses' were almost all single story and not built to last. This picture shows a sod house from which state?
a) Nebraska
b) Wyoming

7. What's the general term for this kind of Victorian townhouse or apartment block seen in many east coast American cities?

8. The Prairie School is a late-19th- and early-20th-century architectural style often attributed to Frank Lloyd Wright, typified by horizontal lines, hipped roofs with broad overhanging eaves and windows grouped in horizontal bands. It was an attempt to integrate design ideas from the Arts and Crafts Movement into a North American style. The best-known example is the Robie House. Where would you find it?
a) Chicago
b) Westchester
c) Kansas City

9. Houses with timber beams on their fascia and plaster in between are known as...
a) Old Englishe
b) Queen Anne
c) Tudor Revival

10. This building style is often associated with the South. It is characterized by grand, symmetrical designs, classical architectural elements such as large columns supporting a portico. What is it known as?
a) Plantation style
b) Antebellum style
c) Richardson Romanesque style

6. Savannah in Georgia is one of the best architecturally preserved cities in no small part thanks to some feisty Savannah ladies who stepped in to preserve buildings in the 1950s. One of their first saves was this Federal-style home, built by master carpenter Isaiah Davenport for his household, Davenport House. When was it built?
a) 1765
b) 1820
c) 1872

11. Today roof shingles are mostly made of asphalt. What is the most common wood used in wooden shingles?
a) Cedar
b) Oak
c) Walnut

12. Where does the word 'bungalow' originate?
a) A Native American word meaning a single story Pueblo house
b) The Hindi word 'bangla,' meaning a house in the Bengali style

THE BRIDGE

America has built many fine bridges to span its bays and rivers. Try and answer a variety of questions about some of the nation's better known engineering feats.

1. The Ann W. Richards Congress Avenue Bridge in downtown _____ is home to the world's largest urban bat colony. The bats are Mexican free-tailed bats that migrate to _____ from Mexico each spring. What's the missing city name?

2. The William Preston Lane Jr. Memorial Bridge is the official name for this bridge which also incorporates a tunnel section to get across a wide stretch of bay. When it was opened in 1952, with a length of 4 miles it was the world's longest continuous over-water steel structure. What is it commonly known as?
a) Chesapeake Bay Bridge
b) Delaware Bay Bridge
c) Massachusetts Bay Bridge

3. The cargo ship _Dali_ infamously collided with the Francis Scott Key Bridge in Baltimore in 2024 blocking cargo traffic. The writer of _The Star-Spangled Banner_, Key has another bridge named in his honor in Georgetown. Why is this one more personal?
a) He wrote the verses on the banks of the Potomac where it now crosses
b) His historic home was demolished to make way for an approach road

4. When the Brooklyn Bridge opened in 1883 many wary Manhattan and Brooklyn residents thought that it might not hold. Indeed, in a panic on a stairway 12 people were crushed to death and many injured. On the anniversary of its opening, circus owner P.T. Barnum suggested marching 21 elephants and 17 camels across to help restore public confidence. True or False?

5. Despite the wide entrance to San Francisco Harbor, the U.S. Navy were concerned that with the area prone to fog, the new Golden Gate Bridge should be painted what color to help the Navy avoid collisions?
a) Black and yellow stripes
b) Black and white stripes
c) Flashing neon strip lights on bridge piers

6. When it opened in 1953, the Eugene Talmadge bridge in Savannah was viewed as a godsend for those traveling between Georgia and South Carolina. By the mid-1980s a new generation of large container ships were struggling to pass under it to reach Savannah's busy container port. A new, taller bridge duly opened in 1990, but already there's a problem. What is it?

a) The ground around the bridge piers has been eroded by floods
b) The two halves are separating
c) It's still not high enough and some ships need to remove aerials

7. Where would you find the Seven Mile Bridge?
a) The Aleutian Islands archipelago
b) The Kodiak Islands archipelago
c) The Florida Keys

8. There are two main footbridges that cross the Colorado River in the Grand Canyon National Park. The Black Suspension Bridge is part of the South Kaibab Trail. It was built in the 1920s for both mules and hikers. The second connects the Bright Angel Trail from the South Rim to Phantom Ranch and the North Rim. What is that one called?
a) The White Bridge
b) The Silver Bridge
c) The Bright Angel Bridge

9. Which is the most expensive bridge built in America at $6.4 billion?
a) Verrazzano-Narrows Bridge in New York
b) Sunshine Skyway Bridge in Florida
c) Eastern Replacement Span, Oakland Bay Bridge, California

10. What is the name of the first bridge across the Mississippi south of the Missouri River, opened in 1874?
a) The Samuel Clemens Bridge
b) The Chain of Rocks Bridge
c) The Eads Bridge

A BRIDGE OVER...

Listed below is a collection of some of America's most celebrated bridges. Your task is to match the 12 stretches of water that lie underneath each bridge. For this reason we haven't included the Bixby Creek Bridge (CA) on the Pacific Coast Highway or – the Lake Pontchartrain Causeway (LA) on Lake Pontchartrain, where the answer lies in the question...

1. George Washington Bridge (NY)	**Delaware River**
2. Manhattan Bridge (NY)	**Charles River**
3. Tacoma Narrows Bridge (WA)	**Willamette River**
4. Arthur Ravenel Jr. Bridge (SC)	**Snake River**
5. Rainbow Bridge (NY)	**Lake Havasu**
6. Glen Canyon Bridge (AZ)	**Ohio River**
7. Longfellow Bridge (MA)	**East River**
8. Fremont Bridge (OR)	**Puget Sound**
9. Benjamin Franklin Bridge (PA/NJ)	**Cooper River**
10. Perrine Bridge (ID)	**Niagara River**
11. London Bridge (AZ)	**Hudson River**
12. John A. Roebling Suspension Bridge (KY/OH)	**Colorado River**

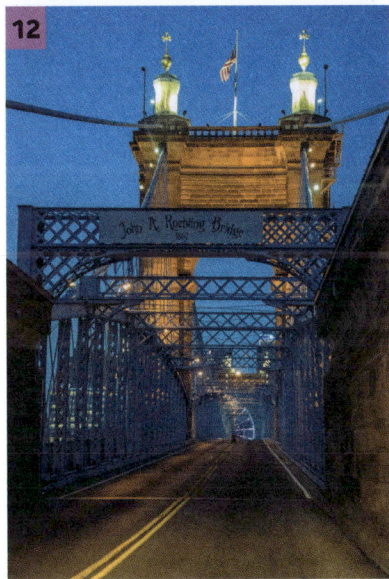

GREAT LOST BUILDINGS

Many great old buildings were lost before their time, the original Palmer House Hotel in Chicago was lost to the 1871 fire only a year after opening. However these particular questions relate to buildings that were razed on purpose, when the preservationists failed to stop the wrecking ball.

1. Penn Station was a Beaux-Arts masterpiece by McKim, Mead & White. It occupied a way-too-valuable 8-acre plot bounded by Seventh and Eighth in Midtown Manhattan. With falling ridership developers saw an opportunity to move the remaining train services underground and build something far more profitable on top. *The New York Times* described it as a 'monumental act of vandalism against one of the largest and finest landmarks of its age of Roman elegance.' What replaced it?
a) Macy's Backstage
b) Midtown Holiday Inn
c) Madison Square Garden

2. Built for the sewing machine company, the 41-story Singer Building had a marble-clad entrance lobby with 16 elevators when it was completed in 1908. It took its place briefly as the world's tallest building. When it was demolished in 1969 it held the record for the tallest building to be razed by its owners, a record it held until what year?
a) 1996
b) 2021

3. The Chicago Federal Building in Chicago, Illinois, was constructed between 1898 and 1905 for the purpose of housing the Midwest's federal courts. Al Capone was tried here for tax evasion. His case was heard in the courtroom of Judge Wilkerson who, fearing that the jury had been bribed by Capone, switched the panel of jurors at the last moment. Capone was found guilty, sentenced to ten years and his crime empire ended. When did the building meet its end?
a) 1957
b) 1965
c) 1974

4. The Metropolitan Opera Company was founded in 1883. Nicknamed 'The Yellow Brick Brewery' for its industrial looking exterior, it was so short of backstage space that scenery and sets were a regular sight propped up against the side of the building on 39th Street. Despite pleas from conductor Leopold Stokowski and many others, the Met management opposed the preservation of its historic opera house. Its new home, the Lincoln Center, was built on the site two years after its demolition. True or False?

5. The Chicago Stock Exchange 1894-1972 was a Chicago School of Architecture masterpiece built in a town not known for its architectural sentiment. Richard Nickel was a photographer who dedicated himself to recording the fast-vanishing work of Dankmar Adler and Louis Sullivan, often removing architectural elements from their buildings that were being destroyed. What happened to him at the Chicago Stock Exchange?
a) He was arrested and imprisoned for theft by the site owners
b) He was killed when part of the building collapsed around him

THE WALDORF ASTORIA NEW YORK

6. The Richfield Tower in Los Angeles was an Art Deco oil company HQ which featured a black and gold façade. The color scheme was intended to symbolize the fact that their business was drilling for 'black gold'. The 12-story building was topped with a 130-foot tower emblazoned vertically with the name 'Richfield'. Lighting on the tower was made to simulate what?
a) A drill bit heading into the 12th floor
b) An oil well gusher

7. The original Waldorf-Astoria originated as two hotels, built side by side by feuding relatives, on Fifth Avenue in New York. The Waldorf went up first as an act of spite by William Waldorf. After his father's death, he built the 13-story to overwhelm the next-door home of his despised Aunt Caroline. Her son, John Jacob Astor IV at first planned to demolish his mother's house and build a stables to stink out

his cousin's fancy hotel. But as their fortunes were tied together he relented and built the even larger Astoria next door, with a connection between the two. The hotel declined during Prohibition and was demolished in 1929. What replaced it?
a) The Rockefeller Center
b) The Empire State Building

8. The Marlborough-Blenheim Hotel was a jewel in Atlantic City's upscale crown. Built at the turn of the century it was constructed of reinforced concrete thanks to a national steel strike, thus making it the largest reinforced concrete building in the world. Atlantic City lost its appeal over the years and the hotel, which once hosted Winston Churchill, declined. It was ultimately bought, demolished and replaced by a casino from which gambling group?
a) Caesars Palace
b) Golden Nugget
c) Ballys

9. There had been a Savannah City Market in Ellis Square since colonial times. Resembling the great market 'halles' of Paris it was a popular meeting place. The market disappeared in 1954 after the city gave permission for the building to be razed and replaced by a parking structure with a 50-year lease. What happened in 2005?
a) The parking garage was demolished to make way for a green space with sculptures and fountains
b) It was transformed into *The Forrest Gump Experience* after much of the film was shot in the city

10. This grand New York building was designed by Stanford White, the philandering architect who was shot dead by his lover's husband. It shows buildings that were demolished in 1925. What was the building?
a) Madison Square Garden
b) The Moravia Hotel
c) Chickering Hall

THE MARKET, SAVANNAH, GA.

THE OLD COLLEGE TEST

Test how much you know about some of the of the top places of learning in the United States, some of which date back almost 400 years. Give our old college test an old college try.

1. Harvard University is the oldest institution of higher learning in the United States, and Massachusetts Hall is the oldest surviving building at Harvard College. Built between 1718 and 1720 it was designed to accommodate 64 students. In the Revolutionary War how many American soldiers did it quarter?
a) 178
b) 490
c) 640

2. Rice University was opened in Houston in 1912 on a 300-acre campus. It was the legacy of Massachusetts businessman William Marsh Rice who made provision in his will that on his death, his fortune would be used to create the Rice Institute. What event almost derailed this plan?
a) His will was forged in favor of his solicitor
b) He was told 'Rice' would make it look like an agricultural college
c) His will was lost in a city fire and the state claimed the money

3. This photo shows University Hall, overlooked by Mount Sentinel, taken from close to a 7-foot, 5,000-pound, bronze statue of a grizzly bear. Which university is it?
a) Wyoming
b) Montana
c) Nebraska

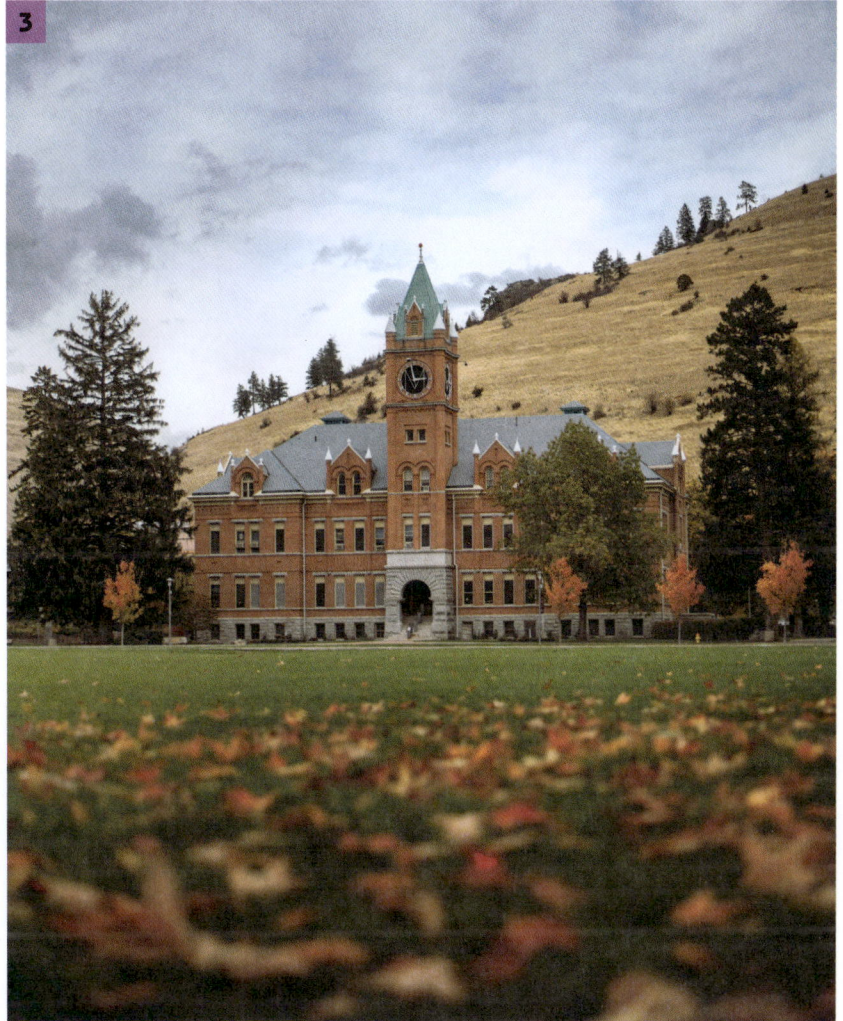

4. The city of Syracuse, in upstate New York, was hoping to bring a university to the city. Ezra Cornell and Andrew Dickson White were looking for a college location. White was a Syracuse resident who knew the advantage of the city's transportation links. However, Cornell had twice been robbed of his wages working as a carpenter in Syracuse, hated the place and argued for his large farm on East Hill, Ithaca, as the site. Cornell won the argument, though Syracuse would get its own university in time. But which one is this?
a) Syracuse
b) Cornell

5. Rutgers University was chartered in 1766 and was originally called Queen's College, affiliated to the Dutch Reformed Church. It is the eighth-oldest college in the United States but has to play second fiddle to its neighbor Princeton. It was re-named Rutgers after donor Henry Rutgers saved the institution from financial ruin and his

donation helped complete this, the oldest building on campus in 1825. What is it called?
a) Old Rutgers
b) Old Queens
c) Old Main

6. Mathey College is one of seven residential colleges at Princeton University. The buildings have been designed in the Collegiate Gothic style, echoing such ancient institutions as Oxford and Cambridge University. When was it built?
a) 1797
b) 1897
c) 1937

7. The College of William & Mary in Williamsburg, Virginia, was one of the original nine colonial colleges. Jefferson attended and George Washington received his surveyor's license from the college in 1749. It has the oldest college building in the States in the Wren Building, built between 1695 and 1700. Who or what was it named after?
a) Sir Christopher Wren
b) Williamsburg Royal Enterprises aka W.R.EN.

8. Columbia University was established as Kings College, a colonial college under royal charter from George II. In 1784 it was renamed Columbia College and in 1787 placed under a private board of trustees headed up by two prominent former students. Who were they?
a) Alexander Hamilton and Aaron Burr
b) Alexander Hamilton and John Jay
c) Aaron Burr and John Jay

9. Sather Tower on the UCLA campus at Berkeley is more commonly known as 'The Campanile' for its resemblance to the Campanile di San Marco in which Italian city?
a) Florence
b) Naples
c) Venice
d) Milan

10. Since 2021 Texas A&M at College Station has enrolled the largest student body in the United States. What does the A&M stand for?
a) Anatomy and Medicine
b) Architecture and Mathematics
c) Agricultural and Mechanical

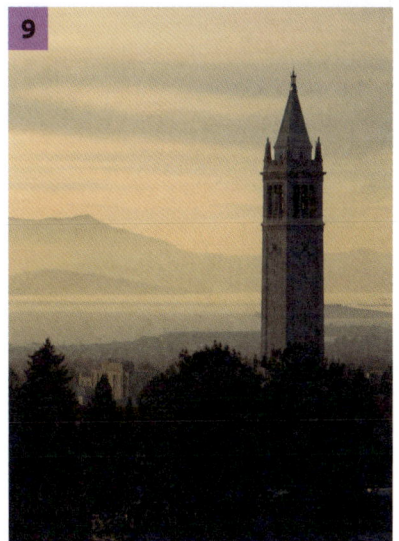

SPORTS STADIUMS

America loves its sports – and over time the arenas where they are played have grown larger and more luxurious (with maybe the exception of Wrigleyville). Try telling a baseball fan from the 1920s that one day you could watch a game from a centerfield swimming pool and they would not believe you. Try answering these questions about the stadia in the three major sports.

1. Which ballpark did writer John Updike describe as: 'a lyric little bandbox of a ballpark. Everything is painted green and seems in curiously sharp focus, like the inside of an old-fashioned peeping-type Easter egg.'
a) Baseball Hall of Fame Field at Cooperstown
b) Fuller Field, Clinton
c) Fenway Park, Boston

2. The state-of-the art SoFi stadium in Los Angeles hosts the Rams and the Chargers, and will also be hosting soccer games in the World Cup as well as the 2028 Olympics. It was built with private capital but a much-quoted figure for its final cost is $6.8 billion. What was the initial cost estimate?
a) $2 billion
b) $3.2 billion

3. When it was opened in 1965 it was known as the Harris County Domed Stadium, which we know better as the Houston Astrodome. Although it has struggled to see sporting action for many years, the sports arena which was once billed as the Eighth Wonder of the World has left a lasting legacy for baseball and football – what?

4. The relatively new (and expensive) Yankee Stadium that opened in 2009, replaced the 'House That Ruth Built'. It had all the elements of a retro ballpark – except with modern seating and perfect sightlines. But was home plate on the same site as the one used by the old Bronx Bombers?
a) Yes
b) No

5. Which is the largest capacity basketball arena in the U.S.?
a) The United Center in Chicago
b) The Chase Center in San Francisco
c) The Barclays Center in Brooklyn

6. In a throwback to baseball of yesteryear, fans of the Chicago Cubs can still watch their team 'live' without walking into Wrigley Field. There are bleachers across the street outside jointly organized as Wrigley Rooftops. Seats on Waveland Avenue overlook left field while those along Sheffield Avenue have a view over right field. How many different properties are there to watch from?
a) 5
b) 7
c) 11

7. Which baseball stadium has a 'touching' experience with an aquarium tank of local fish?
a) Miami Marlins
b) Seattle Mariners
c) Tampa Bay Rays

8. Which old stadium has continually hosted NFL games the longest?
a) Lambeau Field
b) Soldier Field

9. From the 1960s, baseball games were often played in 'cookie cutter' stadiums with no atmosphere (such as RFK Stadium). That all changed in 1992. Which ballpark has been widely hailed as one of the best stadiums in baseball and credited with starting a wave of modern throwback ballparks?
a) Oriole Park at Camden Yards, Baltimore
b) Great American Ballpark, Cincinnati
c) PNC Park, Pittsburgh

10. Which was the first MLB stadium to have a retractable roof?
a) Chase Field (formerly Bank One Ballpark), Phoenix, Arizona
b) Minute Maid Park, Houston, Texas
c) American Family Field (formerly Miller Park), Milwaukee, Wisconsin

STATION TO STATION

The coming of the railroads to America unlocked the vast economic potential of the nation, while making fortunes for the railroad barons. Along the way, they constructed some grand depots and stations for the paying public – cathedrals of transportation. Try these ten questions about rail travel past and present to see if you're on the right track...

1. The Atchinson, Topeka & Santa Fe Railroad was criticized by preservationists when they razed a beloved, old Fred Harvey hotel attached to Albuquerque's station in 1970. A replica building has since been erected on the site – what was the name of the hotel?
a) Alvarado Hotel
b) Silverado Hotel

2. America has some magnificent station concourses that were built in the age when railroad travel was the only game in town. This is the main hall for which union station?
a) Denver
b) Chicago
c) Milwaukee

3. The Art Deco Cincinnati Union Terminal was one of the last union terminals built, only being completed in 1933. Train services were withdrawn in 1972, and the massive terminal building was largely dormant from 1972 to 1980. However Amtrak returned with an intercity train station service in 1991. Today, the occasional transit role is shared

with which major occupant of the space?
a) Land of Oz Shopping Mall
b) Cincinnati Museum Center
c) Les Nessman Laser Quest

4. Washington Union Station was designed by architect Daniel Burnham who was tasked with constructing a station 'monumental in character'. It opened in 1907 and at the height of its ridership in World War II, 200,000 passengers passed through its doors each day. One of the two major railroads that came together to operate from the station was Pennsylvania Railroad and the other was...?
a) Baltimore and Ohio Railroad
b) Atchinson, Topeka & Santa Fe
c) North Carolina and Virginia Railroad

5. The imposing Beaux-Arts Michigan Central Station was the tallest in the world at the time of its construction. It was open for business between 1914 until 1988 when Amtrak relocated services elsewhere. It fell into dereliction and became an embarrassment to the city, playing a part in the 'Decaying Detroit' narrative as the auto industry left town. Thankfully it has been rescued by a major corporation. Who has stumped up the cash?
a) Amtrak Freight
b) Ford
c) Verizon

6. Even without the train and subway passengers included, Grand Central Terminal on 42nd Street in Manhattan is one of the world's top ten tourist attractions. How many are estimated to stroll across what is almost certainly the world's most famous station concourse each year?
a) 11.8 million
b) 21.6 million
c) 39.7 million

7. Like many grand railroad terminals, Kansas City's Union Station hosts many different businesses to pay its way. What annual sporting event took place partly inside and partly outside in 2023?
a) NBA Draft
b) MLB Draft
c) NFL Draft

8. Unlike Kansas, the Los Angeles Union Station is a busy place serving almost 110,000 passengers a day. Given the population of L.A. it's no surprise that it's the busiest train station in the Western United States and the thirteenth-busiest in North America. It is also the destination of the oldest named train service in the United States. The Sunset Limited started off in 1894 run by Southern Pacific and continues with Amtrak. It starts off where…?
a) Chicago
b) New Orleans
c) New York

9. Designed by the company that succeeded Daniel Burnham's architectural practice and opened in 1933, the Pennsylvania Station at 30th Street had a number of innovative features including a reinforced roof with space for small aircraft to land. True or False?

10. Regular wrecking ball wielders, the Atchinson, Topeka & Santa Fe Railroad proposed to demolish the Santa Fe Depot in 1972 and replace it with two 12-story buildings. Mindful of what happened in Albuquerque, the San Diego heritage societies mobilized and prevented them. The station still hosts the 60-year-old train service from Los Angeles to San Diego. It was originally known as The San Diegan but has been renamed as what?
a) Pacific Surfliner
b) Golden State Express
c) California Dreamliner

HIGHER AND HIGHER

America has contributed some inspirational buildings to the portfolio of world architecture. The Chicago School helped establish the skyscraper as the nation's premier form of expression and – judging by the towers along Billionaires' Row overlooking Central Park – they're just getting bigger and bigger. Try answering these questions on some towering structures...

1. The Capitol building in Washington D.C. has acted as an architectural blueprint for many smaller state capitols around the country. The Colorado State Capitol in Denver is a perfect example, and in Austin, the Texas State Capitol's dome is actually taller than the U.S. Capitol and made of Texas pink granite. Which one of the following states/locations does not have a capitol similar to Washington, D.C.?
a) Kentucky
b) Idaho
c) Missouri
d) Havana
e) Massachusetts

2. The Chrysler Building is an Art Deco masterpiece on the East Side of Manhattan. It was completed in 1930, just after the Wall Street Crash, at the intersection of 42nd Street and Lexington Avenue. At 1,046 feet it was the world's tallest building for 11 months. It has now slipped to 12th in New York. Which building took its title?
a) The Empire State Building
b) 40 Wall Street
c) The Rockefeller Center

3. The unmistakeable outline of Los Angeles City Hall is an item of civic pride. Completed in 1928, it adorns LAPD badges. The peak of the pyramid at the top of the building is an airplane beacon named in honor of which former aviation pioneer.
a) Howard Hughes
b) Charles Lindbergh
c) Wiley Post

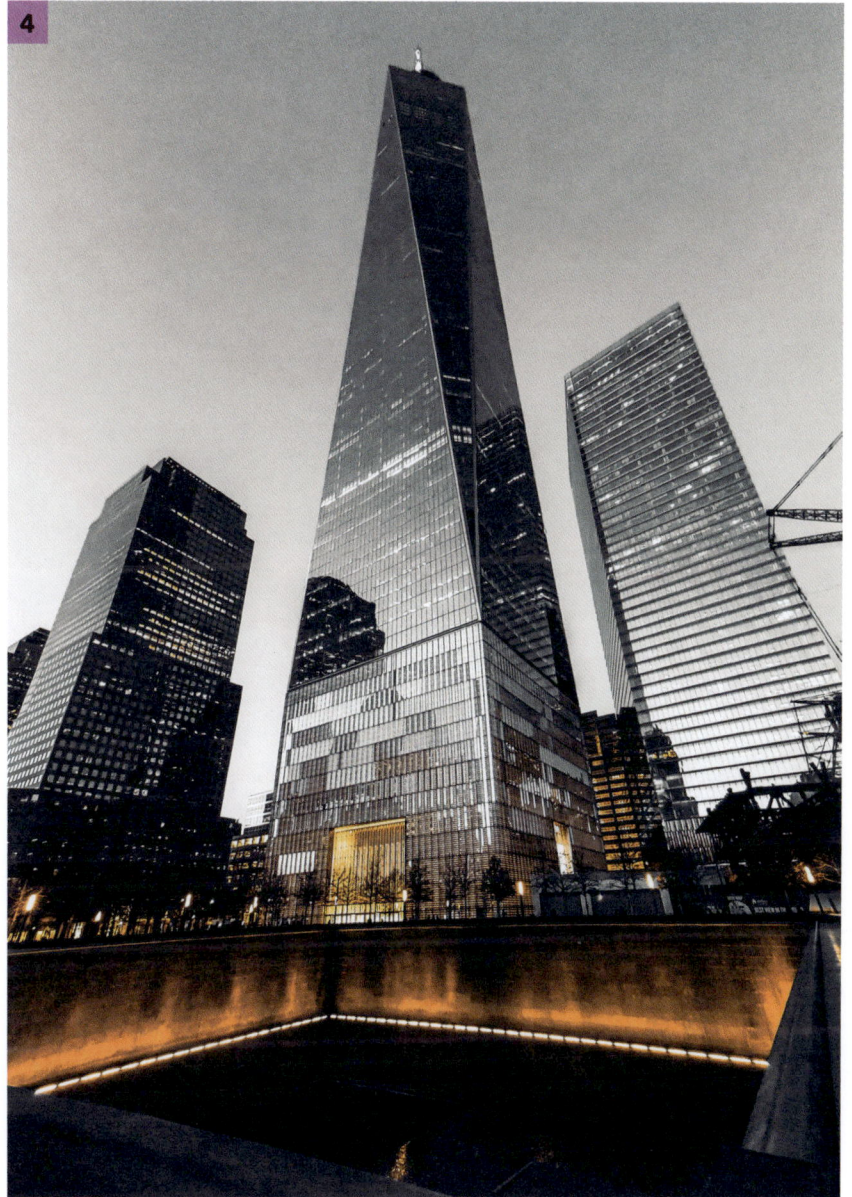

4. One World Trade Center, also known as One WTC, has the same name as the North Tower of the original World Trade Center. It gained its official name from the New York and New Jersey Port Authority in 2009. What had it been known as before?
a) Liberty Tower
b) Freedom Tower

5. The Transamerica Pyramid is a distinctive, pyramid-shaped, modernist skyscraper in San Francisco's financial district. When was it completed?
a) 1972
b) 1982
c) 1992

6. The 1960s heralded some dismal functional buildings, but this twin-tower complex in Chicago, which opened between 1963 and 1967, was a hit with the public. It had 65-story apartment towers, a 10-story office building (now a hotel) and an auditorium used as a cinema. Beneath the platform, at river level, there was a small marina. Its nickname is the corn cobs, what is the official name?

a) One Chicago River
b) Twin Peaks
c) Marina City

7. The 102-story Empire State Building gets its name from the state of New York, known as the 'Empire State'. It enjoyed a long run as the world's tallest building from 1931 until the first of the Twin Towers was topped off in 1970. Times have moved on – where does it stand in the pecking order of New York's tallest buildings today?

a) 3rd
b) 5th
c) 7th

8. The Space Needle in Seattle was built for the 1962 World Fair. All large buildings have a sway factor built in. The Space Needle was built to withstand Category 5-plus wind speeds, double the requirements in the building code of 1962. Thus the Space Needle can withstand wind speeds of … what?

a) 130mph
b) 170mph
c) 200mph

9. Formerly known as the Stratosphere Tower, now known as plain old 'The Strat' Las Vegas's observation tower is the second-tallest in the Western Hemisphere, overlooked in height only by the CN Tower in Toronto. Apart from nerve-jangling thrill rides, including Sky Jump where you literally jump off the edge of the building, what else awaits you at the top?

a) A planetarium
b) An exhibition of the world's ten most expensive Fender Stratocaster guitars, or 'Strats'
c) A revolving restaurant

10. The 110-story Willis Tower in Chicago has its famous glass-floored, knee-tremble-inducing Skydeck, the highest in America. It's one of the city's most popular tourist destinations – how many people are estimated to visit each year?

a) 950,000
b) 1,200,000
c) 1,700,000

6

THEATERS AND PICTURE PALACES

How much do you know about the exceptional showplaces of America? Try and fathom out the answers to these questions on the biggest, oldest and most luxurious of theaters.

1. The 'Fabulous' Fox Theater at 660 Peachtree Street NE in downtown Atlanta opened as a movie theater in 1929. Like many of the Fox venues it was lavishly decorated with an enormous capacity of 4,655 and a jaw-dropping interior that is still intact today. What is the theme?
a) An English castle
b) Moorish Palace
c) Great Wall of China

2. Carnegie Hall is one of New York's most prestigious music venues and 'live' performance recordings have provided landmark moments in American culture. These include bluegrass kings *Flatt and Scruggs: Live at Carnegie Hall* (1963). But one album tops them all. Recorded in 1961 it featured an artist still at the top of their game whose LP went on to win multiple Grammy awards. Who was the singer?
a) Burl Ives
b) Frank Sinatra
c) Judy Garland

3. In the fall of 1896, down in the basement of the Ellicott Square Building in Buffalo, New York, brothers Mitchel and Moe Mark opened a 72-seat theater solely to show motion pictures to a paying public. What new machine enabled them to do this?
a) Edison's Vitascope

b) The Lumière Brothers' Cinématographe

4. Detroit has an equally fabulous Fox Theatre that has escaped the wrecking ball to take its place on the National Register of Historic Places. The Fox has 5,048 permanent seats, making it the largest surviving movie palace of the 1920s. It has leant its name to the surrounding entertainment district which is known as...?
a) Foxborough
b) Foxton
c) Foxville

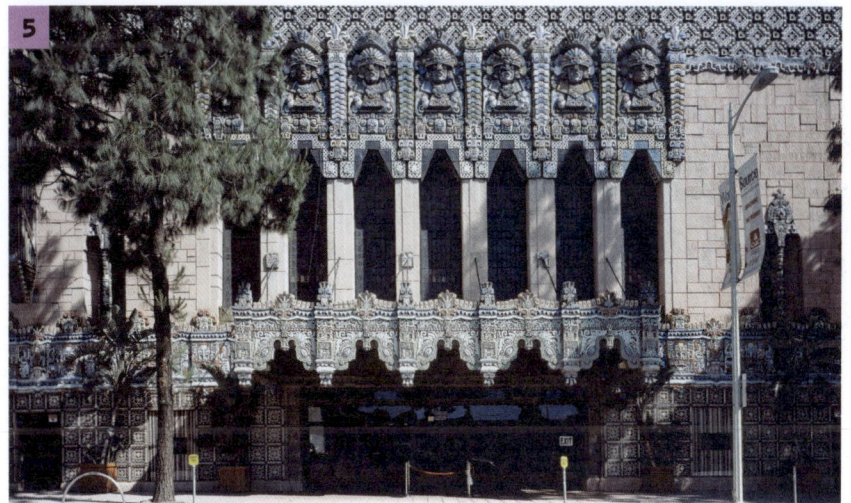

5. This 1927 Los Angeles theater took its name from the architectural styling. In a city with Grauman's Chinese and The Egyptian it paid to be different.

It has since become a nightclub. What was the name of the original theater?
a) The Mayan
b) The Indonesian
c) The Mexican

6. Once there were a string of Orpheum theaters across the country. The Orpheum Circuit began in the late 1890s in California with the mission to provide wholesome family entertainment; singers, dancers, magicians, comedians and animal acts, the whole vaudeville card. Once there were 45 Orpheums, now there are fewer than 20. Which is this one?
a) Phoenix
b) New Orleans
c) Memphis

7. The Hollywood Pantages Theatre, formerly known as RKO Pantages, was the last built by the vaudeville impresario Alexander Pantages. Opening in 1930 the venue had the advantage of 'extra leg room'. Though designed as a 'live' theater the Depression forced its hand into becoming a movie house for many decades. One of the highpoints in its history was hosting the Academy Awards. From which year?
a) 1941
b) 1950
c) 1968

8. Radio City Music Hall forms part of the Rockefeller Center in Midtown Manhattan. The 5,960-seat, four-tiered auditorium was the world's largest when it opened in December 1932. One of the highlights of the Christmas show was the impressive line of high-kicking Radio City Rockettes. Which English dance troupe were they based on?
a) The Tiller Girls
b) The Bluebell Girls
c) The Windmill Girls

9. The Chicago Theatre was originally known as the Balaban and Katz Chicago Theater. It's a nationally famous theater located on North State Street in the Loop. Who owns it?
a) Ticketmaster
b) The City of Chicago
c) Madison Square Gardens Inc

10. Sid Grauman's Chinese Theatre built on the exotic success of the nearby Grauman's Egyptian Theatre. Today it has been converted into an IMAX and is known as the TCL Chinese Theatre. It originally opened in 1927 with the premiere of Cecil B. DeMille's epic *The King of Kings*. Fifty years later it premiered one of the highest-grossing films of all time. What was the film?
a) *Close Encounters of the Third Kind*
b) *Saturday Night Fever*
c) *Star Wars*

TRANSPORT

ON THE ROAD...

From questions on gas guzzlers of the 1950s to the EVs of the 2020s, try and navigate your way through a series of obstacles to reach your destination at Q20.

1. When the U.S. financial system crashed in 2008/2009, following the collapse of Lehman Brothers Bank, auto sales fell off a cliff. In 2007 there had been over 16 million sales. What was the figure in 2009?
a) 13,754,000
b) 11,976,000
c) 10,402,000

2. In 2008, Tesla released its first electric car – sixteen years later and it was the world's top-selling car brand, trouncing the established names of Ford, Toyota, Volkswagen and Honda. What kind of car did Tesla start off with?
a) CitiCar – a two-seat city runabout
b) The Roadster – a sports car
c) Tesla Model Z

3. The *Blade Runner*-inspired Tesla Cybertruck has a revved up version with three motors, 834 horsepower, capable of 0-60 in 2.6 seconds. What is it known as?
a) Cyberbeast
b) Cyberdemon
c) CyberRaptor

4. Texas has the highest permanent speed limit in the United States. It can be found on Texas State Highway 130, a toll road that bypasses Austin. What is the speed limit?
a) 80mph
b) 85mph
c) 90mph

5. Although volumes of sedan sales have fallen off in recent years, with the demand for SUVs and pickup trucks increasing, what was the best-selling sedan between 2003 and 2017?
a) Toyota Camry
b) Honda Accord
c) Toyota Prius

6. The all-time best-selling pickup truck is the trademarked Ford F-150® (Ford once made the Ferrari Formula 1 team rename their car when they called it an F-150!) The F-Series was first introduced in what year?
a) 1948
b) 1953
c) 1957

7. Henry Ford reportedly said that customers could have a Model T in any color 'as long as it was black'. Black was the fastest drying paint finish. However the Model T was available in a variety of colors before 1914 and after 1925, including red, blue, green, and gray. True or False?

8. The fastest street-legal car made by an American auto manufacturer is the 2025 Chevy Corvette ZR1. The standard showroom model ZR1 is the fastest factory stock Corvette ever built. What's the top speed?
a) 210mph
b) 220mph
c) 230mph

9. Which unofficial and unsanctioned auto road race starts at New York City's Red Ball Garage and runs across the country to the Portofino Hotel in Redondo Beach, California. The record time is 25 hours 39 minutes, a highly illegal average speed of 112mph.
a) The 3,000-Mile Dash
b) The Race Across America
c) The Cannonball Run

10. The earliest versions of this classic sportscar can sell for up to $750,000. When it first went on sale in 1953 how much would you pay for a new, polo white Chevrolet Corvette?
a) $3,490
b) $4,290

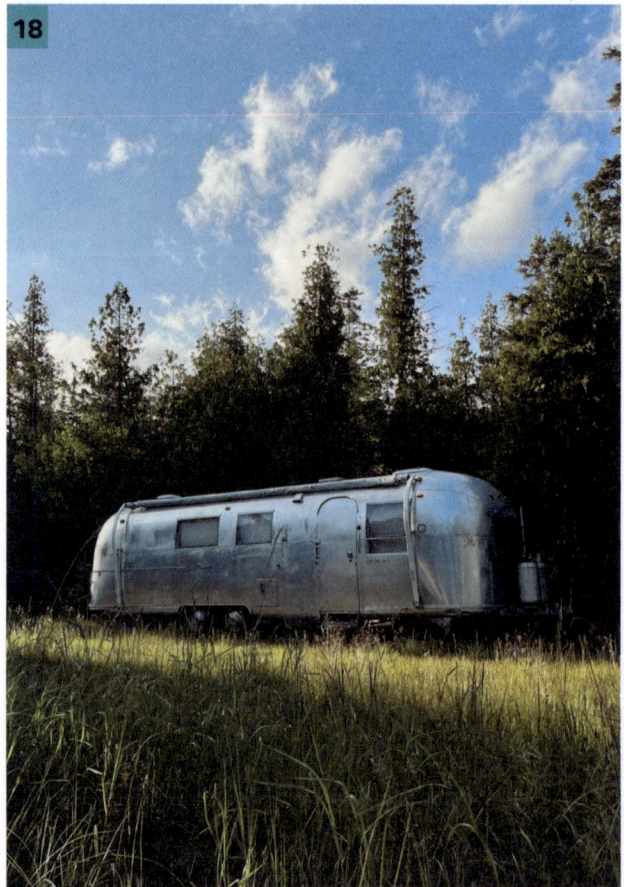

11. Oldsmobile was once an important part of the General Motors roster, along with Chevrolet, Pontiac, Buick and Cadillac. In 1981, the Oldsmobile Cutlass, was America's best-selling automobile for the fourth successive year ... and then sales declined. When it shut down, it was the oldest American automobile marque to fail. Which year?
a) 1992
b) 2004
c) 2012

12. It was a decade after the Corvette launch that Ford introduced the Mustang. It proved to be a marketing triumph for the blue oval badge. It had been budgeted to sell 100,000 a year from 1964 and was up against the new Plymouth Barracuda in a hotly contested market. Within two years it had sold how many?
a) 400,000
b) 750,000
c) 1 million

13. Around the same time, Ford targeted the prestigious Le Mans 24 Hours race. Ferrari had won the race since 1960 with their Ferrari 250, but after challenging in 1965, Ford won it in 1966 and 1967 – and then twice in 1968 and 1969 with a privately-entered Gulf-sponsored car. What was the triumphant model?
a) Ford GT
b) Ford GT40
c) Ford Mustang Shelby GT500

14. The U.S. Army was a major customer for the High Mobility Multipurpose Wheeled Vehicle. It was a design that would soon be adapted for commercial use on American roads. What was it better known as?
a) Willy's MB Jeep
b) Humvee

15. The Jeep Wagoneer was a luxury 4x4 that motoring journalists attribute to being the first sport-utility vehicle (SUV). Jeep stopped making the Grand Wagoneer in 1991 – when was the original Wagoneer first on sale?
a) 1963
b) 1969
c) 1974

16. In the pantheon of classic American autos there is a special place for the Cadillac Eldorado. Produced from 1952 to 2002 there were 12 generations of Eldorado. Can you date the model pictured with its rocketship taillights and flamboyant fins?
a) 1956
b) 1959
c) 1963

17. The Winnebago was one of the first recreational vehicles (RV). Drawing on American Indian heritage some of the early models were named 'Chieftain' and 'Brave'. What does Winnebago mean?
a) It's the name of an American Indian tribe
b) It's the name of the horse-drawn sled
c) It's the name of a sacred mountain

18. Wally Byam had been designing trailers and selling $5 plans for them since the 1920s, before coming up with one that followed an auto 'like a stream of air'. What was the name of his first Airstream model?
a) Silver bullet
b) Clipper
c) Conestoga

19. The launch of the Cybertruck was going very well with the audience wowed by the futuristic styling ... until ... there was an embarrassing failure. What went wrong?
a) The armor-plated glass shattered in a test
b) The battery had run flat
c) The car would not engage first gear

20. It's been almost a century since Henry Seagrave broke the world land speed record at Daytona Beach, taking the mark above 200mph for the first time. Since 1963 the record has only been beaten in the United States – in 1997 it reached 760mph (and broke the sound barrier) with Thrust SSC piloted by Andy Green. Where was the record set?
a) Bonneville Salt Flats
b) Black Rock Desert

AMAZING AVIATORS

The sceptical French did not believe that Orville and Wilbur Wright had made the first powered flight, but when Wilbur demonstrated their Kitty Hawk Flyer in Paris it was a sensation. How much do you know about America's great – and sometimes unsung – aviators?

1. Charles 'Chuck' Yeager was a WWII fighter ace and record-setting test pilot. Through the National Aeronautics program he became the first person to officially break the sound barrier in 1947. What was the name of his record-setting aircraft?
a) Bell X-1
b) Lockheed Thundercat
c) North American Aircraft XP12

2. During WWII, the Women's Auxiliary Ferrying Squadron was used to fly aircraft around the country to free up male pilots. Betty Gillies (pictured) and Nancy Love were the first women to fly which aircraft?
a) Consolidated B-24 Liberator
b) Martin B-26 Marauder
c) Boeing B-17 Flying Fortress

3. Aviation hero Charles Lindbergh was sidelined by Roosevelt during WWII because of his alleged pro-German stance. After his death in 1974 this affection for the Motherland was exposed by what incredible fact?
a) Glowing correspondence between Lindbergh and Luftwaffe chief Herman Goering uncovered at Goering's house in 1945
b) He had three German mistresses in the 1950s and fathered seven German children, none of whom knew who their father was

4. In 1937, Amelia Earhart's attempt to become the first woman to circumnavigate the globe ended in her mysterious disappearance. Along with navigator Fred Noonan, her Lockheed Electra airplane went missing in the Pacific Ocean. Where were they last seen?
a) Fiji
b) New Guinea
c) Midway Island

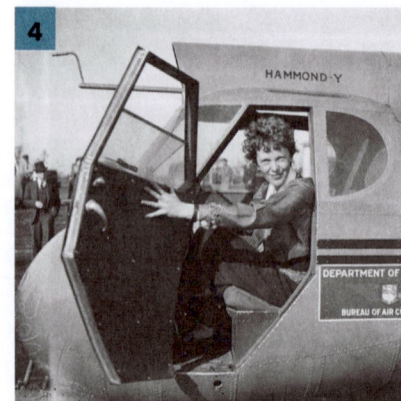

5. James 'Jimmy' Doolittle was an outstanding airman, a Schneider Trophy-winning pilot who pioneered the use of flying 'blind' using instruments. He led a daring raid on Japan early in the Pacific War, the Doolittle raid. Where were his 16 aircraft supposed to land after the raid?
a) Back on the USS *Hornet*
b) Behind Allied lines in China

6. Elizabeth 'Brave Bessie' Coleman was the first Black woman to hold a pilot license. Born to a family of sharecroppers in Texas, she worked several jobs and obtained sponsorships in Chicago to go to France for flight school, where she graduated from the Fédération Aéronautique Internationale in 1921. She earned a living as a stunt pilot in airshows but was killed in a 1926 crash. What went wrong?
a) She failed to execute a barrel-roll safely, the wing tip caught the ground
b) Her Curtiss airplane controls jammed and she was thrown from the cockpit

7. The Wright Brothers' place in aviation history is unquestioned today, but in the early 20th century S.P. Langley, secretary of the Smithsonian Institution from 1887 until 1906, maintained that his 'Aerodrome' was the first heavier-than-air craft 'capable' of manned powered flight. The feud lasted for decades and Orville Wright responded to the Smithsonian's 'perverted view of aviation history' by lending the restored 1903 Kitty Hawk Flyer to which museum in 1928?
a) The Science Museum in London
b) The Musee Aeronautique, Paris

8. Eileen Collins became the first woman to pilot a space shuttle in 1995. Which of the six shuttles did she pilot?
a) Discovery
b) Atlantis
c) Endeavor

9. Howard Hughes was almost killed in 1946 while flying one of his own prototype XF-11 reconnaissance aircraft. He was attempting to crash-land at the Los Angeles Country Club golf course but the plane came down short in Beverly Hills. He was badly injured, but rescued by U.S. Marine Sergeant William L. Durkin. What happened after he recovered?
a) He made Durkin an executive director of the Hughes Aircraft board
b) He sent Durkin a check for $200 a month for the rest of his life

10. Many think Wiley Post was the greatest American aviator of the interwar period. He had been injured in a serious oil rig accident in 1926 and used the compensation to buy his first aircraft. He helped discover the jet stream and in 1933 became the first pilot to fly solo around the world. What disability did he fly with?
a) He had lost sight in his left eye in the oil rig accident
b) He had lost the lower part of his right leg in the accident

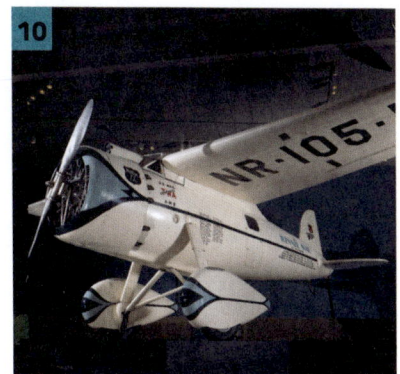

MOTORCYLES

Harley-Davidson is one of the great automotive brands that has survived in an industry that has seen boom and bust. How much do you know about motorcycles and the famous 'hogs'?

1. Harley-Davidson is the dominant American motorcycle brand. It was established in 1903 in the city where it is still headquartered. Where is that?
a) Cleveland
b) Buffalo
c) Milwaukee

2. Harley's great rival, the Indian Motorcycle company, started up in 1901 in Springfield, Massachusetts. During the 1910s Indian were the world's largest manufacturer of motorbikes. When did they cease production first time round?
a) 1946
b) 1953
c) 1961

3. Harley-Davidson have a range of touring models. Which of the following is not in the current range?
a) Road Glide
b) Street Glide
c) Avenue Glide
c) Electra Glide

4. What percentage of the American bike market do Harley hold?
a) 12%
b) 16%
c) 20%

5. The three-wheeled Servi-Car was designed during the Great Depression when Harley-Davidson wanted to expand its customer base. They were used as police patrol vehicles and also for delivering cars, where the car being delivered would tow the stable three-wheeler behind. How long did they make it for?
a) 1932-1946
b) 1932-1964
c) 1932-1973

6. Many Harleys have had long production runs. The Low Rider has been in production since 1977, the Softail since 1984 and the Fat Boy made its debut in 1990. Another classic Harley is the Sportster, a favorite for bike customizers. When was that first available?
a) 1957
b) 1966
c) 1970

7. Who was the last American Moto GP champion?
a) Kenny Roberts Jr.
b) Kevin Schwantz
c) Nicky Hayden

8. The Harley-Davidson XR750 was once the dominant force in flat track racing. It was also the machine of choice for which daredevil stunt jumper?

9. Harley-Davidson shook up their image with the launch of the futuristic and highly influential V-Rod, produced between 2001 and 2017. It was a design collaboration with which auto manufacturer?
a) Ferrari
b) Porsche

10. Harley-Davidson's first all-electric bike was introduced in 2019 but wasn't a roaring success. They have now spun off electric bikes into a separate company and named it after the first model. What was that called?
a) Electron Glide
b) LiveWire
c) Fuse

TRAINSPOTTING

A vast railroad network was the engine behind America's rapid industrial growth. Although the two locomotives that helped celebrate the Golden Spike have gone, many of the classic engines have been preserved. Try and answer questions on these remarkable giants of the rails.

1. The first locomotive built entirely within the United States was completed by the West Point Foundry of New York in 1830 and went into service in South Carolina. It carried passengers at a dizzying 15 to 25mph. What was its unofficial name?
a) The Best Friend of Charleston
b) The Carolina Tornado

2. A Western & Atlantic Railroad 4-4-0 steam locomotive known as #3 General was the subject of the 'Great Locomotive Chase of 1862'. Union raiders led by James J. Andrews, hijacked the Confederate train and took it north for 87 miles, cutting telegraph wires as they went. The failed raid inspired a silent movie, *The General*. Who was the star?
a) Harold Lloyd
b) Buster Keaton
c) Charlie Chaplin

3. Perhaps the greatest day in United States railroad history was in 1869 when the east coast was linked to the west coast at Promontory Summit in Utah. Sadly, the two locomotives present for the Golden Spike ceremony were both scrapped in the early 20th century and so replicas take their place at the site today. One was Union Pacific No. 119, the other was named...?
a) Jupiter
b) Neptune
c) Uranus

4. The Hiawathas were a fleet of Art Deco-styled passenger trains operated by the Milwaukee Road. The most famous was the Twin Cities Hiawatha, which shuttled between St. Paul and Minneapolis and Chicago. Some of the Hiawathas had an observation car (before the Skytop Lounge was introduced). What was it called?
a) The beaver tail observation car
b) The moose head observation car

5. Another Art Deco locomotive, the 80-foot-long Pennsylvania Railroad Class GG1, was a 100mph streamlined electric

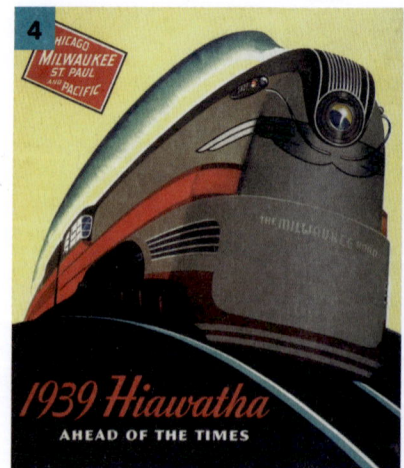

1939 Hiawatha
AHEAD OF THE TIMES

locomotive. They were built between 1934 and 1943 and run by Pennsylvania Railroad, Penn Central, Conrail, Amtrak and New Jersey Transit. When were they retired from service?
a) 1963
b) 1973
c) 1983

6. There are only two remaining Southern Pacific 4449 streamlined steam locomotives. They were built at the Lima Locomotive Works in Ohio. This one, Daylight, was built in 1941, retired in 1957 and was restored between 1974 and 1976. In 1983, where did a poll of Trains magazine readers place No. 4449

in its table of greatest U.S. locos?
a) Sixth
b) Third
c) First

7. The career of the Pennsylvania Railroad (PRR) class T1 duplex-drive 4-4-4-4 steam locomotive was short-lived. Introduced in 1942, by 1948 the PRR had replaced it on all passenger express trains with diesel units. What was its major bugbear?
a) Too much wheelslip
b) Too much smoke
c) Too much water consumed

8. The EMD FT was a 1,350-horsepower diesel-electric workhorse built between

March 1939 and November 1945 by General Motors. The demonstrator loco ran on an epic 83,000-mile tour across 20 railroads in 1939/1940 and showed off the advantages of diesel power. It was known as what...?
a) The 'engine that helped kill steam'
b) 'Casey (Jones) wouldn't like it'

9. The GE Dash 9-44CW has been a major freight shifter of the Burlington Northern Santa Fe (BNSF) railroad. When was it introduced?
a) 1978
b) 1986
c) 1993

10. The Acela is Amtrak's flagship passenger train service along the northeast corridor, running between Washington, D.C. and Boston via Baltimore, New York City and Philadelphia. It uses active tilting to take bends at speed. How fast can it go on the flat?
a) 135mph
b) 150mph
c) 165mph

AIR TRAVEL

In just over a hundred years, air travel has gone from one-seat planes to 853 seats – and the United States now has a vast array of flying options. Take our flight check.

1. The first scheduled air service in the United States was established between St. Petersburg and Tampa on January 1, 1914. The flight distance of 18 miles took 23 minutes in the single-passenger Benoist plane. That was a colossal 11 hours less than traveling between St. Petersburg and Tampa by rail. How much did it cost?
a) $1
b) $5

2. Transatlantic travel between the USA and Germany could be enjoyed in style in the 1930s using Zeppelins. The airship era came to a dramatic end at Lakehurst, New Jersey, in May 1937 when the *Hindenburg* caught fire while docking. Despite the inferno of the hydrogen filled airship people escaped as the incandescent skeleton fell to earth. Of the 36 passengers and 61 crewmen – how many reached safety?
a) 12 passengers and 24 crew
b) 23 Passengers and 39 crew

3. Founded in 1924, Delta Air Lines is the oldest airline still operating in the United States. Its first aerial enterprise was not transporting passengers, though. What was it?
a) Air mail delivery
b) Crop dusting
c) Aerial acrobatic shows

Opening St. Petersburg-Tampa Air Boat Line

4. Pan American was the largest international air carrier and unofficial overseas flag carrier of the United States for much of the 20th century. What did it call every jet in its inventory?
a) Clipper
b) Spirit
c) Speedbird

5. The Boeing 747 'jumbo jet' was a gamechanger in the aviation industry. The first 747 commercial flight took place on January 22, 1970, with a Pan Am flight from New York to London. With rising fuel prices, airlines have moved on to producing more efficient twin-engined aircraft. When did Boeing complete their final 747?
a) August 2009
b) December 2022

6. The Boeing B-314 clipper was the ultimate in transatlantic or transpacific air travel in the late 1930s. Pan Am had set U.S. aircraft manufacturers a challenge: to build the perfect seaplane and Boeing of Seattle beat both Sikorsky and Martin. The seaplanes were large, luxurious, reliable and phenomenally expensive — what

8. Which is America's busiest airport based on passenger traffic?
a) Hartsfield Jackson Atlanta International Airport
b) Chicago O'Hare International Airport
c) Newark Liberty International Airport

9. What was the first commercial jet used in the United States for passenger service, making its debut in 1957?
a) Boeing 707
b) Douglas DC8
c) Lockheed Tristar

was their flying range?
a) 2,300 miles
b) 3,000 miles
c) 3,500 miles

7. According to the U.S. Pilots Association, which airport is considered the most difficult airport to land a jet? Commercial passenger flights must be flown by crews with special qualifications to fly the steep approach to the airport and perform the difficult go-around procedure during an aborted landing.
a) Aspen-Pitkin County Airport, Colorado
b) Flagstaff Pulliam Airport, Arizona
c) Telluride Regional Airport, Colorado

10. Which is the longest domestic airline flight that U.S. passengers can take?
a) Boston to Honolulu
b) New York to Honolulu
c) Anchorage to Miami

DEPARTURES AND ARRIVALS

How much of your life have you spent in airports staring up at Departure or Arrival boards? Try these 20 questions on the three-letter airport codes from across the United States. Some are logical, a few come from left field, and some are just the first three letters of the city.

1. Birmingham International Airport
a) BAL
b) BHM
c) BIR

2. Bill and Hillary Clinton National Airport, Little Rock in Arkansas
a) BHC
b) BCN
c) LIT

3. Long Beach Airport
a) LGB
b) LOB
c) LNG

4. Oakland International Airport
a) OAX
b) OAK
c) OCA

5. Denver International Airport
a) DCO
b) DCL
c) DEN

6. Tucson International Airport
a) TUC
b) TAR
c) TUS

7. Daytona Beach International Airport
a) DAB
b) DAY
c) DBE

8. Chicago O'Hare International Airport
a) COH
b) CHX
c) ORD

9. Grand Rapids Airport in Michigan
a) GRA
b) GRM
c) GRR

10. San Francisco International Airport
a) SAN
b) SFO
c) SFR

11. Orlando International Airport
a) MCO
b) ORX
c) ORL

12. La Guardia, New York
a) NYL
b) LGA
c) LAG

13. Raleigh/Durham International Airport
a) RAD
b) RDU
c) RAL

14. Hector International Airport in Fargo
a) FAX
b) FIA
c) FAR

15. Dallas/Fort Worth International Airport
a) DAF
b) DFO
c) DFW

16. Salt Lake City International Airport
a) SLC
c) MOR
d) SAL

17. Houston George Bush Intercontinental
a) GBH
b) IAH
c) HGB

18. Memphis International Airport
a) MEM
b) BLU
c) MIA

19. Washington, D.C., Dulles International Airport
a) IAD
b) VID
c) DUL

20. Ted Stevens Anchorage International Airport
a) ANC
b) ANA
c) ALA

21. For the following ten airports, guess the city that goes with the three-letter code, starting with a very glamorous MGM?
a) Montgomery, AL
b) Modesto, CA

22. Or how about PIE in the sky?
a) Providence, RI
b) St. Petersburg, FL

23. This destination is not at all flattering: FAT?
a) Fresno, CA
b) Fayetteville, AL

24. This PUB is not in England.
a) Pueblo, CO
b) Pasadena, CA

25. Fairies and elves sometimes might fly to: FAY?
a) Fayetteville, NC
b) Fort Wayne, IN

26. No delay? Have a nice DAY. But where?
a) Davenport, IA
b) Dayton, OH

27. Something to mutter if you miss your flight: CRP?
a) Cedar Rapids, IA
b) Corpus Christie, TX

28. And let's hope no one on the plane needs: CPR?
a) Casper, WY
b) Cape Coral, FL

29. Where do you get a SEA view?
a) Seaford, DE
b) Seattle, WA

30. Finally, this not a great omen if your destination is: END?
a) Endeavour, FL
b) Endicott, NY

THE FINAL FRONTIER

It is no surprise that the nation which first pioneered powered flight is the one that has led the world in exploring space. How much do you know about the American space program?

1. The early Mercury space missions were propelled by which family of rockets?
a) Redstone
b) Saturn
c) Atlas

2. *The Right Stuff* was Tom Wolfe's eye-opening book about the selection of the first seven NASA astronauts. The risks associated with the program were grave, but the experienced airmen tried to make light of the risk. What phrase did they use for a fatal crash?
a) He bought the farm
b) He went to Kansas

3. The original seven NASA astronauts introduced to the public on April 9, 1959, were Scott Carpenter, Gordon Cooper, John Glenn, Wally Schirra, Alan Shepard, Deke Slayton and who else...?
a) Neil Armstrong
b) Buzz Aldrin
c) Gus Grissom

4. Who was the first American in space?
a) Alan Shepard
b) John Glenn
c) Scott Carpenter

5. Who was the first American astronaut to orbit the earth?
a) John Glenn
b) Gordon Cooper
c) Deke Slayton

6. Which Apollo mission crewed by Frank Borman, Jim Lovell and Bill Anders was the first to orbit the moon?
a) Apollo 6
b) Apollo 8
c) Apollo 10

7. Indisputably the greatest moment in human history was the first footstep on the Moon. Neil Armstrong's words that day were: 'One small step for man, one giant leap for mankind'. Is that exactly what he intended to say?
a) Yes, he thought it up once the lunar module had landed
b) Almost. He meant to say 'for a man'

8. When Neil Armstrong guided the lunar module down he was looking for a safe, flat surface to put down on. How much fuel did he have left when the Eagle finally did land?
a) Four minutes
b) One minute, fifteen seconds
c) Twenty-five seconds

9. Where did Apollo 11 touch down on the Moon?
a) The Fra Mauro Highlands
b) The Sea of Tranquility
c) The Ocean of Storms

10. Which was the first Apollo mission to take the Lunar Roving Vehicle?
a) Apollo 13
b) Apollo 14
c) Apollo 15

11. Commander Gene Cernan and Lunar Module Pilot Harrison Schmitt of Apollo 17 were the last to tread on the earth's surface after the cancellation of Apollos 18, 19 and 20. What year was it?
a) 1971
b) 1972
c) 1974

12. The Voyager probes, Voyager 1 and Voyager 2 were launched in 1977. Having accomplished their mission of flybys of Saturn, Titan, Uranus and Neptune they have reached interstellar space and are the furthest manmade objects from Earth. How many miles (relative to the Sun) will Voyager 1 travel in a year?
a) 129 million
b) 325 million

13. Earlier probes Pioneer 10 and Pioneer 11 were launched in 1972. They will be overtaken by the speedier 2006-launched New Horizons probe. Scientists predict that it will pass Pioneer 10 in 2143. When will it pass Pioneer 11?
a) 2197
b) 2275
c) 2314

14. The Space Shuttle Discovery was launched in 1981. The commander of the flight was an astronaut from that rare dozen who had walked on the surface of the moon. Who was it?
a) John Young
b) Charles Duke
c) Gene Cernan

15. Space Shuttle Atlantis completed its 33rd and final mission landing at Kennedy Space Center in July 2011. How many Shuttle missions had there been?
a) 103
b) 135
c) 167

16. NASA's first Mars rover was launched in 2011 and landed inside Gale Crater in August 2012, within 1.5 miles of its target. What was the first car-sized rover called?
a) Carl Sagan Rover
b) Curiosity Rover
c) Enterprise Rover

17. The 2020 Mars Perseverance Rover landed on the planet with a helicopter strapped to it which completed 72 historic flights. What was the helicopter called?

a) da Vinci
b) Ingenuity
c) Orville

18. The James Webb Telescope was launched in 2021 and has provided amazing and insightful views of deep space. Who was James Webb?
a) NASA chief from 1961 to 1968 during the Mercury, Gemini, and Apollo programs
b) The lead designer of the Space Shuttle
c) The inventor of Teflon

19. SpaceX uses the Cape Canaveral launch facility for its Starlink satellites. It also uses the Boca Chica launch site. Where is Boca Chica?
a) Nicaragua
b) Mexico
c) Texas

20. What is the name of the NASA mission intended to revisit the moon in 2027?
a) Artemis
b) Hermes
c) Daedalus

HISTORY

EARLY SETTLERS

They came, they saw... and they relied on Native American cooperation to survive. Getting a foothold in the New World was not as easy as many settlers thought it might be, but battle on they did. Try these questions on the early arrivals.

1. Florida was one of the earliest Spanish colonies in North America. In 1763 to whom did they trade Florida, in exchange for Cuba?
a) Great Britain
b) France
c) Netherlands

2. France's early colonization was double-headed: in the north, along the St Lawrence river and the Great Lakes, and from the south from New Orleans up the Mississippi. How far to the northwest did French Louisiana claim?
a) Modern-day Colorado
b) Modern-day Wyoming
c) Modern-day Montana

3. England's first successful settlement was at Jamestown in Chesapeake Bay in 1607. But what was the name of the English colony which vanished without trace in 1590?
a) Croatoan
b) Roanoke
c) Carolina

4. The wealth of the English colonies came eventually from growing tobacco. But what were the first settlers at Jamestown hoping to find?
a) Exotic furs (valuable beavers had been hunted to extinction for their pelts in England by then)
b) Timber
c) Gold

5. The capital of the English colonies moved in 1699 from Jamestown to Middle Plantation, which was then renamed in honor of the English king at the time. What did it become?
a) Charleston
b) Williamsburg
c) Georgetown

6. Lutheranism was introduced to America by a short-lived seventeenth-century colony – New Sweden. Along which river did it flourish from 1638 to 1655, when it was captured by the Dutch?
a) The Delaware
b) The Hudson
c) The Potomac

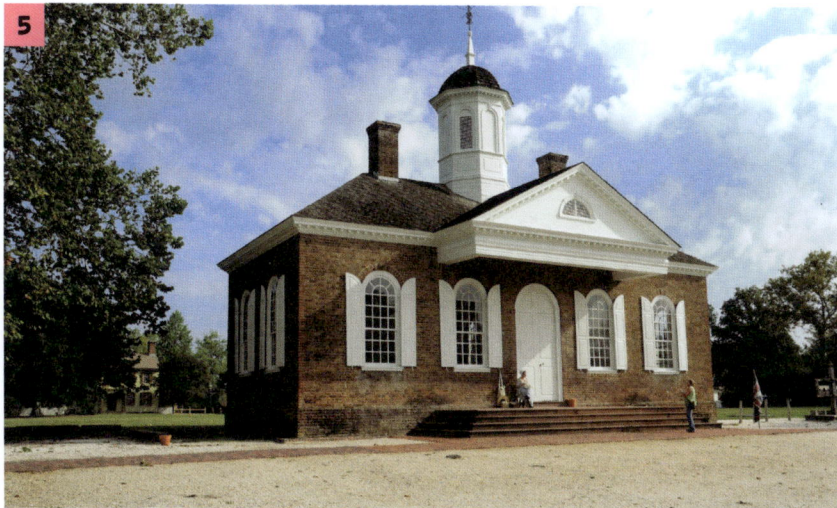

PORTICO OVER PLYMOUTH ROCK, PLYMOUTH, MASS.

landing location was made

c) 1880, when it was moved from Pilgrim Hall Museum back to Plymouth Harbor

10. Russia was a latecomer in the history of colonial America. It claimed Alaska in 1741, and controlled an important trading hub in California. What was its name?

a) Fort Ross, from the Russian word for 'Russian'

b) Fort Low, from the Russian word for 'fishing'

c) Fort Bragg, from the Russian word for 'enemy'

7. New Netherlands, the Dutch colony in North America, was in turn taken over by the English in 1674. What governor of the New Netherlands would eventually be used as a brand of cigarette?

a) Johannes Marlborough

b) Peter Stuyvesant

c) Willem van Chesterfield

8. The Pilgrim Fathers who arrived in Massachusetts in 1620 first fled from England to the Netherlands. On which ship did they sail to England to meet up with the *Mayflower*?

a) The *Speedwell*

b) The *Godspeed*

c) The *Cornflower*

9. The Plymouth Rock is the site of the Pilgrims' arrival in America. When was the date 1620 inscribed upon it?

a) 1620, soon after the Pilgrims arrived

b) 1741, when the first claim for the rock as the *Mayflower*

REVOLUTIONARIES

The colonists in the New World had no appetite to be governed by a parliament that denied them a voice. It was time for a change! How much do you know about those turbulent years and the history of the Continental Army's supreme commander?

1. Much is made of America choosing a president over a king after success in the Revolutionary War. However Britain had long been a constitutional monarchy. King George III was obliged to sign off whatever laws parliament passed. When had the English king become a figurehead?
a) 1689 (four years after Charles II's death)
b) 1727 (after death of George I)

2. Which Native American tribe did the Boston Tea Party raiders imitate in their disguise?
a) Massachusett people
b) Mohawk people
c) Huron people

3. The controversial Stamp Act of 1765 was brought in by the British to pay for the Seven Years War which they had waged against the French and various American Indian tribes battling for possession of North America. Representatives of the 13 colonies met for the Continental Congress of 1765. Where was it held?
a) Philadelphia
b) New York
c) Boston

4. The 1776 Declaration of Independence was primarily signed where?

a) Federal Hall, New York
b) Pennsylvania State House
c) Poughkeepsie Courthouse

5. Because John Hancock's name appeared at the top, in the center, in very large letters and elaborate script, what has 'John Hancock' become a synonym for?
a) Being at the center of affairs
b) Being the first on the list
c) A signature

6. Which significant signature is missing from the document?

7. *Paul Revere's Ride* was immortalized by Longfellow's epic poem. But was it just Revere who warned citizens around Boston that 'the Regulars are out!'?
a) Revere alone
b) Revere and William Dawes
c) Revere, William Dawes, Samuel Prescott and Israel Bissell

8. Alexander Hamilton (the subject of Ron Cernow's outstanding biography) came to prominence in the Revolutionary War. What was his role?
a) Financier of the Continental Army
b) Liaison Officer with the French Army and Navy
c) George Washington's aide-de-camp

9. Exiled Polish cavalry officer Casimir Pulaski became a Revolutionary War hero when he helped George Washington escape capture during which battle?
a) Brandywine
b) Long Island
c) The Clouds
d) Germantown

10. Which was the first country to recognize the new nation of the United States of America?
a) Russia
b) France
c) The Netherlands

11. Countless places, buildings and institutions are named after the first president of the United States. But where is the place from which his ancestors took their family name?
a) Washington Old Hall in the northeast of England
b) Washington Manor in Northamptonshire in the English midlands

12. George Washington was the eldest of six children and had three half-brothers and a sister from his father's previous marriage. But he and Martha had no children of their own. True or False?

13. Washington was a skilled surveyor and mapmaker, and something of a wordsmith. What book did he publish in his teens?
a) *A Survey of the Waterways of Connecticut*
b) *The Rules of Civility*
c) *A Scheme for Irrigating the Tobacco Plantations of Virginia*

14. Washington left mainland USA only once in his lifetime, in 1751. Where did he go?
a) The Bahamas, to recover from a bout of smallpox
b) Cuba, as a special envoy to New Spain
c) Barbados, seeking a cure for his brother's tuberculosis

15. George Washington cut his military teeth in the French and Indian War, which he was partly responsible for starting. How did he do that?
a) He attacked and killed a party of Frenchmen who were on a diplomatic mission
b) Unable to speak French, he accidentally insulted a French officer
c) He mistakenly entered a French fort in the belief that it was a British one

16. The war nevertheless made his reputation. He fought a dramatic rearguard action at the Battle of the Monongahela which allowed his troops to retreat. What was his own fate?
a) He escaped discovery in the aftermath by hiding beneath the body of his horse
b) Having run out of bullets, he swung his rifle butt like a club, killing six Frenchmen
c) Two horses were shot from under him, and six bullets pierced his clothing – but not him

17. The Washington family home was Mount Vernon, a tobacco and wheat farm which he doubled in size, becoming one of the wealthiest men in Virginia. Why was he £1,800 in debt in 1764?
a) He had a gambling problem

b) He spent all his income from tobacco on luxury goods from London
c) He insisted on building decent accommodation for his slaves

18. Which future president of the U.S. appointed Washington as Commander-in-Chief of the Continental Army at the start of the Revolutionary War?
a) John Adams
b) Thomas Jefferson
c) James Madison

19. There were no precedents for the first President of the United States, and Washington was left to define the role himself. What alternatives to addressing him as Mr President were suggested?
a) Your Highness, and Protector of The Liberties of the United States
b) Your Excellency, or Your Electoral Highness
c) Your Highness the President of the United States and Protector of the Rights of the Same
d) All of the above

20. In his retirement at Mount Vernon, how did George Washington supplement his income?
a) He charged the steady stream of visitors for guided tours of the house
b) He gave some of the tobacco plantation over to crops of pumpkins
c) He built a distillery in the grounds

THE WAR OF 1812

President Madison seized an opportunity to take control of Canada after worsening trade relations with Britain.

1. After defeat in the Revolutionary War, Britain supported Native Americans who resisted American expansion into provinces of Canada. Who was the Shawnee leader of that resistance?
a) Tecumseh
b) Sitting Bull
c) Blue Jacket

2. Britain, which was at war with France, blockaded French ports and hence hampered America's international trade. How else did the Royal Navy irritate the United States?
a) It shot holes in the sails of American ships
b) Like France, it boarded American-flagged ships and pressganged their crews
c) It cut through the anchor ropes of American ships

3. Given the distraction of a war with France, America, led by James Madison, reasoned it was the perfect time to claim Canadian territory as their own and declared war on Britain on June 18, 1812. What was remarkable about the vote to do so?
a) It remains the narrowest majority in favor of war ever recorded by Congress
b) It remains the widest majority in favor of war ever recorded by Congress
c) The largest part of the votes was from abstentions

4. Britain, unaware of the declaration, was already making concessions to the U.S. for the sake of better trade relations. Too late – how long did it take at the time for news to cross the Atlantic?
a) Two weeks
b) Three weeks
c) Six weeks

5. Much of the early action centered in Upper Canada, along the Niagara river and toward Montreal. The U.S. assumed that the invasion would be easy because they outnumbered the unprepared Canadian forces, however they had tried to invade once before and it was unsuccessful. When?
a) 1775
b) 1780
c) 1789

6. What was the position of New England in the conflict? They had led in the Revolutionary War...
a) They began an intensive program of ship-building to boost warships on the Great Lakes
b) New England states threatened to secede as the war wrecked their economy

7. Turning its attention to Chesapeake Bay, Britain captured Washington, D.C., burning down the Capitol and the White House. This was in response for what American act of war?
a) The burning of public buildings in York, Upper Canada's capital,
b) The destruction of Niagara-on-the-Lake in December 1813

8. Britain marched on Baltimore but could not break its defenses. The unsuccessful siege of the city's Fort McHenry inspired which celebrated poem?
a) *The Stars and Stripes Forever*
b) *The Defence of Fort McHenry*
c) *America the Brave*

9. Peace negotiations began in Belgium in August 1814. What was the outcome of the war?
a) The U.S. was awarded a nominal 100 square miles of territory in Upper Canada
b) The borders remained exactly where they had been at the start
c) Britain was awarded a nominal 100 square miles of Maine

TAKING MEXICO

With settlers spreading west into the Louisiana territories, the lands of Mexico looked rife for exploitation.

1. Mexico was the largest part of the Kingdom of New Spain which stretched from California to Colombia. Who did the Kingdom support during the Revolutionary War?
a) America
b) Great Britain

2. Spain and the U.S. disagreed about the ownership of Texas, which America thought it had bought as part of the Louisiana Purchase. The U.S. relinquished its claim on Texas, in return for what?
a) Louisiana
b) Iowa
c) Florida

3. Mexico abolished slavery in 1829, but American settlers in Texas wanted to retain it. Volunteers from the U.S. flocked to Texas and threw out its

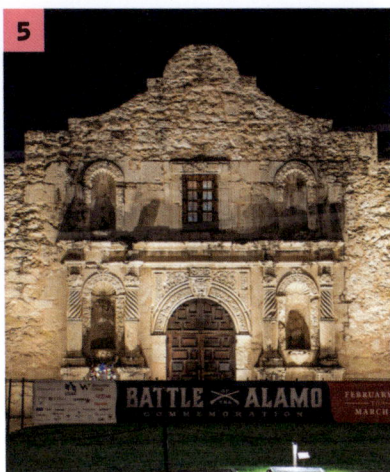

Mexican garrisons in 1836. What else did they do?
a) They enslaved the captured Mexican troops
b) They offered to become the 28th state of the USA
c) They declared an independent country, the Republic of Texas

4. To regain its honor and its province, the Mexican army advanced on San Antonio before laying siege to the Alamo Mission. How many of the 260 people in the Alamo did they kill?
a) 254
b) 257
c) 260

5. Which of these heroes of the Alamo wrote a letter during the siege requesting reinforcements and concluding with the phrase 'Victory or Death!'?
a) James Bowie
b) William B. Travis
c) David Crockett

6. Texas took its revenge at the Battle of San Jacinto, with a war cry of 'Remember the Alamo'. Mexican General Santa Anna was captured. Where had he been hiding?
a) In a Texas bar, disguised as a Texan
b) In a pig sty, disguised as a Mexican peasant
c) In a ditch, disguised as a private of the Mexican army

7. The U.S. annexed Texas in 1845, precipitating the Mexican-American War. After Mexico City fell to America, what was Santa Anna, now President, forced to sell?
a) The Mexican Army's weapons so that he could pay his officers
b) Alta California and Nuevo Mexico, to the U.S.
c) The furniture in his presidential suite

8. At the same time as the Mexican-American War, the U.S. was negotiating its northwestern border with Canada at the 49th parallel. Finally, its southern border was settled in 1854. How?
a) It bought another piece of Mexico to enable the Sunset railroad route to California
b) It returned the Baja California peninsula to Mexico
c) It abandoned claims of a right to a port on the Gulf of California

9. France invaded Mexico in 1861 and installed a puppet king, Maximilian I of Mexico. President Lincoln supported the Mexican president, however, and France withdrew. Who was Maximilian?
a) An illiterate goatherd from Honduras
b) The younger brother of Habsburg Emperor Franz Josef I of Austria
c) The eldest son of disgraced president Santa Anna

NATIVE AMERICAN HISTORY

More than half of state names are derived from Native American words or tribes, and countless rivers and mountains. See how much you know about the earliest founding fathers of the nation.

1. It is believed that the first inhabitants of North America migrated there in three waves between 60,000 and 12,000 years ago. How did they get there?
a) They rowed from northern Scandinavia via Greenland
b) They walked, when Siberia was connected by land to Alaska

2. Native Americans developed sophisticated societies and built impressive earth mounds for burials and ceremonies. The earliest such mound has been dated to 3500 BCE. Where is it?
a) Pinson Mounds TN
b) Serpent Mound OH
c) Watson Brake LA

3. They were still building when Europeans first arrived in the fifteenth century. One mound city, occupied from 900 CE to 1600 CE, had a population of up to 20,000. What was its name?
a) Cahokia
b) Choctaw
c) Chickasaw

4. Native Americans had no resistance to the diseases brought by people from the Old World. By how much is it estimated that the population was reduced by communicable diseases from Europe?
a) 40-55%
b) 60-75%
c) 80-95%

5. Gold often meant trouble. What happened when gold was discovered in the sacred Black Hills in 1874?
a) The Sioux refused to sell the land and their rights were respected
b) The Sioux refused to sell the land so the U.S. Government confiscated it
c) The Sioux agreed to sell the land on condition that they be allowed to manage it

6. The Battle of Little Bighorn in 1876 can be seen as the last stand of both American Indians as well as that of U.S. General George Armstrong Custer. His wife, Libby, who did her best to

burnish her husband's reputation after his demise, found her family decimated after the event. Who did she lose?

a) A husband and a brother

b) A husband, a brother and two brothers-in-law

7. Attitudes began to change in the 20th century, and in 1924 the Snyder Act was passed by Congress. What did that introduce for the first time in American history?

a) Guaranteed citizenship for all Native Americans born in the USA

b) Indemnity for past crimes committed in defence of their culture

c) A fair market for agricultural produce grown by Native American farmers

8. Apache chief Geronimo finally surrendered to General Miles on September 4, 1886, at Skeleton Canyon, Arizona, having been worn down by constant pursuit. He was 57 at the time. His real Apache name was 'Goyathlay' What does 'Goyathlay' translate to?

a) Keen eye of eagle

b) Fetches bad water

c) The one who yawns

9. After the 1830s eviction of five tribes from their southeastern homelands, a small band of Seminole managed to remain in Florida. What icon of popular culture did they buy in 2007?

a) Planet Hollywood

b) Hard Rock Café

c) Wendy's

10. How did some Navajo serve their country during World War II?

a) They passed on traditional hunting skills to soldiers of the U.S. Army

b) They taught their understanding of cloud formations to U.S. Navy navigators

c) They joined the U.S. Marines and used their language in codes to baffle the enemy

ABOVE: Chiefs assembled circa 1877 and photographed by Mathew Brady. Standing: Red Bear, Young Man Afraid of his Horse, Good Voice, Ring Thunder, Iron Crow, White Tail, Young Spotted Tail. Seated: Yellow Bear, Jack Red Cloud, Big Road, Little Wound, Black Crow.

OPPOSITE: Some of the survivors of the Battle of Wounded Knee, huddled in the cold.

JOURNEYS WEST

From the moment the British were thrown out of the thirteen colonies, the starting pistol was fired for expansion west. Some of the journeys were both epic and perilous. See how much you know about these arduous migrations.

1. After the Louisiana Purchase of 1803, President Jefferson sent former military men Merriwether Lewis and William Clark to explore the new territory. What was their team called?
a) The Exploration Corps
b) The Corps of Discovery
c) The Louisiana Territories Expedition

2. Lewis and Clark did not find a route between east and west suitable for wagons. But the discovery of South Pass in Wyoming in 1812 opened the way for which transcontinental route?
a) The North California Trail
b) The Mormon Trail
c) The Oregon Trail

3. The fur trappers who discovered South Pass worked for which German immigrant whose descendants became one of the richest families in the U.S.?
a) John Jacob Astor
b) William Rockefeller
c) Cornelius Vanderbilt

4. Not all travelers westwards went willingly. How has the forced removal in the 1830s of 60,000 Native Americans, 'the five civilized tribes' from the southeastern states to the Indian Territories, become known?
a) The Road of Perdition
b) The Path of Sorrow
c) The Trail of Tears

5. In the same spirit as the Pilgrim Fathers, the Mormons pushed westward to escape persecution. What was the name of the elder who led them from Illinois to a new future in Utah territory in 1847?
a) Hyrum Smith
b) Brigham Young
c) Joseph Smith

6. The discovery of gold in California in 1848 lured many Americans westward. What was the name of the site on the South Fork American River where gold was first discovered in the state?
a) Angel's Camp
b) Sutter's Mill
c) Sonora

9. The two million acres of Oklahoma offered in 1889 were claimed within what time frame?
a) Two weeks
b) Nine days
c) Twelve hours

10. New forms of transport eased transcontinental travel. The first railroad was completed in 1869 when east met west at Promontory Summit. Is the line still in commercial use today?
a) Yes, but the main line has moved 100 yards further north away from the replica locos
b) No, it was abandoned in 1904 and the original rails removed in 1942 to serve the war effort

7. To reach California pioneers had to get their wagons over the Sierra Nevada mountain range. In 1844 the Stephens-Townsend-Murphy Party followed the Truckee River into the mountains. They found a low notch in the mountains and became the first overland settlers to use the pass. Who failed to get over it before the snows in 1846?
a) John C. Fremont party
b) Donner-Reed party
c) The Baker-Fancher party

8. As the country's population grew, the U.S. government released more Native American Land to the west of the Mississippi for settler occupation. How many folk joined the Oklahoma Land Rush of 1889?
a) 10,000
b) 20,000
c) 50,000

THE CIVIL WAR

It was the War Between the States that left bitter memories for decades and a wound that the South struggled to get over. What do you know about America's most devastating conflict?

1. The election of President Lincoln in 1861 raised the possibility of the complete abolition of slavery. Which was the first state to secede from the Union in protest?
a) Virginia
b) North Carolina
c) South Carolina

2. The Confederate takeover of Fort Sumter, South Carolina, is generally considered the start of hostilities in the Civil War. The first large battle was at Bull Run/Manassas. What is Bull Run?
a) A small village
b) A small stream
c) An area of broad meadows

3. The Civil War is considered the first industrial war because of its use of railroads, the telegraph and mass-produced armaments. How did the Battle of Hampton Roads illustrate this?
a) It was the first battle in which reinforcements arrived by train
b) It was fought between two of the new ironclad monitors
c) It was the first battlefield use of rifled cannon

4. At the start of the war the Confederacy placed an embargo on cotton exports to Europe, to persuade nations of the Old World to back its cause. How did that work out?
a) Britain and France promised a safe haven for all Confederate-flagged vessels
b) Union forces hijacked cotton cargoes in vessels flying European flags
c) Europe discovered cheaper, better cotton from Egypt and India

5. Once the U.S. Navy began to blockade Confederate ports, the South's economy crashed. It had contributed 70% of the country's exports before the war. What was the figure at the end?
a) 2%
b) 23%
c) 31%

6. In March 1863 Congress passed the Enrollment Act to establish a draft for the first time. In New York City newly arrived Irish immigrants and the white working class learned that they were expected to fight for their country, while the rich had ways to dodge the draft. What was the result?
a) The worst riots in U.S. history
b) An exodus to Canada
c) An exodus of new arrivals to work the mineral mines of the west

7. The Confederates invaded Maryland in 1862 with the intention of taking Washington. The resulting Battle of Antietam is still the bloodiest single day in U.S. history. How many casualties were there?
a) 12,727
b) 17, 727
c) 22,727

8. West of the Mississippi, the Confederacy fought a guerilla war. Bands of violent pro-slavery outfits harassed Union sympathizers. Why is one gang, Quantrill's Raiders, better known?
a) Two of its members, Frank and Jesse James, went on to form their own gang
b) One of its members was Thomas 'Stonewall' Jackson
c) Its leader William Quantrill had been a Baptist minister

9. After Virginia seceded from the Union, the citizens of the state's western and northern counties seceded from Virginia, forming West Virginia. When was West Virginia admitted to the Union?
a) 1863
b) 1873

10. After his March to the Sea in December 1864, what telegram did William T. Sherman send to President Lincoln?
a) 'I beg to present you as a Christmas gift the city of Savannah'
b) 'Georgia is broken. They cannot turn the tide from here'

11. Aware of the profits to be made from such a trade, European investors paid for the construction of small, fast, lightweight ships which evaded the U.S. Navy's blockades. What were they called?
a) Bullet boats
b) Blockade runners
c) Federal dodgers

12. Andersonville, the notorious prisoner-of-war camp run by the Confederates in Georgia helped introduce a word into the English language. What was it?
a) Deadline
b) Trenchfoot
c) Skedadle

13. Richmond, Virginia, was chosen as the capital of the Confederate States. Jefferson Davies was its first and only president. What was his former role in the U.S. government?
a) Secretary of War
b) Secretary of Foreign Affairs
c) Secretary to the Treasury

14. Many drummer boys signed up for duty at 11 and 12 years of age. But George Penfield Bennett enlisted in 1861 at the age of 9 years and 7 days. He served on the ship his father commanded, the USS *Cossack*. What was his role?
a) He was a powder monkey
b) He was a crow's nest lookout
c) He was a cabin boy

15. In all of the war, twice as many men died of disease as died in action. The greatest risk of fatality, about 10% of all casualties, was among one particular category of combatant. Which was that?
a) Artillery troops
b) Prisoners of war
c) Message couriers

16. XXV Corps of the U.S. Army at last captured the Confederate capital Richmond in April 1865. What was remarkable about XXV?
a) It was composed almost entirely of Black Americans
b) It was composed almost entirely of men from West Virginia
c) It was composed of Zouaves

17. When General Robert E. Lee surrendered to General Ulysses S. Grant in April 1865, how did Grant show his respect for Lee's brilliance as a soldier?
a) They exchanged revolvers, having first unloaded them
b) He accepted Lee's surrender in private
c) He allowed Lee to keep his sword and his horse

18. Once news of Lee's surrender spread, other Confederate officers began to follow suit. Who was the last Confederate general

to surrender?
a) Brigadier General William Wirt Adams of the Army of the Republic of Texas
b) Brigadier William N. Pendleton, chief of artillery of the Army of Northern Virginia
c) Brigadier General Stand Watie of the Cherokee Mounted Rifles

19. News of the end of the war could not be communicated to ships at sea. The last Confederate ship to surrender, CSS *Shenandoah*, finally did so in November 1865. Where?
a) Baltimore, MD
b) Liverpool, England
c) Savannah, GA

20. Former slave trader and cavalry officer General Nathan Bedford Forrest had a controversial war record fighting for the CSA. He was nicknamed 'Wizard of the Saddle'. After the war ended he became Grand Wizard of what organization?
a) Richmond Inner Temple of Law?
b) Mount Ararat Lodge of 44th Virginia Freemasons
c) The Ku Klux Klan

CITY FOUNDERS AND TYCOONS

Many towns can trace the history of their name to a man or woman instrumental in the founding of that settlement. Try working out the backstory for these places and some questions on filthy rich tycoons.

1. Carson City, the Nevada state capital, is named after all-American mountain man Kit Carson. Other places and parks are named after him in California, New Mexico, and which other state?
a) Arizona (Carson Pass)
b) Washington (Carson National Forest)
c) Colorado (Kit Carson Peak)

2. Three different men called Nash have given their names to American centers of population. But which one is associated with the Home of Country Music in Tennessee?
a) Simon Nash, a local judge
b) J. Nash, the community's first postmaster
c) General Francis Nash, killed during the Revolutionary War

3. There are towns in Virginia, North Carolina, Alabama, Mississippi, Louisiana, Oklahoma, Texas and Kentucky named after this Confederate general. Which one?
a) Lee – after Robert E. Lee
b) Stonewall – after Stonewall Jackson

4. William Penn gave his city a name that combined the Greek words for love (*phileo*) and brother (*adelphos*), setting up the enduring civic nickname: the City

of Brotherly Love. What else did he give the city?
a) Two ships named *Phileo* and *Adelphos*
b) An eagle
c) The city street grid

5. The boomtown formerly known as Last Chance Gulch grew up to become Helena, Montana's capital. It is not named after a person but after another place – which one?
a) Helena in Arkansas.
b) St Helena – where Napoleon was exiled
c) St Helena – the South Carolina island

6. Denver City's founder hoped to gain favor with the governor of the territory in 1858 by using his name. What was James Denver's reaction when he returned to the city 24 years later?
a) 'I never asked for my name to be ascribed to this godless city'
b) 'My visits receive little affection from the residents of the city named after me'
c) 'Where have all these people come from? '

7. Horrified at England's jail system – where men were imprisoned for going into debt and even had to pay their jailers – James Oglethorpe founded a new city for ex-debtors in the New

World in 1732. Which one?
a) Wilmington (North Carolina)
b) Beaufort (South Carolina)
c) Savannah (Georgia)

8. Which Oregon town did John Jacob Astor establish as a fur trading post in 1811?
a) Astoria
b) Beaverton
c) Eugene

9. In 1710, Englishman John Harris established a trading post and ferry service on the Susquehanna River where the Shawnee and Delaware tribes' paths met. Today, this is Harrisburg Pennsylvania. However for a time it was renamed as what?

a) Louisburg (After Louis XVI of France)
b) Lafayetteville (residents complained it was too long)

10. In the first presidential election of the new Republic of Texas in 1836, Sam Houston easily defeated Henry Smith, who edged out Stephen Austin. Austin and Houston both have cities named after them. What happened to Smith?
a) He founded Smith, Indiana
b) He died in the California gold rush

11. The Astor family's early fortune was made by John Jacob Astor IV who saw the opportunity for fur trading as the United States expanded westward. What other trade was he involved in?
a) Logging
b) Selling firearms to Native Americans
c) Exporting opium to China

12. John Jacob Astor IV was the first American millionaire. Who was the first U.S. billionaire?
a) Cornelius Vanderbilt
b) John Paul Getty
c) John D. Rockefeller

15

13. Cornelius Vanderbilt built an empire of river and railroad transport across the U.S. He ruthlessly established and exploited monopolies. He was the first modern tycoon to be given what medieval name?
a) Highway robber
b) Robber baron
c) Black knight

14. John D. Rockefeller's prodigious wealth was founded on Standard Oil's anti-competitive practices. By 1900 he controlled what percentage of the United States' oil industry?
a) 70%
b) 80%
c) 90%

15. Pittsburgh steel tycoon and philanthropist Andrew Carnegie gave away about 90% of his wealth. As a young man he had been glad to have access to books. How many libraries did he fund?
a) 909
b) 1,609
c) 2,509

16. Henry Ford built his first car in 1892 and launched the Ford Motor Company in 1903. Which famous inventor had encouraged him to experiment and develop his ideas?
a) Alexander Graham Bell
b) Thomas Edison
c) Henry Singer

17. Along with brothers Lamar and William Herbert Hunt, billionaire oil executive Nelson Bunker Hunt tried and failed to corner the world market for which commodity in the late

1970s and early 1980s?
a) Copper
b) Silver
c) Platinum

18. When J. Paul Getty's grandson J. Paul Getty III was kidnapped for a ransom of $17 million, why did the grandfather, the world's richest man, refuse to pay more than $2.2 million?
a) He said it was all he could afford
b) It was the maximum tax-deductible amount
c) The kidnappers cut off the boy's ear, so Getty said he wasn't getting his money's worth

19. Eccentric Howard Hughes first found success with Hughes Tools before moving into aviation and movie-making. In his later years he lived in Las Vegas hotels – when one asked him and his entourage to leave, he bought the hotel. Which one?
a) El Rancho Vegas
b) Caesars Palace
c) The Desert Inn

20. The richest American in the 1980s shunned publicity and is almost unknown. He developed the supertanker, which increased the profitability of the oil trade. Who was he?
a) Adler von Lubeck
b) John H. Kellogg
c) Daniel K. Ludwig

GREAT FIRES AND OTHER DISASTERS

The ability to bounce back from adversity and come back stronger has always characterized America. These disasters may have seemed ruinous at the time, but just like the Chicago fire of 1871, the response has led to improved safety and more secure buildings. See what you know about these setbacks of the past.

1. The English colonies nearly didn't get off the ground at all. How many times was Jamestown, the first settlement, burned down in the seventeenth century?
a) Twice
b) Three times

2. The hot summer of 1871 caused a high number of fires. On the same day that the Great Chicago Fire broke out, which forest fire, the most deadly in the U.S., claimed five times as many lives?
a) Smokehouse Creek, Texas
b) Unalakleet, Arkansas
c) Peshtigo, Wisconsin

3. The Washburn 'A' flour mill in Minneapolis was the world's largest, until it exploded in 1878 taking eighteen lives and also destroying five neighboring mills. What was the cause?
a) A cigar left smouldering on a wooden handrail
b) A spark from two millstones ignited flour dust in the air
c) Sabotage by one of the neighboring mills

4. The South Fork Dam in Pennsylvania burst in 1889 and unleashed a flood of water equivalent to the average flow of the Mississippi, on Johnstown.

How did they clear the 30-acre mountain of debris afterwards?
a) With dynamite
b) By hand and horse
c) By fire

5. Excluding terrorism, the fire at Chicago's Iroquois Theatre in 1903 is the worst building fire in U.S. history. It led to reforms in fire safety for public buildings. What was missing at the Iroquois?
a) A fire alarm or a telephone
b) Exit signs
c) Unlocked, outward-opening fire doors
d) All of the above

6. Two huge underground explosions caused America's worst mining disaster, at Monongah WV, in 1907. How many of the 367-strong, mostly immigrant workforce survived?

a) One Polish miner and four Italians
b) Seven Irish miners and twenty-three Germans
c) Fourteen Frenchmen and twenty-eight Canadians

7. The SS *Eastland*, a pleasure steamer on the Great Lakes, had a history of listing while underway. In 1915 she capsized in the Chicago River while docked and boarding over two thousand day-trippers, employees of which large employer?
a) Western Electric in Cicero
b) Armour & Company, Chicago stockyards
c) Pullman coachbuilding works

8. The crash of American Airlines Flight 191, seconds after take-off from Chicago's O'Hare International Airport in 1979, is

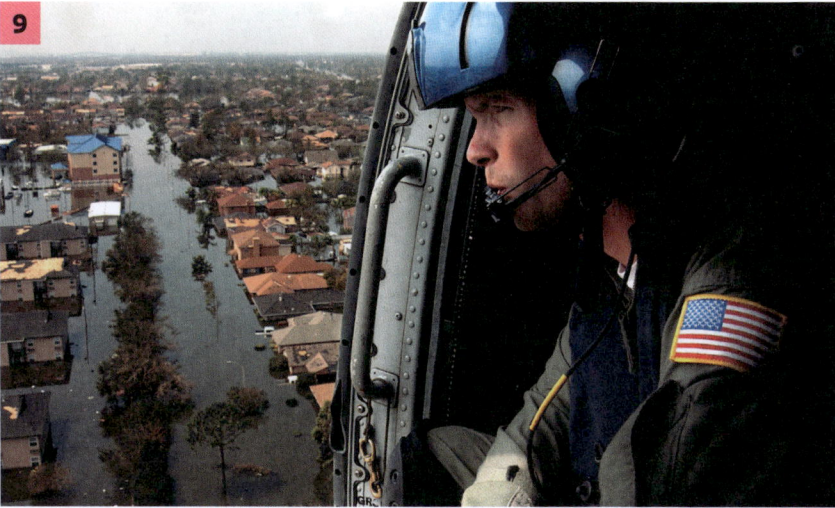

the worst on U.S. soil. What failure caused the accident?
a) A wing fell off during take-off
b) The tailfin fell off during take-off
c) One of its engines fell off during take-off

9. Hurricane Katrina devastated New Orleans when storm surges broke down the levees and flooded 80% of the city. At its height, what was the diameter of the hurricane?
a) 240 Miles
b) 170 miles
c) 100 miles

10. Both Hurricane Katrina and Hurricane Harvey (2017) were estimated to have cost $125 billion of damage. What is the name of the hurricane that devastated Puerto Rico in 2017 causing damage of $95 billion?
a) Hurricane Blanca
b) Hurricane Maria
c) Hurricane Esmerelda

11. The Great Molasses Flood of 1919 occurred in Boston when a large molasses storage tank burst, sending 2.3 million gallons

of the stuff through the streets. It caused 21 deaths and 150 injuries and residents claimed to smell it around the streets for years afterwards. What is molasses?
a) A noxious byproduct of heavy oil refining
b) A thick syrup, the byproduct of sugar refining

12. Riverboat accidents were common in the 19th century, with boats hitting submerged trees or their boilers exploding. When the *Sultana* steamboat went down in the Mississippi in 1865 in America's worst maritime disaster there was an extra level to the tragedy. What was it?
a) It was full of newly arrived immigrants, seeing America for the first time
b) It was packed with paroled prisoners-of-war who had survived wretched Confederate camps
c) The crew included Henry Clemens, Mark Twain's brother

13. The destruction of the Twin Towers was a national tragedy

with frightening scenes. It also brought some inspiring stories of courage and survival. Despite the high death toll, how many people had been in the World Trade Center when the planes hit?
a) 9,500
b) 12,750
c) 17,400

14. The deadliest earthquake in the history of the United States hit San Francisco in April 1906, rupturing gas mains and causing a fire that swept the city. How much of the city was destroyed?
a) 35%
b) 50%
c) 80%

15. The deadliest U.S. avalanche occurred in Wellington. For nine days at the end of February 1910, the Wellington area experienced severe blizzards. Two trains, a passenger train and a mail train were stuck in the depot when a wall of snow a half-mile wide came down the mountain and crushed the trains. It was not until 21 weeks later (July) that the last of the victims could be removed. In which state is Wellington?
a) Vermont
b) Colorado
c) Washington

WORLD FAIRS

There have been many world fairs over the years, but few could match the scale of those held in the United States. Try and answer these questions on some of the more popular events.

1. America's first World Fair was held in New York in 1853, only two years after the groundbreaking Great Exhibition in Britain. What building from the British event inspired its central hall?
a) The Crystal Palace
b) Buckingham Palace
c) Palace of Westminster

2. A World Fair was held to celebrate the centenary of U.S. independence. The 1876 fair showcased recent inventions and introduced the public to popcorn, bananas and root beer. Where was it held?
a) Memphis
b) Philadelphia
c) Baltimore

3. What was the star exhibit of the 1876 World Fair?

a) A recreated Hopi village with Hopi people and a Snake Dance
b) The Centennial Monorail
c) George Ferris's steam-powered Observation Wheel

4. As part of its cultural program, what did the 1904 World Fair in St Louis exhibit for the first time?
a) Art by women
b) Art by Native Americans

5. The Panama Expositions of 1915 celebrated the completion of the Panama Canal. Confusingly, there were two large-scale expositions in California. Which was the one with U.S. government backing?
a) Panama-Pacific International Exposition, San Francisco
b) Panama-California Exposition, in Balboa Park, San Diego

6. ...and which lasted the longest?
a) San Francisco
b) San Diego

7. The 1939 World Fair, held in New York, was titled 'The World of Tomorrow'. Most of its futuristic structures were demolished within 120 days of the end. But why did some exhibitors leave early?
a) Hurricane Daniel temporarily closed the site
b) An outbreak of Spanish Influenza amongst exhibitors
c) The start of World War II

8. The 1964 World Fair was held in New York. What has part of the site been used for since?
a) Columbia University Science and Technology Park
b) Billie Jean King National Tennis Center and Citi Field

9. Enthusiasm for world fairs declined after the war. Attendances did not match expectations and few were profitable. A rare exception was Knoxville in 1982. How much did the expo make?
a) $3,456
b) $1,707
c) $57

10. The last U.S. World Fair was held in New Orleans in 1984. What significant first did it achieve?
a) The first World Fair mascot, a pelican called Seymour D. Fair
b) The first ever cable car operated by water power, known as the WASP

LAWLESS AMERICA

True crime in America has helped give the movie industry a ton of storylines. Although the reality is far grimier than anything on screen. See how much you know about these real-life perpetrators.

1. Al Capone's Chicago criminal empire flourished with the supply of alcohol during Prohibition. What was he finally convicted for?
a) Bribery of city officials
b) Tax evasion
c) Defrauding the U.S. Post Office

2. Determined to take down Capone's crime empire, police officer Eliot Ness was in charge of a nine-man team known by what name?
a) The Invincibles
b) The Untouchables
c) The Dukes of Hazard

3. Bank robber Butch Cassidy claimed never to have shot a man; but the Sundance Kid and the rest of his gang certainly did. What was the gang called?
a) The Wild Boys of Wyoming
b) The Banks Gang
c) The Hole-in-the-Wall Gang

4. Amiable bank robber Willie Sutton stole an estimated $2m in a 40-year career. He said he always brought a gun because: 'You can't rob a bank with charm and personality' but it was never loaded because 'someone might get hurt'. When asked why he robbed banks he replied: 'Because that's where the money is.' True or False?

5. What film was assassin Lee Harvey Oswald watching when he was picked up at the Texas Theatre in Dallas?
a) *War is Hell*
b) *101 Dalmatians*

6. Legendary outlaw of the Old West, Billy the Kid, made newspaper headlines for six years before his inevitably violent death in 1881 aged 21. What was his name at birth?
a) William H. Bonney
b) Henry McCarty
c) Pat Garrett

7. The 1974 kidnap of Patty Hearst, heir to the Hearst newspaper fortune, took an unexpected twist when she began helping her captors in armed robberies. What was the name of the group?
a) The Simbionese Liberation Army
b) The Bay Area Research Collective
c) The Liberal Crime Squad

8. 'The Teflon is gone. The don is covered with Velcro, and all the charges stuck.' About whom was James Fox of the FBI talking at the end of a trial in 1992?
a) Michael 'Mikey Scars' Leonardo
b) Salvatore 'Sammy the Bull' Gravano
c) John 'The Dapper Don' Gotti

9. Rose Dunn learned to ride and shoot with her outlaw brothers. But when they gunned down her outlaw boyfriend in 1895, she quit outlawin' and married a politician. What was her nickname?
a) Rose of Oklahoma
b) San Antonio Rose
c) Rose of Cimarron

10. 'D. B. Cooper' hijacked a Northwest Airlines flight, threatening to blow up the plane. He got hold of a $200,000 ransom, a choice of parachutes and thirty minutes out of Seattle jumped from the rear door of the Boeing 727. What happened next?
a) He broke his leg in the jump and was apprehended by law officers in Oregon
b) He was picked up in Ohio two months later depositing $10,000
c) Nobody knows for certain. It's the only documented unsolved case of air piracy

MONUMENTS

There are many monuments in America, the majority dedicated to defining moments in the nation's history. See how much you know about them.

1. The State House Bell in Philadelphia was removed during the Revolutionary War and taken to Allentown to save it being melted down for cannon. According to the National Constitution Center, when did it assume the name Liberty Bell?
a) The Declaration of Independence 1776
b) The Surrender of British forces in 1781
c) In the 1830s with the gradual abolition of slavery

2. On Liberty Island, Liberty carries a torch to enlighten the world, and a tablet with the date of U.S. Independence carved on it. What lies symbolically under her left foot?
a) A bent and battered British crown, representing the end of colonial rule
b) A broken shackle and chains, representing the abolition of slavery
c) An anchor, representing a safe haven for weary travelers

3. What monument, begun in 1948 and still unfinished, was commissioned by Lakota elder Henry Standing Bear in response to the sculptures of U.S. presidents on Mount Rushmore?
a) The Crazy Horse Memorial
b) The Geronimo Memorial
c) The Sitting Bull Memorial

4. The Lincoln Memorial has been a focus for campaigns on civil rights and race relations since its inauguration in 1922. Which powerful speech did Martin Luther King Jr. deliver from its steps?
a) 'I have been to the mountaintop'
b) 'Our God is marching on!'
c) 'I have a dream'

5. The Gateway Arch in St Louis, Missouri, celebrates American expansion westward. At least ten pilots have flown (illegally) through it: what happened when a hot-air balloon tried it?
a) It struck the arch and fell 70ft before regaining control
b) Wind currents around the arch briefly trapped it in a spin around one of the legs
c) It caught fire, forcing its pilot to parachute to safety

6. The Martin Luther King Jr. Memorial in Washington, D.C. is not the first raised to a Black American. To whom does that honor belong?
a) Harriet Tubman
b) Frederick Douglass

7. The obelisk of the Washington Memorial was briefly the world's tallest structure, taking over from Lincoln Cathedral in England in 1884. To what did it lose its crown in 1889?
a) Cologne Cathedral, Germany
b) The Eiffel Tower, Paris, France

8. Building work on the Washington Memorial started in 1848 but was halted from 1854 till 1877. What was the reason for the delay?
a) The project ran out of funds
b) A dispute with the marble quarry owners in Baltimore County, Maryland
c) The Washington Society planned to move the location

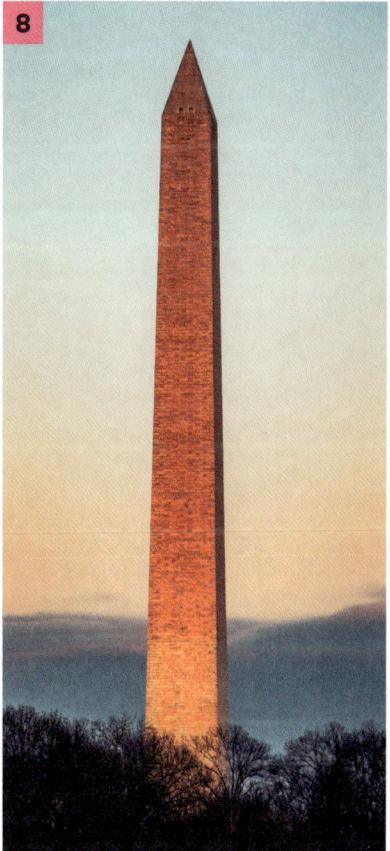

9. The Marine Corps War Memorial is an iconic sculpture inspired by a 1945 photograph of U.S. Marines hoisting an American flag. Where was the photograph taken?
a) Okinawa
b) Iwo Jima
c) Midway

10. Arlington National Cemetery in Virginia honors fallen military personnel and includes the Tomb of the Unknown Soldier. Which of these presidents is also buried there?
a) Woodrow Wilson
b) Harry S. Truman
c) John F. Kennedy

11. The Tomb of the Unknown Soldier originated with a serviceman from which conflict?
a) The Civil War
b) The Spanish-American War
c) World War I

12. Which sunken U.S. battleship is central to the Pearl Harbor National Memorial in Hawaii?
a) USS *Arizona*
b) USS *Texas*
c) USS *Alabama*

13. The Vietnam Veterans Memorial in Washington, D.C. is a somber, black granite wall inscribed with the names of fallen soldiers. How many names are etched in this hallowed place?
a) 46,000
b) 58,000

14. The striking Korean War Veterans Memorial in Washington, D.C., honors those who served in the Korean War, and features soldiers on patrol. How long did the conflict last?
a) 1950–1953
b) 1953–1956

15. Mount Rushmore and the Black Hills are considered sacred by American Indians such as the Arapaho, Cheyenne, and Lakota Sioux. They called the mountain 'Six Grandfathers' symbolizing ancient gods in the form of: north, south, east, west – and which two others?
a) Water and Forest
b) Mountain and Valley
c) Sky and Earth

16. Funding the giant sculptures at Mount Rushmore was always limited by budgetary issues. What was the original plan?
a) To feature five presidents, including Ulysses Grant
b) To sculpt them as full figures, not just heads

17. The sinking of the USS *Maine* in Havana Harbor was the flashpoint that started the 1898 Spanish-American war (even though it was very likely an accident). The ship was brought to the surface and many artifacts

from it were distributed around the U.S. as memorials. The foremast of the *Maine* resides where today?
a) East Battery, Charleston
b) Annapolis, Maryland
c) Bangor, Maine

18. Echoing a trend to more linear memorials and monuments – which former president does this Washington memorial honor?
a) John F. Kennedy
b) Dwight D. Eisenhower
c) Franklin D. Roosevelt

19. In the post-Civil War period the level of bitterness directed towards the North from the defeated South can be gauged by the people of Savannah. Tasked with creating a Confederate war memorial they refused to use architects from the North and settled on Welshman Robert Reid. Pre-cut sandstone blocks from Nova Scotia were shipped from Canada to Savannah using a British vessel to avoid transporting the monument through Northern states. True or False?

20. Polish cavalry officer Casimir Pulaski was likely killed by friendly fire at the Siege of Savannah, but the city has remembered his bravery in many different ways. There are many reminders around the city, but which one of the following is yet to be created in Chatham County?
a) Pulaski Square
b) Pulaski Monument
c) Fort Pulaski
d) Pulaski Hotel
e) Pulaski Expressway

CIVIL RIGHTS HISTORY

The Constitution guarantees many different rights to American citizens. How much do you know about the building blocks of America?

1. Some delegates thought the resolution passed at the Seneca Falls Convention organized by Elizabeth Cady Stanton in 1848 was too extreme. What shocking idea did it contain?
a) That women should be allowed to wear trousers
b) That women need not obey their husbands
c) That women should be allowed to vote in elections

2. Lincoln's Emancipation Proclamation (1863) was the first major piece of Civil Rights legislation, but segregation persisted. Why was African American Kate Brown beaten and kicked in 1866?
a) She boarded 'the white people's car' of a train bound for Washington, D.C.
b) She attempted to use a 'whites only' rest room in Virginia
c) She tried to buy food from a grocer who displayed a 'white trade only' sign

3. Jim Crow Laws were introduced in the former

Confederate States of the U.S. to perpetuate segregation. What was the origin of the term 'Jim Crow'?
a) It began as an affectionate name for any big black bird
b) It was an 1828 stage routine by white actor Thomas D. Rice wearing blackface
c) Jim Crow was a plantation owner known for his harsh treatment of slaves

4. Which group of citizens was not allowed to vote until 1924?
a) Women
b) African Americans
c) Native Americans

5. The principle of 'separate but equal' was used to justify segregation, although provision for each race was rarely equal. Why did Black American Oliver Brown challenge it in 1954 in the landmark Brown vs Board case?
a) His daughter was made to travel to a distant Black-only school instead of her local one
b) He entered a white-only school and saw the difference in facilities

6. Rosa Parks was an NAACP officer in Montgomery, Alabama. She was asked to give up her Black-section bus seat to a white

passenger because the white-only section was full. Did she?
a) Yes, but vowed never to travel on a Montgomery bus again
b) Yes, but then sat in white-only seat that became available
c) No, and her arrest inspired a year-long boycott of the buses

7. Meetings were held in the Montgomery church of a local pastor, whose leadership and oratory surrounding the incident made him a national figure. Who was he?
a) Howard Thurman
b) Martin Luther King Jr.
c) Malcolm X

8. The right to protest cannot always be taken for granted. Thirteen unarmed students were shot (4 dead) on the campus of Kent State University by the National Guard in 1970? What news event had sparked this particular protest?
a) The expansion of the Vietnam War into Cambodia
b) The U.S. National Draft
c) The depiction of napalm-strafed children on television

9. The Stonewall Inn in Manhattan was a safe haven for homosexuals. A police raid in 1969 sparked riots, and gave new impetus to the gay rights movement. When did same-sex marriage become legal across 50 states?
a) 2010
b) 2015
c) 2020

10. Polygamy (multiple partner marriage) has been regarded as a felony in all 50 states since 1882. Which state downgraded it to a misdemeanor in 2020 (i.e. the same as a parking ticket)?
a) Utah
b) Nevada
c) California

AMERICAN MUSEUMS

The custodians of history, America has some of the largest and most inspiring museums, along with some very specialized ones as well (two museums to barbed wire). How much do you know about our custodians of the past?

1. The museum in Charleston, South Carolina, is the nation's oldest, founded in 1773. Among its broad range of exhibits from the arts and sciences, one is unique. What is it?
a) A fossilized skeleton of the largest bird ever discovered
b) A silver fountain pen left by George Washington when he visited the city
c) A pair of dueling pistols once owned by Alexander Hamilton

2. The mining town of Superior, Arizona, is home to two museums, including America's smallest, which covers only 134 sq ft. What is its roof made of?
a) Wheelbarrows
b) Recycled drinks cans
c) Dried pumpkin rinds

3. The Smithsonian Castle on the National Mall was the first building and remains the headquarters of the Institute, which today numbers 21 museums and 21 libraries, 14 research centers and a zoo. When was it built?
a) 1824
b) 1847

4. Ellis Island now houses the National Museum of Immigration. Who was the first person to be processed at the Ellis Island immigration center?
a) Annie Moore from Ireland, who was given a $10 gold coin
b) Samuel Ellis from Wales, who was given a passport
c) Michiel Pauw from the Netherlands, who was given a hen

5. New York's Metropolitan Museum of Art is the largest museum in the U.S. Who painted one of its most famous exhibits, Washington Crossing the Delaware?
a) French-American artist Robert Colescotte
b) German-American artist Emanuel Leutze
c) English-American artist David Shulman

6. The Country Music Hall of Fame (Nashville) and the Rock and Roll Hall of Fame (Cleveland) were joined in 2000 by the Museum of Pop Culture in Seattle. Who founded it?
a) Google co-founder Larry Page
b) Apple co-founder Steve Wozniak
c) Microsoft co-founder Paul Allen

7. The National WWI Museum is in Kansas City. Where is the National WWII Museum?
a) New Orleans
b) Pearl Harbor
c) Washington, D.C.

8. The exhibits of a museum in Indianapolis, Indiana (the largest of its kind in the world), include the Dinosphere, the Beyond Spaceship Earth gallery and an antique carousel. What is the museum?
a) The Museum of Movie Special Effects of Indianapolis
b) The Children's Museum of Indianapolis

c) The TV History Museum of Indianapolis

9. The Musical Instruments Museum in Phoenix, Arizona, is the largest of its kind with over 15,000 items in its collection. What is notable about the piano in the John Lennon exhibit?
a) Lennon scratched a self-portrait on the piano lid
b) Lennon painted the words Yoko and Ono on either side of the music holder
c) Lennon wrote the song *Imagine* on it

10. The U.S. has many museums dedicated to the exploration of flight. What is distinctive about the one in San Diego, California?
a) It's housed in the USS *Midway* – once the biggest aircraft carrier in the world
b) Unlike the carrier museum in NYC, it's dedicated to plane designs which never got off the ground
c) Visitors can be taken on flights in a limited number of exhibits

HISTORY OF TECH

Since the 1970s, Silicon Valley has led the world in expanding the tech horizon. How much do you know about this rapidly evolving sector?

1. Bell introduced the first non-rotary telephone dial – i.e. a push-button phone. When?
a) 1954
b) 1963
c) 1970

2. Micro Instrumentation and Telemetry Systems (MITS) launched the first personal computer, the Altair 8800, and advertised it in *Popular Electronics*, in what year?
a) 1975
b) 1977

3. Two young tech bros, Bill Gates and Tim Allen (of Microsoft fame) contacted the makers of the Altair 8800 and told them they could write a BASIC program for it – were they interested? Even though they hadn't used one and didn't own one. True or False?

4. Even before the PC got adopted by consumers, there were gremlins creeping into mainframe computers. What was the name of the first virus detected in 1971?
a) Trojan
b) Creeper
c) Blue screen

5. Who sent the first email using ARPANET in 1971?
a) Steve Jobs
b) Ray Tomlinson

10

6. What was considered to be the first smartphone introduced in 1992?
a) IBM Simon, Personal Communicator
b) Apple Newton
c) Blackberry Mk1

7. The first social media network was in business from 1997 to 2000. What was it called?
a) Contax.com – it called itself 'the first interactive digital Rolodex'
b) SixDegrees.com – a play on the phrase 'Six degrees of separation'

8. What was the first modern web browser, the forerunner to the browser everyone had in the 1990s, Netscape Navigator?
a) Mosaic (1993)
b) Spider (1993)
c) Burrow (1992)

9. Through her work with the 'frequency-hopping spread spectrum' in the 1940s, this former Hollywood screen actress pioneered the technology later used for Wi-Fi. Who was it?
a) Claudette Colbert
a) Katharine Hepburn
c) Hedy Lamarr

10. The first commercial automatic self-driving taxi was introduced by Google spin-off company Waymo. What year did it stop running tests and start taking passengers?
a) 2020
b) 2021
c) 2022

BUYING AMERICA

Ever since 1803 America has been looking to make real estate investments. Try and answer these questions on the inventory.

1. The Louisiana Purchase was a massive investment for the young nation – especially when critics pointed out that Napoleon couldn't defend it and it could be got for nothing. It cost 20% of the federal budget. How much was that?
a) $5m
b) $10m
c) $15m

2. At the time – the United States didn't have the money. Where did they get it from?
a) Loans from Russia
b) Loans from British and Dutch banks
c) Loans from Spanish and Vatican banks

3. Why did France's Emperor Napoleon agree to sell to Thomas Jefferson in 1803?
a) He had received a rival bid from the Netherlands, Great Britain's ally
b) He was planning to invade Great Britain and needed his troops back from Louisiana

4. Most of the U.S. Virgin Islands were acquired by America in a single purchase in 1917. Before the deal, what were the islands known as?
a) The Danish Virgin Islands
b) Dutch Virginia
c) Les Isles de Virginie

5. One last U.S. Virgin Island was purchased in 1944 for a bargain price, $10,000. Blessed with several freshwater ponds, it was a valuable stop for pirates and other travelers. What is its name?
a) Fill-The-Barrel Island
b) Red Beard's Island
c) Water Island

6. The Panama Canal Zone was created in 1903, under U.S. authority to build a canal. The U.S. paid $10,000,000 for it, and an annual rent of $250,000. What was the zone's state code?
a) PC
b) CZ
c) PZ

7. The Canal Zone reverted to full Panamanian control in 1979. During U.S. control, how were Americans living and working in the zone known?
a) Panamericans
b) Zonians

8. Many former Spanish territories have come under U.S. control. Which of the following was *not* purchased from Spain?
a) The Philippines
b) Puerto Rico
c) Florida

9. It may seem strange that the capitalist U.S. is allowed to control a small piece of communist Cuba. What has the country been paying Cuba in annual rent for Guantanamo Bay since 1934?
a) $400,050
b) A token $5
c) $4,085.00

10. What forced Russia to sell its Alaskan territory to the U.S. in 1867?
a) Costly defeat by the British in the Crimean War
b) The difficulty of supplying Russian bases in Alaska through frozen Arctic seas

INVENTIONS

American ingenuity has brought the world some striking innovations. Equally, there are some inventions that people *think* are American, but actually originated elsewhere...

1. Following their successful powered flights of 1903 the Wright Brothers hired a patent attorney to protect which invention?
a) Their self-built engine, the Wright Vertical 4
b) Their novel use of bracing in the super-light wings
c) Their three-axis control system that used wing-warping, a rudder, and an elevator

2. Nikola Tesla was an American-based Serb who took on Thomas Edison in 'the Battle of the Currents' to determine which electricity supply system would be adopted in America. Which current did Tesla champion?
a) Direct Current DC
b) Alternating Current AC

3. Businessman and inventor Garrett Morgan invented the first traffic signal in 1923. How did it work?
a) Manually-operated traffic signal arms featuring 'Stop' and 'Go' signs
b) Automatic lights – Red for 'Stop' and Green for 'Go'

4. The polio vaccine prevents the crippling disease poliomyelitis by introducing a weakened form of the virus into the body. The physician who invented it tested the vaccine on himself and his family in 1953. It was licensed in 1955. Who was it?

a) Dr. Jonas Salk
b) Dr Benjamin Spock

5. Percy Spencer invented the microwave oven in 1945 after seeing the effect of magnetrons he was working with on radar defense systems, melt a nearby candy bar. His employer, Raytheon, patented the device. How much did they pay Spencer?
a) $2
b) $20,511

6. American inventor Willis H. Carrier built the first modern electrical air conditioning unit. What was it used for?
a) John D. Rockefeller's New York private office
b) A lithographing and publishing company in Brooklyn to keep paper dimensions accurate
c) Delmonico's restaurant to keep diners cool

7. Who invented Tupperware in 1946?
a) Earl Tupper
b) Kitchen Aid's research department
c) Frigidaire

8. Stephanie Louise Kwolek was a Polish-American chemist who worked for the DuPont company. In 1995 she became only the fourth woman to be added to the National Inventors Hall of Fame. What did she invent?
a) Teflon
b) Kevlar
c) Glyphosate weedkiller

9. The Manhattan Project was a collaborative effort by Allied scientists during World War II to create a nuclear weapon before the Axis scientists achieved the feat. The team, led by Robert Oppenheimer, created a prototype

bomb which was first detonated in 1945. What was the bomb called?
a) Thin Man
b) Fat Man
c) Little Boy

10. Robert Hutchings Goddard was an American engineer, physicist and inventor who is credited with creating and building the world's first what?
a) Electron telescope
b) Liquid fueled rocket
c) Sonar submarine detection device

11. Baseball was first played in England before crossing the pond. It is referenced in a classic English novel where the children of the village go off to play 'Base Ball'. Who was the author?
a) Jonathan Swift
b) Jane Austen
c) Daniel Defoe

12. Poker Nights are still going strong and Las Vegas rakes in a ton of money from its blackjack tables. Where did playing cards originate?
a) China
b) Greece
c) Italy

13. Actor David Schwimmer – Ross in *Friends* – once spent a summer as a roller-skating waiter in Chicago. Where were roller-skates invented?
a) Belgium
b) Poland
c) Czechoslovakia

14. Everyone loves the occasional Dunkin' donuts. Who brought the donuts?
a) The French
b) The Dutch

15. The iconic Marlboro Man was a western cowboy who spent all day in the saddle, riding the range and relaxing with a 'cool smoke' at the end of the day. Who were the first cowboys?
a) Argentinian *gauchos*
b) Mexican *vaqueros*
c) French *gardians* of the Camargue

16. Apart from expensive leather chaps, cowboys are associated with leather boots and hard-wearing denim pants. Where did denim originate?
a) Nimes in France
b) Buttenheim, Bavaria, home town of Levi Strauss

17. Who invented (and patented) peanut butter?
a) An Egyptian
b) A Canadian

18. Football, as played in the NFL, is derived from the game of rugby, which originated as ... soccer. Rugby only started when a young soccer player picked up the ball and ran with it. Where was that?
a) Eton School
b) Oxford University
c) Rugby School

19. 'French Fries' is an American term for slender fried potato wedges. But food historians believe they were first cooked where?
a) Belgium
b) Austria
c) Prussia

20. The Liberty Bell in Philadelphia has been recast twice since it got to America. Where was it originally manufactured?
a) Dresden, Germany
b) Whitechapel, London
c) St. Denis, Paris

ACROSS THE 50 STATES

AMERICAN 'CAPITALS OF THE WORLD'

There is no law against calling yourself the 'Penguin Capital of the World', even if, like Cut Bank in Montana, you don't have any live penguins. What they *do* have, is one of the largest penguin statues in the world celebrating how cold it gets. We have assembled ten 'Capitals of the World' and your task is to match their claim to fame with the town or city. Some are famous places, and for others, it's all in the name...

1.	UFO Capital of the World	**New Orleans, Louisiana**
2.	Most Boring Capital of the World	**San Antonio, Texas**
3.	Groundhog Capital of the World	**Pinehurst, North Carolina**
4.	Weed Capital of the World	**Greenfield, California**
5.	Dog-Friendly Capital of the World	**Perry, Georgia**
6.	Golf Capital of the World	**Boring, Oregon**
7.	Beekeeping Capital of the World	**Punxsutawney, Pennsylvania**
8.	Puffy Taco Capital of the World	**Hershey, Pennsylvania**
9.	Honeymoon Capital of the World	**Newport, Rhode Island**
10.	Cowboy Capital of the World	**Niagara Falls, New York**
11.	Peach Capital of the World	**North Pole, Alaska**
12.	Choo-Choo Capital of the World	**Cuba, Missouri**
13.	Chocolate Capital of the World	**Roswell, New Mexico**
14.	College World Series Capital of the World	**Westminster, Colorado**
15.	Gilded Age Mansion Capital of the World	**Weed, California**
16.	Cajun Music Capital of the World	**Beeville, Texas**
17.	Broccoli Capital of the World	**Bandera, Texas**
18.	Voodoo Capital of the World	**Omaha, Nebraska**
19.	Christmas Capital of the World	**Chattanooga, Tennessee**
20.	Route 66 Mural Capital of the World	**Lafayette, Louisiana**

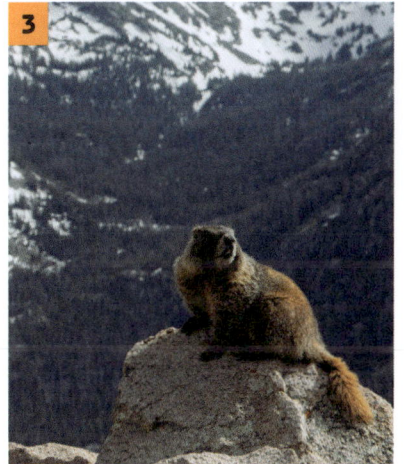

21. Gibsonton in Florida gained fame as the favorite overwintering spot for performers from the carnival and circus world. At one time the Post Office operated a special, low counter, built for entertainers of restricted height, and zoning laws allowed elephants and circus trailers on residents' front lawns. What was the town billed as?
a) The Sideshow Capital of the World
b) The Circus Trailer Capital of the World

22. In northern Wisconsin, Mercer stakes its claim to be the Loon Capital of the World. It has a showpiece 16-foot-high statue known as 'Claire d'Loon'. What are we celebrating here?
a) People highly affected by the lunar cycle
b) People who enjoy wearing loon pants
c) Ducks

23. Keeping it in the same state, Jefferson, Wisconsin, hosts an annual festival for a familiar animal. Among other celebrations, they hold races. Making it what...?
a) The Goat Racing Capital of the World
b) The Weasel Racing Capital of the World
c) The Skunk Racing Capital of the World

24. Mackinac Island in Michigan is known as the Fudge Capital of the World. Tourists who come to sample the amazing variety of fudge on sale are known as...?
a) Fudgers
b) Fudgies

25. Scottsboro, Alabama, is the Lost Luggage Capital of the World. Why?
a) There is a large retailer selling unclaimed baggage from U.S. airports
b) It is the holding depot for United, Delta, Jet Blue and American Airlines

26. The Last Blockbuster Capital of the World is attributed to the city hosting the sole surviving Blockbuster store. As such it's a popular tourist attraction selling Blockbuster memorabilia and still renting out movies. Where would you find it?
a) Bend, Oregon
b) Lewiston, Maine

27. Superior, Arizona, regards itself as the Apache Tears Capital of the World. What are Apache tears?
a) Pear-flavored sweets in the shape of a teardrop
b) Rounded pebbles of obsidian, a volcanic glass

28. Many towns claim to be the Cowboy Capital of the World but only one has a major claim for being the Cowboy Poetry Capital of the World. The National Cowboy Poetry Gathering takes place in Elko, Nevada, each year, a tradition that includes ballads, songs, and other verse. It was founded by the great cowboy philosopher Will Rogers. True or False?

29. Havre de Grace located on the Susquehanna River in Maryland is known as the Decoy Capital of the World. It has a museum dedicated to waterfowl and the carving of decoy ducks, used to lure wild ducks. Where did the town get its name?
a) Le Havre, France
b) Grâce-Hollogne, Belgium

30. One of the largest natural springs in the world emerges at Mammoth Spring in Fulton County, Arkansas. The pure constant flow makes it the perfect recipient of the title...?
a) Striped Bass Fishing Capital of the World
b) Trout Fishing Capital of the World

31. It may not be an Olympic event yet but Cow Chip Tossing has been held in Beaver County, Oklahoma, since the 1960s, giving it the enviable claim of Cow Chip Tossing Capital of the World. What is a cow chip?
a) Dried cow dung
b) Disks of concentrated cow feed

32. The Barbed Wire Capital of the World is La Crosse in Kansas, which has a barbed wire museum. But is it the only one in the USA?
a) Yes
b) No, there's also one in Texas

33. Casey, Illinois, is known as the Big Things Capital of the World because of ... well, the very big things it has built. These include

BLOCKBUSTER

the world's largest rocking chair, the largest wind chimes and what else?
a) World's largest mailbox
b) World's largest banana
c) World's largest plaster sock

34. Olney, Illinois, known as the White Squirrel Capital of the World, is home to the world's largest known white squirrel colony. How many were there in 2022?
a) 64
b) 940

35. Frog fans in Louisiana know what they'll be doing on the second weekend in May. The annual festival in Rayne, the Frog Racing Capital of the World, has a whole variety of frog-based activities in a family-friendly event. But it's not *totally* frog friendly as there's also a frog-eating competition. True or False?

36. Sweetwater, Texas, is known as the Rattlesnake Capital of the World because of its annual rattlesnake roundup, held since 1958. Rattlesnakes are milked for their venom, bought and sold and used to create snakeskin products as well as deep-fried rattlesnake. The roundup once featured in an episode of which TV series?
a) *Family Guy*
b) *The Simpsons*
c) *American Dad*

37. Kearney, Nebraska, is known as the Sandhill Crane Capital of the World because 80% of the world's sandhill crane population funnels through Nebraska as they migrate. How many visit?
a) 50,000
b) 500,000

38. Fans of the perfect watermelon will be well aware that Cordele, Georgia, produces the largest and sweetest watermelons. How is its status as World Capital celebrated?
a) It has an annual watermelon festival in June
b) It hosts a watermelon marathon. Contestants carry a 20lb watermelon over a 3-mile steeplechase course

39. What reinforces New Mexico's boast to be Chilli Capital of the World ?
a) License plates with red and green chillis
b) The state flag is a red and a green chilli pepper

40. Clarksdale, Mississippi and Jackson, Mississippi, both claim to be Blues Capital of the World, but a major American city hosts multiple venues playing Blues 365 days of the year. Which one?
a) Chicago, Illinois
b) Austin, Texas
c) Phoenix, Arizona

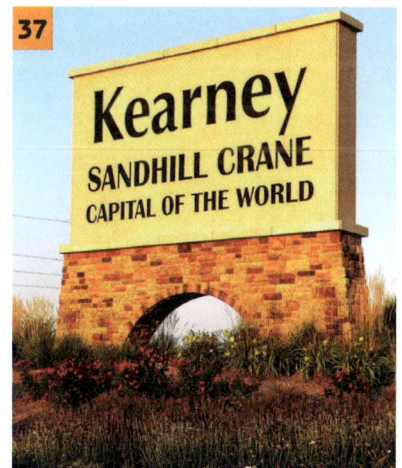

ALABAMA

If New England is the cradle of the Revolutionary War then Alabama is certainly the Cradle of the Civil Rights Movement

1. What is the state capital of Alabama?
a) Huntsville
b) Birmingham
c) Montgomery

2. When was Alabama admitted to the Union?
a) 1802
b) 1819

3. Which is Alabama's largest city?
a) Huntsville
b) Mobile
c) Tuscaloosa

4. The highest point in Alabama is Cheaha Mountain at 2,413 feet. Though nowhere near as high as North Carolina's Mount Mitchell (6,684 feet) it is still part of the Appalachian mountain range. True or False?

5. Where does Alabama rank in the most populated states in the U.S.?
a) 24th
b) 35th

6. What is the name of the world's largest cast-iron statue in Birmingham that commemorates the city's steel heritage?
a) Mars
b) Titan
c) Vulcan

7. In 1836 Alabama was the first state to give its citizens an official holiday on which day?
a) 4th July

b) George Washington's birthday
c) Christmas Day

8. Mardi Gras was first celebrated by French settlers in Mobile in 1703. It pre-dated New Orleans' celebrations by how many years?
a) 56
b) 104
c) 154

9. What famous sporting venue is located in Talladega?
a) The longest NASCAR oval, the Talladega Speedway
b) The Crimson Tide's Saban Field at Bryant-Denny Stadium

10. Celebrated Civil Rights advocate Rosa Parks instigated the Montgomery bus boycott. What was the route she was traveling (on the bus's sign board)?
a) Cleveland Avenue
b) Polk Avenue

11. Another astonishing woman, Helen Keller was born in Tuscumbia in 1880 and became one of America's leading campaigners for disability. What was hers?
a) She was blind
b) She was deaf
c) She was deaf and blind

12. What world-leading technology was developed in Huntsville?
a) The Saturn V rocket
b) The Lockheed SR-71 Blackbird spy plane

13. What is the state reptile?
a) Alabama red-bellied turtle
b) Alabama green-footed cooter
c) Alabama spiny-tailed iguana

14. The Alabama coat of arms has the flag of which nation in a quadrant?
a) Spain
b) France
c) Britain

15. Alabama has more species of freshwater _____ than any other state in the U.S.?
a) Frogs
b) Snails
c) Crayfish

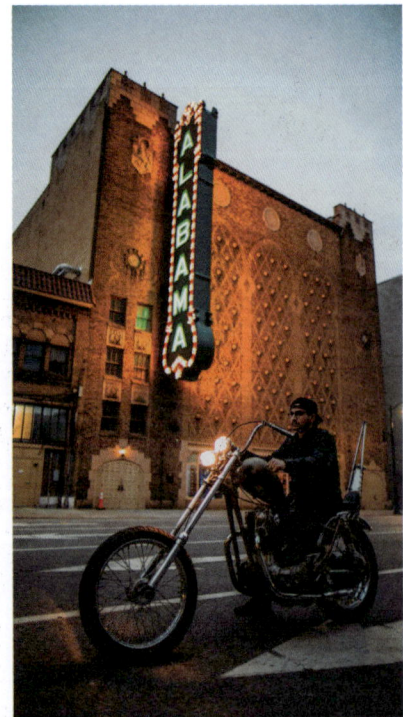

ALASKA

Once known as 'Seward's Folly' Alaska cost two cents an acre. It was cheap at ten times the price when they struck gold in the Klondike

1. What is the state capital of Alaska?
a) Badger
b) Ketchikan
c) Juneau

2. When was Alaska admitted to the Union?
a) 1942
b) 1959

3. Which is Alaska's largest city?
a) Fairbanks
b) Sitka
c) Anchorage

4. Mount McKinley is the highest peak in Alaska at 20,310 feet. What is it also known as?
a) Denali
b) Tanana
c) Mount Bering

5. Where does Alaska rank in the most populated states in the U.S.?
a) 48th
b) 50th

6. How much did Alaska cost William Seward when he bought it for the U.S. from Tsar Alexander II in 1867?
a) $7.2m
b) $15.6m
c) $12m + 14 Pacific islands

7. In 1971, a weather station at Prospect Creek, Alaska, recorded the coldest U.S. temperature. How cold did it get?
a) -45F
b) -60F
c) -80F

8. The Trans-Alaska Pipeline stretches 800 miles between Prudhoe Bay to Valdez. Which is the southerly port?
a) Prudhoe Bay
b) Valdez

9. What is the state's official sport?
a) Ice hockey
b) Dog mushing
c) Cross-country skiing

10. During the diphtheria outbreak of 1925 the isolated town of Nome was saved by sled dogs carrying a vaccine through. One is commemorated with a statue in Central Park – which one?
a) Togo
b) Balto
c) Bono

11. Author Jack London based many of his novels in the wilds of Yukon territory. Which of the following is *not* a Jack London novel
a) *Call of the Wild*
b) *Dances with Wolves*
c) *White Fang*

12. Which city was at the heart of the 1890s Klondike Gold Rush?
a) Dawson City
b) Chilkoot City
c) Angels Camp

13. The Kodiak bear is found where?
a) The Kodiak archipelago
b) The Aleutian archipelago

14. What is the state mammal of Alaska?
a) Moose
b) Kodiak bear
c) Beaver

15. The city of Sitka gave its name to which popular forestry tree?
a) Sitka pine
b) Sitka larch
c) Sitka spruce

ARIZONA

Historically part of Alta California, explorers through the centuries have been awed by their first sight of the Grand Canyon

1. What is the state capital of Arizona?
a) Tucson
b) Phoenix
c) Flagstaff

2. When was Arizona admitted to the Union?
a) 1896
b) 1912

3. Phoenix is the state's largest city – which of the following is not in the Phoenix Metropolitan Area?
a) City of Scottsdale
b) City of Glendale
c) City of Allendale

4. The highest peak in Arizona is a dormant volcano – Mount Humphreys at 12,633 feet. Despite the vulcanicity it is also a ski resort with 55 ski runs. True or False?

5. Where does Arizona rank in the most populated states in the United States?
a) 6th
b) 14th

6. Arizona is one of the four states that meet at a corner, celebrated with the Four Corners Monument. Three of the states are Arizona, Colorado and New Mexico. What is the fourth?
a) Nevada
b) Utah
c) Idaho

7. The state hosts one of the world's oldest rodeos. In which town?
a) Tombstone
b) Tucson
c) Prescott

8. Arizona's economy is based on 'The 5 Cs' – cattle, citrus, climate, cotton and...?
a) Computer chips
b) Copper
c) Cadillac

9. Which planet was first discovered at the Lowell Observatory in Flagstaff in 1930?
a) Pluto
b) Neptune
c) Saturn

10. The Gunfight at the OK Corral in Tombstone involved which famous gunslingers?
a) Frank and Jesse James
b) Billy the Kid and Wild Bill Hickok
c) Wyatt Earp and Doc Holiday

11. The state of Arizona could have been named Montezuma. Of the following three choices, two are genuine contenders, one is false – spot the imposter.
a) Arizuma
b) Gadsonia
c) Navajonia

12. Located near Tucson, the massive ecological project to create a self-sustaining environment that could be used on another planet is called...?
a) Biosphere 2
b) Planet Eco

13. What is the state fish of Arizona?
a) Apache trout
b) Navajo roundtail chub
c) Flathead catfish

14. What is the state amphibian?
a) Arizona lurking toad
b) Arizona tree frog
c) Western tiger salamander

15. You can find the real London Bridge over Lake Havasu, though there was a long-held belief that Robert Paxton McCulloch thought he was buying which bridge?
a) Westminster Bridge
b) Tower Bridge
c) Blackfriars Bridge

ARKANSAS

The Natural State – Arkansas is known as The Natural State due to its stunning mountains, rivers, and forests

1. What is the state capital of Arkansas?
a) Fayetteville
b) Bentonville
c) Little Rock

2. When was Arkansas admitted to the Union?
a) 1805
b) 1836

3. Largest city Little Rock was named in 1722 by a French explorer. However, in 1920 there was a move to change to a name which appears on early maps from the U.S. Geological Survey. What was it?
a) Arkville
b) Arkburgh
c) Arkopolis

4. Arkansas is unusual in that it has a state pronunciation law. It is illegal to pronounce the state's name as Ar-kan-sas. It must be pronounced Ar-kan-saw. True or False?

5. The highest mountain in Arkansas rises to 2,753 feet. What is it called?
a) Mount Magazine
b) Mount Newspaper
c) Mount Broadsheet

6. Bentonville hosts a bizarre but popular annual cooking contest featuring dishes made from what?
a) Groundhogs
b) Squirrels
c) Mice

7. One of the nation's largest stores started up in Bentonville. Which one?
a) Walmart
b) Home Depot
c) Trader Joe's

8. America's 42nd president Bill Clinton was born where in Arkansas?
a) Little Rock
b) Pine Bluff
c) Hope

9. What does Arkansas produce more than any other U.S. state?
a) Avocados
b) Squash
c) Rice

10. The University of Arkansas Razorbacks are the state's beloved college football team, known for their unique chant, which is...?
a) 'Wooo Pig Sooie'
b) 'Gooo Piggy Pig Pig'

11. Arkansas is famous for its duck hunting and Stuttgart, Arkansas, is host to which famous competition?
a) Duck Calling Contest
b) Duck Herding Contest
c) Duck Racing Contest

12. Arkansas shares a border with Missouri to the north, Louisiana to the south, Texas to the southwest, Oklahoma to the west, and Mississippi and which other state to the east?

13. The town of Bauxite, Arkansas, was named after the ore it produced. What metal is derived from bauxite?
a) Magnesium
b) Aluminium
b) Chromium

14. Which unusual state park is located at Murfreesboro, Arkansas (where supposedly you are allowed to take home any gem you find)?
a) Crater of Diamonds State Park
b) Mountain of Emeralds State Park
c) River of Rubies State Park

15. What is Arkansas's state bird?
a) Mockingbird
b) Ruby-throated hummingbird
c) Whistling duck

CALIFORNIA

The Golden State has everything – Hollywood glitz, Silicon Valley tech, beaches, mountains, and majestic redwood forests

1. What is the state capital of California?
a) Pasadena
b) San Diego
c) Sacramento

2. When was California admitted to the Union?
a) 1850
b) 1865

3. Which of these facts about Eureka is *not* true?
a) It's the largest city between San Francisco and Portland
b) It's the state motto
c) Miner 49ers were obliged by state law to shout it if they found gold

4. Which is the highest mountain in California at 14,505 feet (and the whole of the Sierra Nevada)?

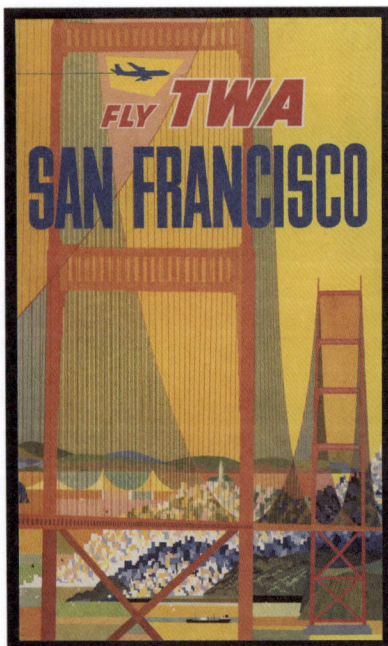

a) Mount Russell
b) Mount Whitney
c) Mount Shasta

5. Where does California rank in the most populated states in the U.S.?
a) 1st
b) 2nd

6. Spanish explorers founded San Francisco in 1776 and named it 'Yerba Buena' which means...?
a) Good anchorage
b) Good water
c) Good herbs

7. A highly destructive wildfire that began burning in the Santa Monica Mountains of Los Angeles County in January 2025 destroyed many homes and businesses. What was it known as?
a) The Malibu Fire
b) The Pallisades Fire
c) The Hollywood Fire

8. The famous Hollywood sign started life advertising a housing division called...?
a) Hollywood Homes
b) Hollywood Villas
c) Hollywoodland

9. California's economy is so strong, if it were a country it would be larger than the UK or India. True or False?

10. The McDonald brothers opened their first fast food restaurant in 1948 in which city?

a) San Bernardino
b) San Diego
c) San Jose

11. The Golden Gate Bridge was the longest suspension bridge in the world when it was completed in...?
a) 1927
b) 1937
c) 1947

12. Which famous transatlantic liner is moored in Long Beach?
a) SS *Normandie*
b) RMS *Queen Mary*
c) SS *United States*

13. What is California's state mammal?
a) Grizzly bear
b) Sonoma chipmunk
c) California deermouse

14. Santa Monica Pier in Los Angeles is the official finishing point of what?
a) The Pacific Coast Highway
b) Route 66
c) Mulholland Drive

15. San Diego has a legacy park from the great 1915 Panama-California exposition. What's it called?
a) Rocky Park
b) Balboa Park
c) Spreckles Park

COLORADO

The Centennial State, Colorado is the gateway to the Rocky Mountains and its world-class ski resorts and hiking trails

1. What is the state capital of Colorado?
a) Aurora
b) Thornton
c) Denver

2. When was Colorado admitted to the Union?
a) 1861
b) 1876

3. What is the height of Colorado's lowest point, the Arikaree River
a) 1,145 ft
b) 3,317 ft

4. The Rocky Mountains within Colorado contain 58 named peaks that are 14,000 feet or higher. What are they collectively known as?
a) The 58-ers
b) Fourteeners

5. Thanks to suppression of the North American tectonic plate Denver is now 2.23 inches short of being 'mile high'. True or False?

6. In 2012 Colorado, along with Washington, became the first U.S. state to legalize what?
a) Recreational marijuana
b) Autonomous vehicles
c) Same-sex marriage

7. Which is Colorado's largest ski resort by area?
a) Aspen
b) Breckenridge
c) Vail

8. What did Denver businessman Louis Ballast, owner of the Humpty Dumpty Drive-In, trademark in 1935?
a) The glazed donut
b) The cheeseburger
c) The banana split

9. Pikes Peak is the highest summit of the southern Front Range of the Rocky Mountains. What world-famous event does it run?
a) The Pike's Peak International Hillclimb
b) The Pike's Peak Mountain Trail Race
c) The Pike's Peak Big Air MTB Challenge

10. Singer John Denver lived in Aspen and wrote the state song *Rocky Mountain High.* What was his real name?
a) Henry Deutschendorf Jr.
b) Schlomo Metzenbaum
c) David Crabbs

11. The world famous Red Rocks amphitheater near Morrison is a regular tour venue for music acts. When was it opened?
a) 1906
b) 1926
c) 1946

12. Telluride is a former silver mining camp on the San Miguel River. What is it famous for today?
a) A biennial eco technology convention
b) A film festival

c) A Harley Davidson owners' camp-out

13. In 1868 an undocumented stowaway from Hamburg arrived in America and eventually started a brewery in Golden, Colorado. What was his name?
a) Frederick Pabst
b) Eberhard Anheuser
c) Adolph Coors

14. What is the Colorado state mammal?
a) Rocky Mountain bighorn sheep
b) Cougar
c) American black bear

15. Can you name the state fish of Colorado?
a) Central stoneroller
b) Colorado pikeminnow
c) Greenback cutthroat trout

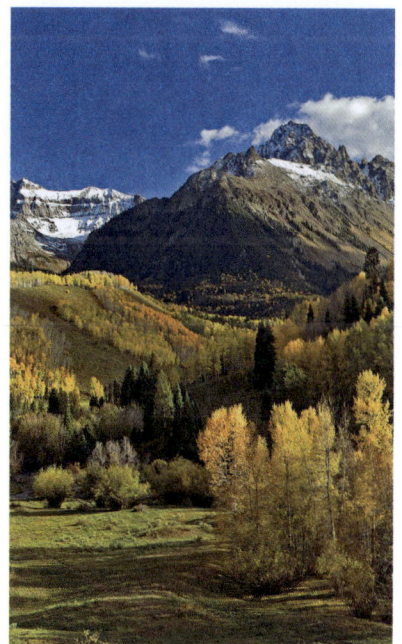

CONNECTICUT

The Constitution State, Connecticut blends historic charm with coastal beauty and the Ivy League prestige of Yale University

1. What is the state capital of Connecticut?
a) Hartford
b) Stamford
c) Bridgeport

2. When was the Colony of Connecticut first established?
a) 1625
b) 1636

3. What did Connecticut claim as part of its colony until 1664
a) The Hudson River
b) The top end of Long Island

4. The highest point in Connecticut is on the lower slope of Mount Frissel on the border with which state?
a) New York
b) Massachusetts
c) Rhode Island

5. Where does Connecticut rank in the most populated states in the U.S.?
a) 29th
b) 41st

6. In 1687, the English governor general came to collect the very liberal royal charter given to the colonists by Charles II in 1662. Where did they hide it?
a) In an oak tree
b) In a church spire
c) In the cellar of the village inn

7. One of the country's great industrialists was born in Hartford, Connecticut. Who was it?
a) George Pullman
b) Samuel Colt
c) John D. Rockefeller

8. When the first telephone directory was published in Newhaven in 1878 how many names did it contain?
a) 5
b) 50
c) 211

9. What did Edwin Land invent in New Haven in 1948?
a) The photo-copier
b) The Polaroid camera
c) The 35mm film canister

10. Mark Twain lived in Hartford from 1874 to 1891 and wrote *The Adventures of Tom Sawyer* there. What profession had he trained as?
a) Lawyer's clerk
b) Optician
c) Riverboat pilot

11. Toy company Wham-O named the Frisbee after the pie tins used by the Frisbie Pie Company of Bridgeport, which were thrown for fun. True or False?

12. Which major U.S. sports network was founded in Bristol, Connecticut, in 1979?
a) Fox Sports
b) ESPN

13. In 1901 Connecticut was the first state to restrict the speed of dangerous, new-fangled motor vehicles. What was the speed limit?
a) 6 mph
b) 12 mph
c) 29 mph

14. New Haven biennially hosts 'The Game', the country's second oldest college football rivalry between Harvard and Yale – whose team is...?
a) The Badgers
b) The Cougars
c) The Bulldogs

15. What is the state bird of Connecticut?
a) Black-capped chickadee
b) Magnificent frigatebird
c) American robin

DELAWARE

Delaware is the first state that companies think of when choosing to register their new business

1. What is the state capital of Delaware?
a) Dover
b) Wilmington
c) Delaware City

2. When was Delaware admitted to the Union?
a) 1787 – it was the first state
b) 1787 – it was the third state

3. Delaware was named after the third Baron De La Warr, a great-grandson of Mary Boleyn. Who was Mary Boleyn's one-time brother in law?
a) Thomas Cromwell
b) King Henry VIII
c) Richard III

4. Delaware has no mountains, the highest point is actually an apartment building at 1201 North Market Street in Wilmington. True or False?

5. Place these states in order of size: New Jersey, Delaware, Rhode Island, Connecticut

6. What does Delaware have in common with Montana, New Hampshire, Alaska and Oregon?
a) No pets over 168lbs
b) No fish farming
c) No sales tax

7. Which U.S. president represented the State of Delaware in the Senate for 36 years?

8. In the 19th century Delaware was known as 'The ___ State' because it had over a million trees. Name the tree.
a) Peach
b) Apricots
c) Gingko

9. Which world-leading company has their headquarters in Wilmington?
a) Lockheed Martin
b) Procter & Gamble
c) DuPont

10. Henry Heimlich was born in Wilmington. What did he invent?
a) The tubeless tire
b) Kevlar
c) The Heimlich maneuver

11. Delaware Bay is home to one of the world's largest populations of...
a) Basking sharks
b) Soft shell crabs
c) Horseshoe crabs

12. The Delaware Water Gap is not in the state of Delaware. True or False?

13. Delaware has no MLB, NBA or NFL team – or a major airport – but it does host...
a) The National Skim-Boarding Championship
b) The ExxonMobil Interstate Kite Challenge
c) NASCAR at the Dover Speedway

14. What is the state bird of Delaware?
a) Delaware blue hen
b) Rehoboth warbler
c) Delaware nightingale

15. Until it ran into legal difficulties Delaware hosted the annual World Punkin Chunkin Championship. What do competitors have to do?
a) Balance on a stack of pumpkins
b) Hurl a pumpkin the farthest distance by catapult
c) Hit a variety of targets with a swinging pumpkin

FLORIDA

The Sunshine State is a vacation paradise, famous for its Art Deco heritage, theme parks and golf courses

1. What is the state capital of Florida?
a) Tallahassee
b) Orlando
c) Naples

2. When was Florida admitted to the Union?
a) 1845
b) 1884

3. Which is Florida's largest city?
a) Miami Beach
b) Jacksonville
c) Tampa

4. The 85-story Panorama Tower in downtown Miami is taller than Florida's highest point, Britton Hill. True or False?

5. Where does Florida rank in the most populated states in the U.S.?
a) 3rd
b) 6th

6. What weather phenomenon does Florida experience more than any other U.S. state?
a) Tornadoes
b) Typhoons
c) Hurricanes

7. Pensacola in Florida is in the same time zone as Chicago, Illinois. True or False?

8. Which Florida city has over 800 Art Deco buildings?
a) Naples
b) St Petersburg
c) Miami Beach

9. Spanish explorer Juan Ponce de Leon landed in 1513 and called the territory 'La Pascua Florida'. What does that mean?
a) Flowering flatlands
b) Feast of flowers
c) The passion flower coast

10. The first in Florida was built at Clearwater in 1897. Now there are around 1,250, the most in the United States. What are they?
a) Golf courses
b) Tennis (and Racket) clubs
c) Ballparks

11. Daytona Beach is famous for its NASCAR speedway created by Bill France in the 1950s. Prior to that, did cars race on the sands?
a) No, it was purely speed trials – up to 276mph for 'Bluebird'.
b) Yes. Occasionally cars got stuck

12. Walt Disney started the Florida theme park gold rush. When did Disney World at Kissimmee open?
a) 1962
b) 1971
c) 1977

13. The first rocket launched at Cape Canaveral in 1950 was a V-2 the same design used to terrorize London in WWII. Who was the designer, who would later build the Saturn V rocket?
a) Wernher von Braun
b) Herman Göring
c) Niels Bohr

14. Which of these is not a state reptile?
a) American alligator
b) Loggerhead turtle
c) Manatee

15. What is the most southerly point of mainland USA?
a) Cape Sable
b) Key West
c) Key Largo

GEORGIA

The Peach State is known for its Southern charm, historic cities like Savannah, and its vibrant capital Atlanta

1. What is the state capital of Georgia?
a) Macon
b) Atlanta
c) Augusta

2. Of the 13 Colonies to be established by England – where does Georgia rank in the chronology?
a) 7th
b) 13th

3. Which is Georgia's oldest city?
a) Savannah
b) Decatur
c) Athens

4. Georgia was named after King George. Which George?
a) George I
b) George II
c) George III

5. Which of these classics is the state song?
a) *Midnight Train to Georgia*
b) *Rainy Night in Georgia*
c) *Georgia on My Mind*

6. Name the major U.S. company headquartered in Atlanta.
a) Microsoft
b) Dell
c) Coca Cola

7. Which major rock band originated in Athens, Georgia?
a) REM
b) Foo Fighters
c) The Eagles

8. Peachtree Road is a major route in Atlanta. It's also an album by a singer who had a residence in Atlanta. Who is it?
a) Taylor Swift
b) Cher
c) Elton John

9. One of golf's 'major' tournaments is held in Georgia each year. The Masters was created by which legendary golfer?
a) Arnold Palmer
b) Bobby Jones
c) Gene Sarazen

10. Which summer Olympic Games was hosted in Atlanta?
a) 1988
b) 1996
c) 2008

11. The founder of the Girl Scouts of the USA, Juliette Gordon Low, was born in which Georgia city?
a) Macon
b) Athens
c) Savannah

12. Moon River, which reaches the Atlantic near Tybee island, featured in the film *Breakfast at Tiffany's*. Can you name the Georgia-born songwriter?
a) Johnny Mercer
b) Harold Melvin
c) Cole Porter

13. In the Civil War – which Union general set the city of Atlanta ablaze?
a) William Tecumseh Sherman
b) Ulysses Grant
c) George Meade

14. Which Atlanta statesman was born on January 15, 1929?

15. What is the state tree of Georgia?
a) Southern live oak
b) Georgia longleaf pine

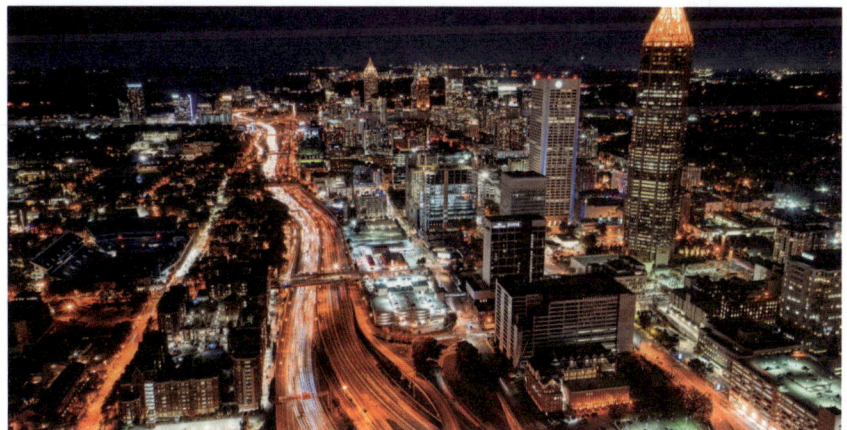

HAWAII

The Aloha State, Hawaii boasts surf-friendly beaches, volcanoes and a distinctive Polynesian culture

1. Who was the first European to set eyes on Hawaii?
a) Captain George Vancouver
b) Captain Francis Drake
c) Captain James Cook

2. What was Hawaii first known as in the West?
a) New Brighton
b) The Sandwich Islands
c) The Vesuvian Islands

3. The highest point in Hawaii is the volcanic Mount Mauna Kea – what kind of volcano is it?
a) Shield volcano
b) Cinder Cone

4. Hawaii was annexed by the United States to protect American business interests, especially in the sugar trade – what year?
a) 1898
b) 1906

5. When did Hawaii become the 50th state?
a) 1942
b) 1959

6. The Hawaiian islands are the western-most territory of the United States. True or False?

7. The United States entered World War II on December 7, 1941 after the unprovoked attack on Pearl Harbor. Who planned the attack?
a) Admiral Yamamoto
b) Prime Minister Hideki Tojo
c) Flight leader Mitsuo Fuchida

8. What is illegal to have as a pet in Hawaii?
a) A parakeet
b) A snake
c) A rabbit

9. Hawaiians and many Polynesians enjoy *he'enalu*. What is it?
a) A feast where only fingers of one hand are used
b) Outrigger canoe racing
c) Surfing

10. Which president was born in Honolulu in 1961?

11. One of the following items is now banned in Hawaii. Which one?
a) Billboards
b) Rental cycles
c) Ukeleles

12. Author Herman Melville visited Hawaii in 1843. At that time it was at the center of which important industry?

13. Hawaiian shirts can be traced to the 1920s when the Honolulu-based Japanese shirtmaker 'Musa-Shiya' started making shirts with colorful Japanese prints. True or False?

14. There are four larger Hawaiian islands. What is the nickname of the main Hawaii island?
a) The Big Island
b) The Strong Island
c) The Brave Island

15. And the smaller Maui...?
a) Little Brother
b) The Valley Isle
c) The Sacred Isle

IDAHO

Known as the Gem State thanks to the variety of gemstones found within its borders, including the rare Idaho Star Garnet

1. What is the state capital of Idaho?
a) Boise
b) Twin Falls
c) Pocatello

2. When was Idaho admitted to the Union?
a) 1863
b) 1890

3. Which government department manages 38% of Idaho land?
a) Department of Defense
b) National Park Service
c) National Forestry Service

4. The deepest river gorge in North America, Hells Canyon, is 7,993 feet deep, which is deeper than the Grand Canyon. True or False?

5. Idaho produce around a third of all America's...?
a) Swedes
b) Potatoes
c) Turnips

6. Idaho's state fruit also appears in the title of Mark Twain's greatest novel. What is it?

7. Which *Breaking Bad* star is a native of Idaho?
a) Bryan Cranston
b) Aaron Paul
c) Bob Odenkirk

8. In 1955 Arco, Idaho, became the first city in America to be powered by what kind of energy?
a) Hydro-electric
b) Solar
c) Nuclear

9. Idaho has more white-water river miles than any other state – a paradise for rafting and kayaking. But how many?
a) 1,400 miles
b) 2,300 miles
c) 3,100 miles

10. Apart from the white-water rivers, what does Idaho have more than any other state?
a) Cave systems
b) Hot springs
c) Box canyons

11. The Shoshone Falls, located on the Snake River, is actually a higher drop than Niagara Falls. True or False?

12. Idaho shares a border with six states – Washington, Oregon, Nevada, Utah, Montana and... which is the sixth?

13. The lakeside golf course at Coeur d'Alene has a unique hole. What makes it special?
a) It is a monster par-8
b) It is a par-3 with a floating green, accessible by boat
c) It is a par-4 with a resident colony of otters

14. How many different gemstones are found in Idaho, including the rare star garnet?
a) 11
b) 29
c) 72

15. Which great writer spent his final two years at Ketchum, Idaho, and is buried in the local cemetery?
a) Henry James
b) Raymond Chandler
c) Ernest Hemingway

ILLINOIS

Known as the Prairie State, yet much of the original grassland has gone, now cities like Chicago drive its economy

1. What is the state capital of Illinois?
a) Chicago
b) Batavia
c) Springfield

2. When was Illinois admitted to the Union?
a) 1801
b) 1818

3. Nauvoo, Illinois, on the banks of the Mississippi River, was once the hometown of which Utopian religious group?
a) Church of the Latter Day Saints
b) Plymouth Brethren
c) Lutheran World Federation

4. Route 66 starts its journey close to Lake Michigan, by Grant Park in Chicago. What is its nickname?
a) The Grand Tour
b) The Greatest Highway
c) The Mother Road

5. Once the tallest building in the world, the Willis Tower still has the highest observation deck. What was the tower's previous name?
a) The Citicorp Tower
b) The FedEx Tower
c) The Sears Tower

6. Born in Tampico, Illinois, which is the only U.S. president to be born in the state?
a) Ulysses Grant
b) Ronald Reagan
c) Abraham Lincoln

7. The Chicago Bears NFL team played for 50 seasons at Wrigley Field, home of the Chicago Cubs baseball team. True or False?

8. On December 2, 1942, a group of 49 scientists led by Enrico Fermi created the world's first controlled, self-sustaining nuclear chain reaction. Where did it take place?
a) The Field Museum storage shed
b) Chicago University physics lab
c) Underneath the Chicago University football stadium

9. In the gangster wars of the 1920s, Al Capone ran the Italian Chicago Outfit while the rival Irish North Side Gang was led by...?
a) John Dillinger
b) 'Bugs' O'Hare
c) 'Bugs' Moran

10. What caused the ruinous fire of 1871 which devastated the city?
a) Catherine O'Leary's cow
b) Sparks from a steam locomotive
c) A kitchen fire at the Palmer House Hotel

11. Is Lincoln Park in Chicago bigger than the 1,017-acre Golden Gate Park in San Francisco?
a) Bigger
b) Smaller

12. Illinois is bordered by six states: Wisconsin, Iowa, Missouri, Kentucky, Indiana, and which other...?

13. Which comic book hero cites Metropolis, Illinois, as his home town?
a) Spider-Man
b) Superman

14. Which pizza was created in 1943 at Pizzeria Uno in Chicago?
a) Neapolitan thin crust pizza
b) Calzone pizza
c) Chicago deep dish pizza

15. Architect Frank Lloyd-Wright is most associated with which Chicago suburb?
a) Forest Park
b) Oak Park

INDIANA

At the Crossroads of America, Indiana boasts the Indianapolis Motor Speedway, the cathedral of American motorsport

1. What is the state capital of Indiana?
a) Indianapolis
b) Franklin
c) Hammond

2. Which is Indiana's largest city?
a) Fort Wayne
b) Evansville
c) Indianapolis

3. At a not-too-lofty 1,257 feet the highest point in Indianapolis is...?
a) Hoosier Hill
b) Round Knob

4. You will find Indiana Dunes State Park on Lake Michigan. How long is the Indiana shoreline?
a) 7 miles
b) 45 miles
c) 173 miles

5. In 1880 what did Wabash, get before the rest of the world?
a) The first telephone system
b) The first electric streetlights
c) The first supermarket

6. In 2023, Indiana was the 2,021st most popular name given to babies in the U.S. Girls or boys?

7. Which pop act from Gary, Indiana, scored four No.1 hits for Tamla Motown on debut?
a) The Supremes
b) Stevie Wonder
c) The Jackson Five

8. The Indianapolis Motor Speedway is one of the world's great sporting venues seating over 250,000. Its nickname is...?
a) The Temple of Speed
b) The Brickyard
c) The Ultimate

9. A crowd of 40,000 turned out to see the first race at Indianapolis in 1909. But it wasn't automobiles they had come to see race. What was it?
a) Helium balloons
b) Longhorn cattle
c) Tricycles

10. In 1849 a community in Spencer County wanted to name their settlement Santa Fe. The Post Office rejected it. What did they choose instead?
a) Santa Monica
b) Santa Claus
c) Santa Ana

11. The city of Gary is famous for what major product?
a) Paint
b) Flat-rolled steel

12. The official tree of Indiana, *liriodendron*, has unusual flowers. What is its common name?
a) The tulip tree
b) The handkerchief tree

13. Itinerant, bare-footed nurseryman John Chapman became a rural legend. What was he better known as?
a) Johnny Fruit
b) Johnny Appleseed
c) Johhny Appletree

14. Film star James Dean was born in Marion, Indiana. How old was he when he fatally crashed his Porsche Spider.
a) 24
b) 27

15. West Lafayette in Tippecanoe County is also known as...?
a) 'Firefly Capital of the World'
b) 'Dormouse Capital of the World'
c) 'Unstable Canoe Capital of the World'

IOWA

Iowa is a heartland state known for its vast cornfields and friendly communities. It also plays a key role in elections

1. What is the state capital of Iowa?
a) Cedar Rapids
b) Des Moines
c) Davenport

2. When did Iowa become part of the Union?
a) 1846
b) 1860

3. The largest city in Iowa, Des Moines, was named by the French. What does 'des moines' mean?
a) The monks
b) The mounds

4. Iowa is a prodigious grower of corn and raiser of hogs. It was estimated that the porcine population outnumbers humans by what ratio?
a) 3 to 1
b) 5 to 1
c) 7 to 1

5. The 1989 baseball film *Field of Dreams* was filmed where?
a) Dyersville
b) Urbandale

6. Iowa is traditionally the first caucus state in election year. Trump won for the Republicans in 2024 but who was second?
a) Ron de Santis
b) Nikki Haley

7. Which major manufacturer has their largest factory in Waterloo, Iowa?
a) John Deere
b) Caterpillar

8. Buffalo Bill, was born in Le Claire, Iowa Territory. Before he served his time as a Union soldier, scout, bison hunter, and showman – at age 15 – he worked as what?
a) Dispatch rider for the Pony Express
b) Apprentice gunsmith

9. Which essential addition to modern life was brought to us by Iowan inventor Otto Frederick Rohwedder in the 1920s.
a) The first automatic bread slicer
b) The first upright vacuum cleaner

10. One of the most recognizable artworks in art history, *American Gothic,* was painted by an Iowan. Who was it?
a) Grant Wood
b) Andrew Wyeth
c) Edward Hopper

11. Seven villages made up the Amana Colonies, an Amish-like religious community from the 1850s to the 1930s with their own self-sufficient local economy. From which European nation did they come?
a) Sweden
b) Holland
c) Germany

12. *Star Trek*'s Captain James T. Kirk was/will be from a small Iowa town. Riverside has claimed his future birthplace with a monument to that effect outside the town hall. When will he be born?
a) 2143
b) 2228

13. The Red Delicious apple was first cultivated in Madison County. It was the most produced apple stock from 1968 until 2018, when it was surpassed by which apple?
a) Pink Lady
b) Gala
c) Braeburn

14. Iowa is bordered by six states: Missouri, Nebraska, Minnesota, Wisconsin, Illinois and which other?

15. The Iowa State Fair prides itself on the life-size sculpted cow made from what...?
a) Butter
c) Cheese

KANSAS

The Sunflower State is a land of endless prairies and wheat fields, known for its wild west history and frontier reputation

1. What is the state capital of Kansas?
a) Kansas City
b) Topeka
c) Wichita

2. When was Kansas admitted to the Union?
a) 1823
b) 1861

3. What is special about Lebanon, Kansas?
a) It was the first of the 47 Lebanons founded in America
b) Some view it as the geographical center of mainland USA

4. Kansas is known as the Sunflower State, every county grows them and it is the state flower. The highest peak is Mount Sunflower, there are sunflower ponds and a Sunflower River. True or False?

5. Which major restaurant chain opened its first restaurant in Wichita in 1958?
a) Dairy Queen
b) Pizza Hut

6. Over thirty years earlier, in 1921, the first fast-food hamburger chain had been founded in Wichita. Which one?
a) White Castle
b) Burger King
c) Wendy's

7. NFL team the Kansas City Chiefs are regularly lobbied by Native American groups to change their name. Where do they play?
a) Arrowhead Stadium
b) Tomahawk Stadium

8. Which famous aviator was born in Atchison, Kansas, in 1897?
a) Eddie Rickenbacker
b) Amelia Earhart
c) Amy Johnson

9. Kansas railroad, the Atchison, Topeka and Santa Fe Railroad operated a famous passenger service between Chicago and Los Angeles from 1938 to 1971 headed by a streamliner locomotive. What was it called?
a) El Capitan
b) The Sundowner

10. The Hutchinson Salt Mines extend to 650 feet underground. What are they famous for storing?
a) Seeds for the National Arboretum
b) Hollywood film reels
c) Nuclear warheads

11. One of the great silent movie stars was born in Piqa, Kansas, in 1895. Who was it?
a) Harold Lloyd
b) Buster Keaton
c) Oliver Hardy

12. This photo shows the Milky Way visible over one of the 'Eight Wonders of Kansas'. What is this chalk outcrop known as?
a) Monument Rocks
b) The White Cliffs of Oakley

13. Which outlaw gang regularly holed up in a Meade, KS, hideout?
a) The Dalton Gang
b) The Wild Bunch

14. One of the most famous movie lines ever spoken comes from Dorothy in *The Wizard of Oz*: 'I have a feeling we're not in Kansas any more.' Who was she talking to?
a) Bobo
b) Balto
c) Toto

15. What is the state reptile?
a) Ornate box turtle
b) Plain box turtle
c) Square box turtle

KENTUCKY

The Bluegrass State – Kentucky got its nickname because of the blue-tinted grass that grows in its fertile pastures

1. What is the state capital of Kentucky?
a) Louisville
b) Frankfort
c) Lexington

2. When was Kentucky admitted to the Union?
a) 1792
b) 1821

3. What is the state dance of Kentucky?
a) Line dancing
b) Clogging
c) High step hoofin'

4. Just as Scotland is the home of whiskey, Kentucky is the home of bourbon. What percentage of the world's bourbon is produced with its limestone-filtered water?
a) 72%
b) 95%

5. Thanks to Colonel Sanders, Kentucky is famous the world over. Sanders started off in 1930 running a Shell Oil Company service station in North Corbin, Kentucky, and added a restaurant later on. The 'Colonel' title is a non-military title. What was his first name?
a) Jefferson
b) Harland
c) Jabez

6. In what year did Sanders trademark the famous slogan, 'It's Finger Lickin' Good'?
a) 1937
b) 1951
c) 1963

7. The Mammoth Cave system is justifiably named. It's the world's longest, surveyed cave system with how many miles of mapped passageways?
a) 176
b) 305
c) 426

8. America's most famous horse race has been run since 1875 outside Louisville. Where is the track exactly?
a) Churchill Downs
b) Epsom Downs
c) Newmarket Gallops

9. The Cumberland Falls in Kentucky (sometimes known as Little Niagra) is one of the few places in the world where you can reliably see what feature during full moons?
a) A moonbow
b) A blue halo

10. Fort Knox has become a phrase to describe the tightest of security. Which service looks after over half of the nation's gold reserves at the Kentucky facility?
a) The U.S. Army
b) The U.S. Mint Police
c) Allied Universal

11. Kentucky's early constitution allowed this practise, but now public officials must swear they have never participated before taking office. What is it?
a) Dueling
b) Freemasonry
c) Moonshine distillation

12. The University of Kentucky Wildcats have won more games than any other college team in history. What is the sport?
a) NCAA basketball games
b) NCAA ice hockey games

13. Kentucky shares borders with seven states: Illinois, Indiana, Ohio, West Virginia, Virginia, Tennessee, and which is the seventh?

14. Which famous figure was born in a one-room log cabin in Hodgenville, Kentucky?
a) Dolly Parton
b) Henry Ford
c) Abraham Lincoln

15. Bowling Green, Kentucky, is responsible for the manufacture of which American transport icon?
a) Harley-Davidson Sportster
b) Airstream trailers
c) Chevrolet Corvette

LOUISIANA

The Pelican State, Louisiana is a cultural melting pot with Creole and Cajun influences, best known for New Orleans and Mardi Gras

1. What is the state capital of Louisiana?
a) New Orleans
b) Baton Rouge
c) Lake Charles

2. When was Louisiana admitted to the Union?
a) 1803
b) 1812

3. Before the French lost control to Spain after the Seven Years' War, Louisiana had been named in honor of King Louis. Which one?
a) Louis XIII of France (1601–1643), Louis the Just
b) Louis XIV of France (1638–1715), the Sun King
c) Louis XV of France (1710–1774), Louis the Beloved

4. For how long had France re-possessed Louisiana (trading it for European territory with Spain) before they sold it on to the United States?
a) A year
b) Ten years
c) Twenty-five years

5. France still follows Code Napoleon legal statutes and similarly, Louisiana follows Napoleonic law, making its legal system different from the other 49 states. True or False?

6. The term 'Dixie' is a throwback to the French influence. 'Dix' is the French word for 'ten'. How did it get into common parlance?
a) It was printed on a ten-dollar note issued by a New Orleans Bank
b) New Orleans was divided into ten parishes – hence Dixieland

7. In 1840, New Orleans was the richest city in the U.S. with the largest population. True or False?

8. Louisiana is the birthplace for which distinctive accordion-based music style?
a) Zydeco
b) Bluegrass
c) Ragtime

9. Florida and Louisiana both have large swamp territories: One state has two million wild alligators, the other has 1.3 million. Which state has the most?
a) Florida
b) Louisiana

10. Louisiana produces 90% of America's...?
a) Oysters
b) Soft-shelled crabs
c) Crawfish

11. The McIlhenny family has been making this specialist sauce on Avery Island since the 1860s. What's the sauce?
a) Tabasco
b) Cholula

12. The highest elevation in Louisiana is Driskill Mountain. How high does this *mountain* rise...?
a) 535 feet
b) 964 feet

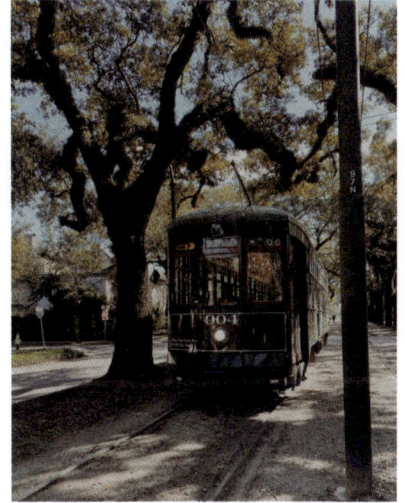

13. The state fish of Louisiana is what?
a) Crappie
b) Hogchoker
c) Sarcastic fringehead

14. Which Pulitzer Prize winning play/novel is set in New Orleans?
a) *A Streetcar Named Desire*
b) *Cat on a Hot Tin Roof*
c) *Midnight in the Garden of Good and Evil*

15. New Orleans' famous Metairie Cemetery used to be a race track owned by the Jockey Club. They refused membership to Charles T. Howard, who earned his fortune from the first state lottery. Howard vowed he would turn the race course into a cemetery, and after the Civil War he was able to buy it and make good his promise. Howard is buried in his cemetery, but how did he meet his end in 1885?
a) He fell off a horse
b) A large marble angel fell on him

MAINE

Maine is the largest of the six New England states, covering as much land as the other five combined, with a single neighbor – Vermont

1. What is the state capital of Maine?
a) Bangor
b) Scarborough
c) Augusta

2. What is the largest city in Maine?
a) Lewiston
b) Brunswick
c) Portland

3. What number state was Maine to join the Union?
a) 12th
b) 23rd

4. What is the state pie of Maine?
a) Apple pie
b) Cranberry pie
c) Whoopie pie

5. The state cat is the Maine Coon, a large, furry, hunting cat adept at surviving outside in Maine's cold winters. What is its nickname?
a) The all-weather cat
b) The gentle giant
c) The furry avenger

6. With all its bays and inlets Maine has more coastline than California's 840 miles. How much more?
a) Double
b) Treble
c) Quadruple

7. Given that it has all those rocky inlets, it is the nation's greatest source of lobsters. How much of the market does it command?

a) 74%
b) 90%

8. The largest peak in the Acadia National Park is one of the first places in the U.S. to see the sunrise each day. What's it called?
a) Mount Chevrolet
b) Mount Cadillac
c) Mount Pontiac

9. The Bay of Fundy stretches from Maine into Canada and boasts a world-beating statistic. What is it?
a) Biggest tidal bore
b) Biggest tidal range
c) Biggest tidal barrage

10. What kind of holiday does the Maine Windjammer Association specialize in?
a) Kite surfing
b) Windsurfing
c) Wooden sail craft

11. Author Steven King often sets his novels in Maine. Which one of the following was *not* set in Maine?
a) *Cuju*
b) *Carrie*
c) *It*
d) *The Green Mile*

12. It's estimated that Maine has 95% of the country's wild...?
a) Goats
b) Blueberries
c) Haggis

13. President George H.W. Bush had a summer residence in which

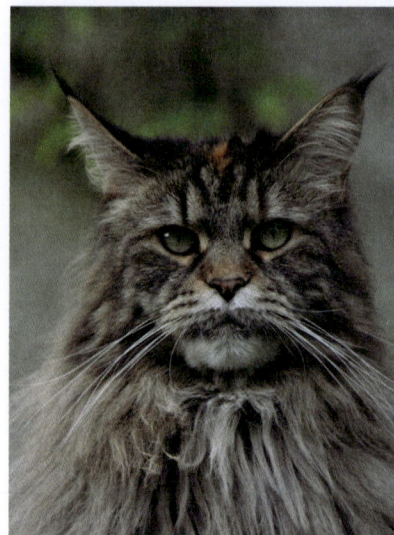

Maine resort (to which he invited Mikhail Gorbachev and Margaret Thatcher)?
a) Old Orchard Beach
b) Kennebunkport
c) Cape Elizabeth

14. What other name is Maine known by?
a) The Rocky Shore State
b) The Pine Tree State
c) The Lobster Pot State

15. Each year Maine records between 500 and 700 vehicle collisions - with what?
a) Migrating crabs
b) Raccoons
c) Moose

MARYLAND

The Old Line State, Maryland is a mix of colonial history, Chesapeake Bay seafood, and scenic waterfronts

1. What is the state capital of Maryland?
a) Baltimore
b) Hagerstown
c) Annapolis

2. What is the state insect of Maryland?
a) Baltimore checkerspot butterfly
b) American lady butterfly
c) Olympia marble butterfly

3. The Battle of Baltimore (1814) inspired Francis Scott Key to write *The Star-Spangled Banner* after seeing which fort withstand a punishing bombardment?
a) Fort Pulaski
b) Fort McHenry
c) Fort McKenzie

4. Which famous literary figure was found in a disheveled state wandering the streets of Baltimore on October 3, 1849. He died four days later.
a) Herman Melville
b) Nathaniel Hawthorne
c) Edgar Allan Poe

5. Maryland was the birthplace of which influential figure in the abolitionist movement?
a) Frederick Douglass
b) Harriet Tubman
c) Sojourner Truth

6. One of the baseball greats was born in Pigtown, Baltimore, and played briefly for the Baltimore Orioles before getting sold on. Who was it?

a) Jackie Robinson
b) Lou Gehrig
c) Babe Ruth

7. Maryland was one of the first states to adopt an official state sport in 1962. What did they choose?
a) Pole-vaulting
b) Logrolling
c) Jousting

8. The National Aquarium in Baltimore opened in 1981 as part of an urban renewal project. It is now the most popular tourist attraction in Maryland. True or False?

9. What was established in Annapolis in 1845?
a) The Welsh Rite Masonic Lodge
b) The Annapolis Crab Canning Company (ACCC)
c) The U.S. Naval Academy

10. Maryland is famous for what kind of crabs?
a) Dungeness crabs
b) Spider crabs
c) Peekytoe crabs
d) Blue crabs

11. One of America's first railroad companies, the Baltimore & Ohio (B&O) was chartered in Baltimore in which year?
a) 1819
b) 1827

12. Baltimore was also the recipient of the first long-distance telegraph message, sent from Washington, D.C., in 1844.

Who sent it?
a) Thomas Edison
b) Samuel Morse
c) Alexander Graham Bell

13. In the Civil War the 1862 Battle of Antietam remains the 'Bloodiest Day in U.S. History'. What is it known as in the Southern states?
a) Battle of Dunker Church
b) Battle of Sharpsburg
c) Battle of South Mountain

14. What happens at NASA's Goddard Space Flight Center in Greenbelt, Maryland?
a) It's the main assembly point for NASA rockets
b) It's where space research and complex instruments are built
c) It's the reserve control center

15. Philanthropist Johns Hopkins founded the University and Hospital that bear his name. The university now has campuses in Baltimore, Washington, D.C., Italy and where else?
a) Argentina
b) Vietnam
c) China

MASSACHUSETTS

The Bay State first welcomed the Pilgrims over 400 years ago, now it's a hub for education

1. What is the state capital of Massachusetts?
a) Boston
b) Worcester
c) Cambridge

2. What should you call someone who lives in Massachusetts? Three of the following are used, one is not. Can you spot it?
a) Bay Stater
b) Massachusite
c) Massachuseteer
d) Massachusettsan

3. Boston is famous for its 1773 tea party in which tea was thrown into the harbor in protest against the Stamp Act taxes. Which city simply turned the ship round and refused to unload it?
a) Charleston
b) Baltimore
c) Philadelphia

4. The Boston Massacre of 1770 was a confrontation between British troops and a hostile crowd of colonists. Five were killed and the soldiers put on trial. Who defended them in court?

a) John Adams, future president
b) Aaron Burr, future vice-president
b) James Madison, future president

5. The Bee Gees' hit song, *Massachusetts*, was a 1967 anti-San Francisco song, lamenting the fact that everyone had rushed off to California to wear flowers in their hair. They had never been to Massachusetts. True or False?

6. The Pilgrim Fathers set off from Plymouth and arrived in ... Plymouth Rock, Massachusetts, aboard the *Mayflower*. What was the year?
a) 1595
b) 1603
c) 1620

7. Harvard college was initially established in 1636 for what purpose?
a) To train farmers
b) To train clergymen
c) To train physicians

8. Canadian-American gym teacher James Naismith invented which sport in Springfield, Massachusetts, in 1891?
a) Ice hockey
b) Netball
c) Volleyball

9. Scottish inventor Alexander Graham Bell made the first successful telephone call in Boston. When did he call?
a) 1852
b) 1876
c) 1894

10. Boston was a pioneer in many ways. In 1897 it built America's first...?
a) Concrete floating pier
b) Subway line

11. Fifty-three years later, in 1950, the first shop of what would become a national chain started up in Quincy. What was it?
a) Taco Bell
b) Dunkin' Donuts
c) Subway

12. What is the scenic region in western Massachusetts known for its hiking, arts, and cultural festival?
a) The Wiltshires
b) The Berkshires
c) The Yorkshires

13. Martha's Vineyard is closest to Cape Cod, MA, but which state does it fall under?
a) Rhode Island
b) New York
c) Massachusetts

14. Every flat city has its own annual marathon these days, but Boston led the way. When was the first?
a) 1897
b) 1963
c) 1979

15. Which U.S. president was born in Brookline, Massachusetts?
a) John Adams
b) Woodrow Wilson
c) John F. Kennedy

MICHIGAN

Surrounded by the Great Lakes, Michigan boasts stunning shorelines along with the auto industry and the birthplace of Motown

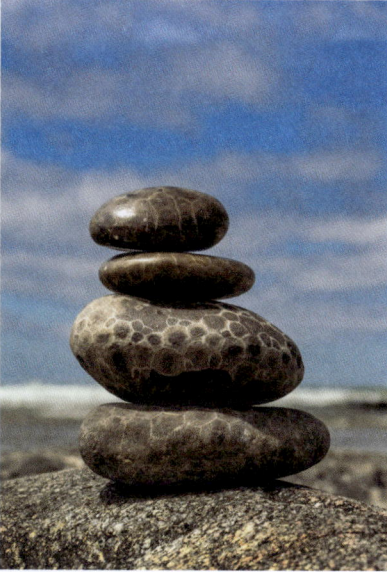

1. What is the state capital of Michigan?
a) Detroit
b) Lansing
c) Flint

2. What is the state motto (translated from Latin)?
a) If you seek a pleasant peninsula, look about you
b) Glory in the expanse of water before your eyes

3. Michigan is rare in that it has a state native grain, manoomin. What is manoomin?
a) Wild rice
b) Wild oats

4. Michigan is the only state that touches four of the five Great Lakes. Which lake does it not touch?
a) Superior
b) Huron
c) Ontario

5. Michigan has about 3,288 miles of freshwater coastline, the most of any U.S. state. It also has one of the following...
a) The most lighthouses
b) The most U.S. Coastguard vessels
c) The most yacht clubs

6. The Mackinac Bridge connecting the two Michigan peninsulas, Upper and Lower, was opened in 1957. What is its nickname?
a) The Mighty Mac
b) The Green gate
c) SuperMac

7. Operating out of Detroit, Michigan, the J.W. Westcott II is the only floating post office in the world, delivering mail to ships in transit. What makes it unique in the U.S. postal system?
a) It can issue its own stamps
b) As a post office it has its own zip code – 48222 – making it the only floating zip code

8. Battle Creek is the world headquarters of which global food brand?
a) Kellogg's
b) Kraft

9. Residents of the Upper Peninsula have a distinct culture and accent. What are they known as?
a) Floopers
b) Yoopers
c) Pooters

10. Leland, Michigan, has a preserved village with buildings dating back over a century. What is it called?
a) Silvertown
b) Fishtown

11. Petoskey stones – Michigan's state stone – can often be found on Michigan beaches. Petoskey stones consist of fossilized what...?
a) Ferns
b) Coral
c) Moss

12. Hell does exist and it's a town in Michigan. As a tourist attraction, visitors can take on what role for a day?
a) Sheriff of Hell
b) Mayor of Hell
c) Parking Officer from Hell

13. In 1879, Detroit became the first big city to do what...?
a) Offer free streetcar rides to veterans
b) Assign individual telephone numbers

14. The Upper Peninsula once proposed becoming a state on its own, but was never granted statehood. What was the proposed name of the new state?
a) Algonquin
b) Superior
c) Forest

15. *Up in Michigan* was a short story in his first published collection by which American writer?
a) Truman Capote
b) Earnest Hemingway

MINNESOTA

The Land of 10,000 Lakes has the vibrant Twin Cities and a behemoth of a shopping mall for some retail therapy

1. What is the state capital of Minnesota?
a) Saint Paul
b) Minneapolis
c) Duluth

2. When was Minneapolis admitted to the Union?
a) 1816
b) 1858

3. Saint Paul and Minneapolis are known as the Twin Cities. Which has the greater population?
a) Saint Paul
b) Minneapolis

4. With 14,420 lakes covering at least ten acres it is known as 'The Land of 10,000 Lakes'. What is another state nickname?
a) Gopher State
b) Otter State
c) Anaconda State

5. The state bird – not surprisingly, given the amount of water – is a waterfowl. What kind?
a) Common loon duck
b) Trumpeter swan
c) Cackling goose

6. Given the frozen lake area in winter (up to -60F), Minnesota can see thousands of … what … put onto the ice each winter?
a) Hockey goals
b) Fishing houses
c) Speed-skating tracks

7. What does Minnesota have more of per capita than any other U.S. state? It's reckoned to be

143 per thousand people.
a) Snowmobiles
b) Huskies
c) Boats

8. Minnesota is the birthplace of Bob Dylan and which other music legend?
a) Tom Petty
b) Madonna
c) Prince

9. Located in Bloomington, the Mall of America (MOA), is the largest shopping mall in America. It has over 500 stores, an indoor amusement park, an aquarium, and what else?
a) A wedding chapel
b) A *hammam* or Turkish bath
c) A strip of Tarmac from the Buckingham Palace Mall

10. The Mall of America was built on the site of what?
a) An American Indian burial ground
b) Bloomington city dump
c) The Minnesota Vikings' former Metropolitan Stadium

11. The Twin Cities have a transport system spanning 9.5 miles. What is it?
a) Skyway for pedestrians
b) Subway for commuters
c) Monorail for connecting office blocks

12. Wolves still roam the wild places of Minnesota. Of the Lower 48 states it has the largest population of which wolf?

a) Timber wolf
b) Gray wolf

13. If you have free time in Austin, Minnesota, and love visiting museums, where could you spend some quality time?
a) The Spam Museum
b) The Barbed Wire Museum
c) The Anorak (parka) Museum

14. Which national transport company can trace its history to Hibbing, Minnesota?
a) Greyhound Bus
b) American Airlines

15. Many believe the Vikings discovered America long before Columbus. In 1927, to celebrate Leif Erikson's trip around 997CE, a wooden replica of his longship was built in Norway and sailed all the way to Duluth on Lake Superior. How long was that journey?
a) 4,900 miles
b) 6,700 miles

MISSISSIPPI

The Magnolia State is rich in blues music history, Southern traditions and unique cypress-tupelo swamp ecosystems

1. What is the state capital of Mississippi?
a) Jackson
b) Biloxi
c) Gulfport

2. Mississippi seceded from the Union in 1861. When was it re-admitted?
a) 1865
b) 1870
c) 1900

3. Mississippi is known as the Magnolia State – what is its alternative nickname?
a) The Azalea State
b) The Hospitality State
c) The Laurel State

4. What is the nickname for the University of Mississippi?
a) Li'l Miss
b) Ole Miss
c) Sweet Miss

5. Belzoni, is known as the 'Catfish Capital of the World' and the obvious place to hold the World Catfish Festival. Mississippi is the largest supplier of Catfish in America. What kind?

a) Wild
b) Farmed

6. Mississippi has more ... what ... per capita than any other state?
a) Canal cruisers
b) Churches
c) Dry Cleaners

7. Legendary blues artists like B.B. King, Muddy Waters, and Robert Johnson were born in Mississippi. But who was born in Tupelo?
a) Jerry Lee Lewis
b) Little Richard
c) Elvis Presley

8. Cat Island in the Gulf of Mexico got its name from early explorers who mistook which animal for cats?
a) Key deer
b) Racoons

9. Vicksburg on the Mississippi was known as the 'Gibraltar of the Confederacy' due to its strategic location during the Civil War. However, unlike Gibralter, a 47-day siege ended its resistance and marked the turning point, coming as it did...
a) One day before the Battle of Gettysburg
b) One day after the Battle of Gettysburg

10. By 1860, slaves accounted for 55% of the Mississippi state population. It was also the top producer of which crop?
a) Tobacco
b) Cotton
c) Rice

11. Prohibition was repealed in 1934. However Mississippians voted to keep it till what year?
a) 1942
b) 1950
c) 1966

12. Hurricane Katrina wreaked havoc on the Mississippi Gulf Coast with high winds, heavy rains and a 30-foot storm surge. Forty Mississippi libraries were damaged beyond repair. What year was Katrina?
a) 2001
b) 2005
c) 2008

13. One Muppet creator was born in Hereford, England, the other in Greenville, Mississippi. Who was the Mississippian?
a) Frank Oz
b) Jim Henson

14. When ranked against other states – where does Mississippi come in the table of median household incomes?
a) 36th
b) 44th
c) 50th

15. Actor James Earl Jones was born in Arkabutla, Mississippi. What was his most famous role?
a) Yoda in *Star Wars*
b) Darth Vader in *Star Wars*
c) Jabba the Hutt in *Star Wars*

MISSOURI

The Show-Me State is known for its barbecues, the Gateway Arch in St. Louis, not forgetting Ted Drewes Frozen Custard

1. What is the state capital of Missouri?
a) Jefferson City
b) Joplin
c) Columbia

2. Which is the largest city in Missouri?
a) St Louis
b) Kansas City
c) Springfield

3. What is the state motto of Missouri?
a) Let the good of the people be the supreme law
b) Our freedom is our opportunity

4. With its strong German heritage Missouri is a major center of beer brewing and home to the world's largest beer producer. Which company?
a) Pabst
b) Molson-Coors
c) Anheuser-Busch

5. It is also a wine producer, centering on an area which echoes an Old World vine growing region...

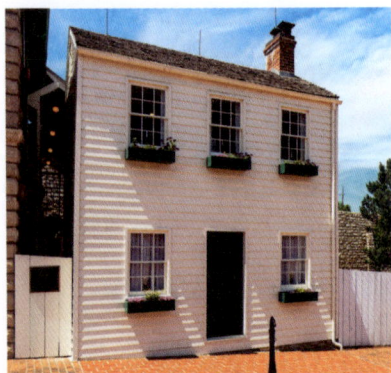

a) Missouri Champagne
b) Missouri Bordeaux
c) Missouri Rhineland

6. The Pony Express, the legendary mail service, began in St. Joseph, Missouri, in 1860. But how long was it in business?
a) 18 months
b) Three years
c) Six years

7. The Jesse James Home Museum in St. Joseph is where the infamous outlaw Jesse James was assassinated in 1882. Who shot him in the back?
a) Robert Ford
b) Emmett Dalton

8. Mark Twain described one of his childhood friends, Tom Blankenship, thus: 'His liberties were totally unrestricted. He was the only really independent person – boy or man – and by consequence he was tranquil and continuously happy and envied by the rest of us.' Who is he describing?
a) Tom Sawyer
b) Huckleberry Finn

9. A cave features in *The Adventures of Tom Sawyer* – Missouri is known as 'The Cave State'. How many does it have?
a) 3,000
b) 6,000

10. The Lake of the Ozarks was created with the construction of the Bagnell Dam in 1931. With 1,150 miles of shoreline that

snake around river valleys it has been nicknamed what...?
a) The Missouri Dragon
b) The Missouri Twister
c) The Missouri Serpent

11. In 1906, when Walt Disney was four, the family moved from Chicago to a farm in Marceline, Missouri. There he developed his interest in drawing when he was paid to draw what...?
a) The horse of the neighborhood doctor
b) His uncle's two farm dogs

12. The Ha Ha Tonka State Park is one of 90 in Missouri. 'Ha Ha Tonka' means what in Osage?
a) Laughing waters
b) Smiling sky

13. At the 1904 Olympics in St Louis, one of the most remarkable athletes was the American gymnast George Eyser, who won six medals on the same day. What was extraordinary about this sportsman – apart from competing and winning six events?
a) He was partially sighted
b) His left leg was made of wood

14. Kansas City boasts 200 fountains – a figure that exceeds which famous European city?
a) Vienna
b) Paris
c) Rome

15. In Missouri, it's against the law to drive with an uncaged bear in your car. True or False?

MONTANA

The Treasure State has vast landscapes, an ocean of wilderness and towering mountains that surround the Glacier National Park

1. What is the state capital of Montana?
a) Billings
b) Helena
c) Bozeman

2. When was it admitted to the Union?
a) 1863
b) 1889

3. There was great debate about the name of the state – 'Montana' came from the Spanish word for mountain and not all of the state is mountainous. At one stage an American Indian name was suggested. Which one?
a) Choctaw
b) Chippewa
c) Shoshone

4. Montana was originally part of which other state?
a) Idaho
b) North Dakota
c) Wyoming

5. The lowest point in Montana is on the Kootenai River at the Idaho border. What height is it above sea level?
a) 975 feet
b) 1,804 feet

6. Montana is the fourth largest state covering 147,040 square miles – bigger than which country?
a) Italy
b) France
c) Neither

7. Montana has more species of what than any other state?
a) Mammals
b) Birds
c) Reptiles

8. The state mammal is the grizzly bear and Montana has more than any in the Lower 48 states. How many?
a) Around 1,200
b) Around 2,000

9. The Battle of the Little Bighorn in 1876 between the 7th Cavalry under George Armstrong Custer was a shocking defeat for the military. What confederacy of American Indians did they take on?
a) Lakota Sioux, Northern Cheyenne, and Arapaho
b) Blackfeet, Chippewa, and Crow

10. The first all-Black regiment, the 25th Infantry were nicknamed 'Buffalo Soldiers' by Native Americans and went into Montana after the conflict to help protect frontier settlers. What did

they use for transport?
a) Ponies
b) Conestoga wagons
c) Bicycles

11. Montana is one of the least densely populated states in America. Leaving aside Alaska, which is the only state less densely populated than Montana?
a) Maine
b) Wyoming

12. The Museum of the Rockies in Bozeman houses the largest collection of what in the U.S.?
a) Stuffed grizzly bears
b) Dinosaur fossils
c) Teepees

13. Yellowstone is mostly located in Wyoming, but the village of West Yellowstone and how much of the national park is in Montana?
a) 4%
b) 12%

14. Butte, Montana was known as 'The Richest Hill on Earth' because of its abundance of minerals, including silver and gold. What other valuable metal was mined in the late 1800s and early 1900s?
a) Lead
b) Aluminium
c) Copper

15. Because of its mining heritage, Butte has the largest population of Irish Americans per capita of any U.S. city. Even Boston. True or False?

NEBRASKA

The Cornhusker State, Nebraska is a land of rolling prairies including the distinctive horizons of the Sand Hills region

1. What is the state capital of Nebraska?
a) Omaha
b) Lincoln
c) North Platte

2. The state's name comes from the Omaha tribe's word 'Ní Btháska', meaning what...?
a) Distant horizon
b) Flat water

3. The city of Lincoln was renamed in honor of the 16th president. What was it called originally?
a) Lancaster
b) Lakota City

4. The Nebraska Badlands is home to a state park with unusual rock formations. What is it called?
a) Top Hat Geologic Park
b) Toadstool Geologic Park

5. Nebraska covers 77,358 square miles, making it larger than which country?
a) Japan
b) South Korea

6. Can you identify this unusual peak (right) in Nebraska's Badlands that was a landmark to those on the Oregon Trail?
a) Devil's Finger
b) Chimney Rock
c) Pawnee Spire

7. Even though it has the largest hand-planted forest in America, Nebraska still has the fewest trees per square mile than any other state except...?

a) New Mexico
b) North Dakota
c) Arizona

8. In Alliance, Nebraska, you can find a replica of which UNESCO monument made out of cars?
a) Carhenge, a copy of Stonehenge
b) The Carfel Tower replicating the Eiffel Tower
c) The 'Car-lesseum' of Rome

9. Nebraska specialty the Runza sandwich consists of a stuffed bread roll filled with beef, onions and what else?
a) Lettuce
b) Cabbage/Sauerkraut

10. Legendary course designers Ben Crenshaw and Bill Coore created one of America's greatest golf courses in the Sandhills of Nebraska. What is it called?
a) Sand Hills
b) Distant Horizon

11. *Nebraska* is a studio album from which U.S. rock star?

a) Jon Bon Jovi
b) Axl Rose
c) Bruce Springsteen

12. Hastings, Nebraska, has a a museum dedicated to this drink invented in 1927. What's the drink?
a) Gatorade
b) Kool-Aid
c) Dr Pepper

13. Thanks to the Ogallala Aquifer the state has more of this/these than any other state. What are we talking about?
a) Water reserves
b) Freshwater springs

14. The state is famous for a particular grass species which can survive extreme droughts. Which one?
a) Bluegrass
b) Buffalo grass
c) Marram grass

15. The village of Monowi became famous for having a population of just one. True or False?

NEVADA

Home to Las Vegas casinos and entertainment. Beyond the neon lights it boasts breathtaking deserts and stunning Lake Tahoe

1. What is the state capital of Nevada?
a) Reno
b) Henderson
c) Carson City

2. Nevada is the seventh-largest state in the U.S., covering 110,577 square miles. Which country is it bigger than?
a) United Kingdom
b) Germany

3. Despite its size, a large part of Nevada is owned by the federal government. How large a part?
a) 63%
b) 85%

4. You want mountains? Nevada has more named mountain ranges than any other state. How many is that?
a) 148
b) 211
c) 314

5. The Valley of Fire State Park is home to 40,000-year-old what?
a) Petroglyphs carved by ancient man
b) Fossilized ferns
c) Stone huts

6. The Fly Geyser in Washoe County is a geothermal feature which sprang into life in 1916 as a result of what?
a) Drilling for a well
b) Dynamiting in a local quarry

7. Nevada has the largest population of wild ... what ... roaming free in the United States?
a) Mules
b) Horses
c) Pigs

8. The desert tortoise is Nevada's official reptile. How long can it live for?
a) Up to 60 years
b) Over 80 years

9. The Black Rock Desert is home to which famous festival?
a) Coachella
b) Burning Man

10. The Comstock Lode, discovered in 1859, was the largest deposit of which metal found in the U.S.?
a) Gold
b) Silver
c) Nickel

11. One of the most secretive U.S. government facilities is located in Nevada's Groom Lake region. What is it known as?
a) Area 47
b) Area 51
c) Area 53

12. Technically, the famous Las Vegas Strip is not in Las Vegas — it's in a CDP (Census Designated Place) called...?
a) Heaven
b) Paradise
c) Joy

13. During his residency in Las Vegas, Howard Hughes was (rightfully) concerned about the proliferation of nuclear tests in the desert nearby. How many tests were conducted between 1951 and 1992?
a) 265
b) 476
c) 928

14. Which casino resort in Las Vegas emits the brightest beam of light in the world?
a) Bellagio
b) Mandalay Bay
c) Luxor

15. Who designed the famous 'Welcome to Fabulous Las Vegas' sign?
a) Bette Davis
b) Betty Hutton
b) Betty Willis

NEW HAMPSHIRE

The Granite State is perfect for a tour of fall foliage and a hike through the White Mountains

1. What is the state capital of New Hampshire?
a) Loudon
b) Concord
c) Manchester

2. New Hampshire has the shortest coastline of any coastal state. How many miles?
a) 7
b) 18
c) 46

3. In 1934, Mount Washington recorded the second-highest wind speed ever recorded on Earth. How fast?
a) 202 mph
b) 231 mph
c) 296 mph

4. Which river forms New Hampshire's entire western border with Vermont?
a) Connecticut
b) Merrimack
c) Ossipee

5. New Hampshire is easy on drivers. It is the only state where what is *not* required?
a) Carrying your driving license in the car
b) Mandatory auto insurance
c) Carrying a spare wheel

6. It is also the only state without a mandatory seat belt law for adults. But what about motorcycles? Do adults need a helmet for riding high-powered Harleys?
a) Yes
b) No

7. What is the state motto?
a) Live free or die
b) Speed is a virtue
c) Believe in ambition

8. Influential newspaper editor Horace Greeley, born in Amherst, NH, coined which famous phrase?
a) 'Live fast, die young'
b) 'Go west, young man'
c) 'Penny wise, dollar foolish'

9. Dartmouth College is one of the nine colonial colleges chartered before the Revolution. What was it originally set up to do?
a) Educate Native Americans in Christian theology
b) Educate colonists on agriculture

10. Portsmouth, USA, is a sea port in New Hampshire. Portsmouth, England, is a sea port in which English county?

11. The first American astronaut in space was from Derry, New Hampshire. Who was it?
a) John Glenn
b) Alan Shepard

12. Sadly one of the most tragic space accidents claimed the life of which teacher from Concord, in the Challenger disaster?
a) Christa McAuliffe
b) Laurel Clark

13. Which one of these movie stars was born in Manchester?
a) Tom Cruise
b) Adam Sandler

14. In 2003 New Hampshire became the first state to legalize...?
a) Marijuana for personal use
b) Same-sex civil unions

15. What happens at the annual Pumpkin Regatta in Goffstown?
a) Small pumpkins fitted with model engines are raced
b) Giant single pumpkins are hollowed out and raced

NEW JERSEY

The Garden State boasts idyllic countryside, some serious industry and a host of music stars from The Boss to Ol' Blue Eyes

1. What is the state capital of New Jersey?
a) Paterson
b) Trenton
c) Elizabeth

2. Which is the largest city by population in New Jersey?
a) Jersey City
b) Paterson
c) Newark

3. How many states are smaller in area than New Jersey?
a) 11
b) 6
c) 3

4. New Jersey is the second most densely populated state in the Union. True or False?

5. Calculated at $99,781, New Jersey is ranked second in median household income. Which state is No.1?
a) Massachusetts
b) New Hampshire
c) Colorado

6. The first college football game was played in 1869 in New Brunswick between Rutgers and which other college team?
a) Princeton
b) Seton Hall
c) Penn State

7. The first officially recorded baseball game this side of the pond took place at Elysian Fields in Hoboken, New Jersey in 1846. The New York Base Ball Club won

23-1. Who were they playing?
a) The Knickerbockers
b) The Redstockings

8. Thomas Edison devised the first efficient incandescent lightbulb at his New Jersey laboratory. Where was it?
a) Paterson
b) Menlo Park
c) Princeton

9. New Jersey has more ... what ... per square mile than any other state?
a) Goats
b) Horses
c) Chihuahuas

10. Home to the oldest lighthouse in America, Sandy Hook has been shining its light since 1764. What is it warning mariners of?
a) Offshore rocks
b) A tidal whirlpool
c) A sandy spit

11. As of 2025 what are you still not allowed to do yourself in New Jersey?
a) Pump your own gas
b) Light a bonfire over 12 feet in height
c) Change any kind of electrical fuse

12. Camden, New Jersey, is the home of Andy Warhol's favorite soup brand. What is it?
a) Heinz
b) Campbell's
c) General Mills

13. What seaside delight originated in Atlantic City in the late 19th century?
a) Cotton candy
b) Boardwalk caramel creams
c) Saltwater taffy

14. The first boardwalk was built at Atlantic City in 1870 to help hotel owners keep sand out of their buildings. In its early years what happened at the end of each season?
a) Another 100 yards was added
b) It was removed for the winter

15. In 1882, James V. Lafferty built what would become America's oldest roadside attraction in Margate City, New Jersey. What was it?
a) A six-story-high elephant called Lucy
b) A five-story-high hippo called Bertha
c) A four-story-high walrus called Walter

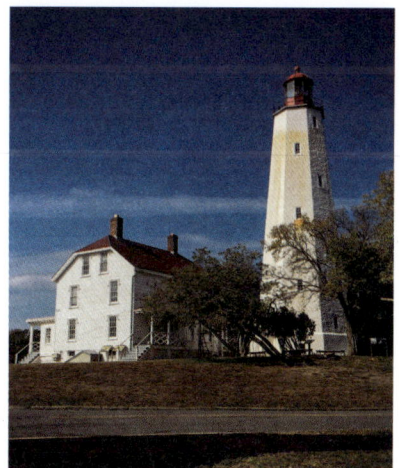

NEW MEXICO

The Land of Enchantment with chilli peppers, known for its stunning desert scenery and eye-watering cuisine

1. What is the state capital of New Mexico?
a) Santa Fe
b) Albuquerque
c) Las Cruces

2. How high is the lowest point in New Mexico?
a) 2,011 feet
b) 2,845 feet

3. What distinguishes New Mexico's capital city, apart from the fact that it's the highest at 7,199 feet above sea level?
a) It's the oldest
b) The most background radiation
b) It has the smallest population

4. The Spanish name Nuevo México was coined in 1581 long before the United States got involved and when Mexico was New Spain. True or False?

5. Which New Mexico state animal is also a Looney Tunes star?
a) State bird: Roadrunner
b) State mammal: Coyote

6. During World War II the first atomic bomb was tested at Jornada del Muerto. Also known as...?
a) The Trinity Site
b) The Los Alamos Site

7. Thanks in part to the presence of the Los Alamos research facility – New Mexico has more ... what ... per capita than any other state?
a) Grand pianos
b) PhDs
c) MBAs

8. The Zia sun symbol is the central feature of the state flag. What does it represent?
a) Harmony and balance
b) Peace and tranquillity
c) Burning desire to succeed

9. Smokey Bear, the wildfire prevention icon for the forest service, was inspired by a real bear cub rescued from a New Mexico forest fire. When?
a) 1936
b) 1950
c) 1967

10. Albuquerque holds an internationally recognized festival that has become the largest in the world. What is the subject?
a) *Breaking Bad* fan convention
b) Hot-air balloons
c) Tamales

11. New Mexico is the only state with an official state question. What is it?
a) 'Red or Green?'
b) 'Mountain or River?'
c) 'Today or Tomorrow?'

12. Many states like to boast of their firsts. New Mexico claims the very first what...?
a) Spaceport America
b) The first UFO reception area
c) The first black bear activity park, Go Bear!

13. The Roswell Incident in 1947 was supposedly a crashed UFO. Although the residents of Roswell like to maintain that it was an

extra-terrestrial, it was in fact...?
a) A hoax by student interns at Los Alamos
b) A crashed army spy balloon
c) An experimental micro-jet

14. Several hot springs are located in one New Mexico tourist town with an unusual name. What is it?
a) Truth or Consequences
b) Hot Hot Hot
c) So Delightful

15. Carlsbad Caverns in the Guadalupe Mountains has a large limestone chamber which is almost 4,000 feet long, 625 feet wide, and 255 feet high at its highest point. What is it called?
a) The Big Room
b) Goliath's bedroom
c) The 747 Hangar

NEW YORK

The Empire State, New York is far more than the five boroughs, stretching north to the Finger Lakes and the colossal Adirondacks

1. What is the state capital of New York?
a) Ithaca
b) Buffalo
c) Albany

2. The Statue of Liberty welcomes ships into New York Harbor. It is the state's most visited (and photographed) attraction. True or False?

3. New York is home to the largest marble cave entrance in the Eastern U.S. Howe Caverns allows visitors to take an underground boat ride, thus giving an easy introduction to spelunking. What is spelunking?
a) The study of stalactites and stalagmites
b) Cave exploring
c) Dropping stones into cave water

4. What world-renowned company did George Eastman found in Rochester, New York?

5. Since 1939 Cooperstown has been the home of the National Hall of Fame for which sport?
a) Basketball
b) Lacrosse
c) Baseball

6. In 1897, a factory in Le Roy, New York, started making this classic of the American dining table. What was it?
a) Betty Crocker cake mixes
b) Swiss Miss Puddings
c) Jell-O

7. New York has the second largest maple syrup production outside of which state?
a) Vermont
b) Maine

8. Where were 'buffalo wings' first served?
a) At the Anchor Bar, Buffalo
b) The Buffalo Hotel, Queens
c) At Buffalo Bill's Shake and Bake Shack, Rochester

9. The Buffalo Bills are the only NFL team to play home games in New York state. True or False?

10. Rochester is home to the National Toy Hall of Fame, showcasing toys such as Hot Wheels, LEGO and Barbie. What is the museum called?
a) The Strong Museum
b) The Museum of Childhood
c) The Mattel Museum

11. Which church was founded in Palmyra, New York, in 1830?
a) National Baptist Convention
b) Reformed Mennonites
c) Latter Day Saints

12. Mark Twain and his family spent summers at Quarry Farm in Elmira from 1871 to 1889. Twain wrote parts of *Huckleberry Finn* and his biographical account *Life on the Mississippi*, in which special room?
a) His octagonal 'pilot's house'
b) His billiard room-come-study
c) The cellar – 'where no visitor could find him'

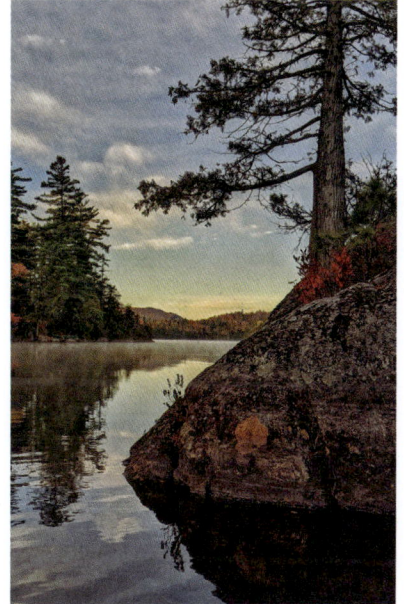

13. Letchworth State Park between Buffalo and Rochester has stunning waterfalls and deep gorges giving it the nickname?
a) 'The Five and Dime Niagara'
b) 'The Grand Canyon of the East'
c) 'The Yellowstone of the East'

14. Cornell University is an Ivy League School in Ithaca. Engineering staff at the university advised on the building of which local auto race track?
a) Watkins Glen
b) Road America
c) Mont Tremblant

15. The Adirondack Park is bigger than Yellowstone and the Everglades National Parks combined – with 6.1 million acres, it is the largest national park in the contiguous United States. True or False?

NORTH CAROLINA

Home to the military, golf at Pinehurst, and fast gaining a reputation as a center for scientific research

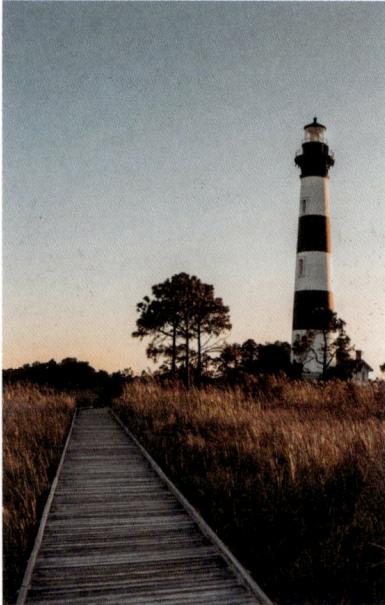

1. What is the state capital of North Carolina?
a) Raleigh
b) Durham
c) Charlotte

2. North Carolina announces itself on Welcome signs as what?
a) 'The nation's most scientific state'
b) 'The nation's most military friendly state'
c) 'The nation's banking friendly state'

3. Why did North Carolina split from South Carolina?
a) North Carolina would not accept slaves
b) It was too large to administer from Charles Town
c) It had valuable gold and did not want the entire state cashing in

4. Charlotte was the location of the country's first gold rush in

1799 when a young boy picked up a gold nugget of what size?
a) 6lbs (today worth $252,000)
b) 17lbs (today worth $714,000)

5. North Carolina is home to the largest U.S. military base – Fort Bragg. What was it briefly called during the Biden administration?
a) Fort Campbell
b) Fort Benning
c) Fort Liberty

6. The state has a unique chain of barrier islands which stretch along the coast for over 200 miles. What are they called?
a) The Outer Banks
b) The Inner Banks

7. What waistline-increasing food chain opened up for business in Winston-Salem in 1937?
a) Dairy Queen
b) Krispy Kreme
c) Cozy Dog

8. Winston-Salem was also the source of a sauce – which one?
a) Texas Pete Hot Sauce
b) Frank's Red Hot Sauce

9. Located in Asheville, Biltmore House is a Château-like mansion with 250 rooms. It is America's largest private house and was built in the Gilded Age. Who for?
a) George Washington Vanderbilt II
b) John D. Rockefeller
c) Jay Gould

10. The Wright Brothers chose Kitty Hawk, North Carolina,

to conduct their early flight experiments. How many flights did Flyer 1 make?
a) One
b) Four
c) Seven

11. Which basketball legend was born in Wilmington and played for UNC?
a) LeBron James
b) Steph Curry
c) Michael Jordan

12. North Carolina State, Duke University, and UNC. combine to form what?
a) Silicon Valley East
b) Silicon Forest
c) The Research Triangle

13. Which resident of Chapel Hill wrote *Carolina in My Mind* about North Carolina?
a) Carole King
b) James Taylor
c) Neil Diamond

14. Bat Cave is an unincorporated community in Henderson County with its own post office. What happened when the movie *Batman Returns* was released in the 1990s?
a) The post office was inundated with letters to Bruce Wayne
b) Local road signs started disappearing

15. North Carolina produces wine What is the most popular grape variety grown?
a) Muscadine
b) Zinfandel

NORTH DAKOTA

The Peace Garden State is home to the rugged Badlands and is rich in Native American history

1. What is the state capital of North Dakota?
a) Bismarck
b) Fargo
c) Billings

2. North Dakota was once part of the Dakota Territory. Dakota itself was considered too big and at the territorial election voters decided to split it in two. When was that?
a) 1870
b) 1887

3. North and South Dakota were admitted to the Union on the same day but such was the rivalry to be first that President Benjamin Harrison did what?
a) Shuffle the papers so no-one could see which he signed first
b) Asked state representatives to wait outside the Oval Office

4. North Dakota is considered the least visited state for what reason?
a) A very high level of state tax
b) No major tourist attraction

5. Mountain bikers love North Dakota because of the Maah Daah Hey Trail, one of the longest MTB trails in the U.S. How long?
a) 96 miles
b) 144 miles

6. North Dakota looks after its wildlife. It has more what than any other state?
a) National Wildlife Refuges
b) National Wilderness Areas

7. North Dakota's highest point is White Butte. Is that higher than South Dakota's Black Elk Peak?
a) Twice the size
b) Half the size
c) An irritating 23 feet lower

8. The Lewis and Clark expedition spent more time camped in (what would become) North Dakota than any other state. How many days?
a) 98
b) 200

9. Which future U.S. president bought a cattle ranch in North Dakota and served as a deputy sheriff in Billings County?
a) Woodrow Wilson
b) Bill Taft
c) Theodore Roosevelt

10. North Dakota is America's top producer of sunflowers and what else?
a) Flax
b) Hemp
c) Maize

11. Tourists will find the World's Largest Holstein Cow Statue standing 38 feet tall in New Salem. What's her given name?
a) Henrietta Holstein
b) Salem Sue
c) Dakota Daisy

12. Not surprisingly the state motto reflects a farming theme. What is it?
a) Strength from the soil
b) Harnessing the good earth
c) Sew, reap and prosper

13. Reflecting the immigrant culture Minot, near Fargo, hosts the largest Scandinavian festival in the U.S. – the Norsk Høstfest, while the town of New Leipzig hosts an annual...?
a) Fasching
b) Oktoberfest

14. ...and talking of Fargo, the Coen Brothers put the city on the map with their movie of the same name. Which actress won an Oscar for her role as Marge Gunderson, a pregnant police chief?
a) Sigourney Weaver
b) Frances McDormand
c) Cameron Diaz

15. North Dakota is America's third highest producer of oil, behind only Texas and New Mexico. True or False?

OHIO

A Midwest powerhouse, known for rock and roll, aviation pioneers, and insanely passionate sports fans. And a big basket...

1. What is the state capital of Ohio?
a) Dayton
b) Akron
c) Columbus

2. What is the largest city by population?
a) Cincinnati
b) Columbus
c) Cleveland

3. What is unique about the Ohio state flag?
a) The only non-rectangular flag
b) The only state flag with muskrats
c) The only state flag with cherubs

4. From north to south, Ohio is 220 miles. How big is it east to west?
a) 220 miles
b) 250 miles

5. The state's name comes from the Iroquois word 'ohi-yo' which means...?
a) Edge of lake
b) Angry river
c) Great river

6. The highest point in Ohio is Campbell Hill. How high is that?
a) 775 feet
b) 1,549 feet

7. The Cuyahoga River in Cleveland once caught fire in 1969. True or False?

8. Which superstar basketball player comes from Akron, Ohio?
a) Caitlin Clark
b) LeBron James

9. Ohio is a sports mad state with the Browns, the Bengals and the Cavaliers. Where do the passionate Cleveland Browns fans hang out?
a) The Junkyard
b) The Backyard
c) The Dawg Pound

10. Apart from rock and roll, Ohio is also home to which sporting Hall of Fame, located in Canton?
a) Pro Tennis
b) Pro Pool
c) Pro Football

11. The first professional baseball team was formed in Ohio in 1869. What was it called?
a) The Cincinnati Red Stockings
b) The Cleveland Knickerbockers
c) The Akron Racer Snakes

12. The Rock and Roll Hall of Fame is in Cleveland. Which Cleveland DJ popularized 'rock and roll' in the 1950s?
a) Dick Clark
b) Wolfman Jack
c) Alan Freed

13. Ohio is home to Cedar Point. What gets tourists flocking there?
a) Ohio's biggest golf resort: 8 courses, plus a floodlit par-3 course
b) Cedar Point State Park and River Rapids
c) A massive amusement park

14. The Longaberger Company manufactured handcrafted maple wood baskets. Its HQ was in Dresden, Ohio, and was built in the shape of a giant basket. At seven stories high this is the largest 'mimetic' structure in the world. True or False?

15. The first Wendy's restaurant opened in Columbus. When?
a) 1935
b) 1969

OKLAHOMA

The Sooner State, Oklahoma's cowboy spirit shines in its rodeos, even though the chance of a box social have long since passed...

1. What is the state capital of Oklahoma?
a) Norman
b) Broken Arrow
c) Oklahoma City

2. Before statehood in 1907, what was Oklahoma known as?
a) Oklahoma Territory
b) Tribal Lands Territory
c) Indian Territory

3. Oklahoma has three official state languages: English, Choctaw and what is the third?
a) Cherokee
b) Spanish
c) Iroquois

4. The area was the destination of Indian tribes relocated from the southeast – the Five Tribes of the Choctaw, Chickasaw, Cherokee, Creek and...?
a) Seminole
b) Lenape

5. The U.S. Army experimented with which animal before releasing it into the wild in the state?
a) Zebras
b) Camels

6. What is the state bird?
a) Scissor-tailed flycatcher
b) The mourning dove

7. Our photo shows a supercell thunderstorm brewing over the Oklahoma prairie. How many kinds of thunderstorms are there?
a) Four
b) Seven

8. The state's sporting hope is the NBA's Oklahoma City Thunder. Which team did they start out as?
a) Seattle Sounders
b) Seattle Mariners
c) Seattle SuperSonics

9. In 1937, American supermarket owner Sylvan Goldman came up with a way to get his customers to spend more at his Humpty Dumpty chain in Oklahoma. What was it?
a) A loyalty card
b) The first shopping trolley

10. The University of Oklahoma has America's largest school of what discipline?
a) Animal science
b) Meteorology
c) Soil science

11. Tulsa was once known as...?
a) 'The Frozen Custard Capital of the World'
b) 'The Cattle Ranching Capital of the World'
c) 'The Oil Capital of the World'

12. In 1927, Tulsa businessman Cyrus Avery began the campaign to create a national route through his town. What had he started?
a) The Lincoln Highway
b) Route 66

13. Oklahoma is part of Tornado Alley. On average, how many tornadoes are expected each year?
a) 47
b) 62

14. *Oklahoma!* is an eternal favorite from Broadway duo Rodgers and Hammerstein. Which was their first hit musical?
a) *South Pacific*
b) *Carousel*
c) *Oklahoma!*

15. The musical was set in farm country outside the town of Claremore, Oklahoma – which just happened to be famous for cowboy superstar...?
a) Roy Rogers
b) Will Rogers

OREGON

The Beaver State has a paradise of lush forests to gnaw into, quirky cities like Portland and the monster Crater Lake

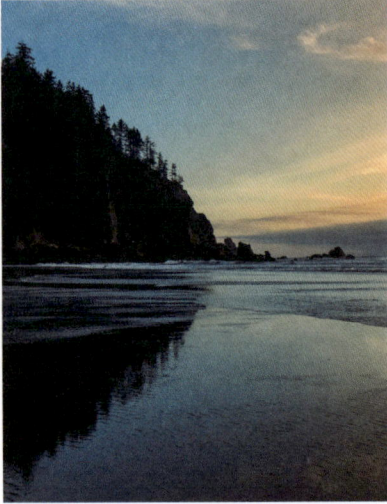

1. What is the state capital of Oregon?
a) Eugene
b) Medford
c) Salem

2. What is unique about the Oregon state flag?
a) It shows a beaver in a top hat
b) It has different designs either side
c) It is an exact copy of Saskatchewan province (Canada)

3. At 11,249 feet, which is Oregon's highest peak?
a) South Sister
b) Mount Jefferson
c) Mount Hood

4. Oregon has the largest living organism living in the Blue Mountains – what is it?
a) A fungus covering 3.4 square miles
b) A stand of aspen trees all linked by root suckers

5. What did the 1967 Beach Bill grant Oregonians?
a) Their right to build sand castles of any size
b) Beach fishing without permits
c) All beaches made public land

6. Oregon is the top producer in the contiguous U.S. of which product?
a) Lumber
b) Farmed salmon

7. Oregon is also one of the top wine producing states. Which variety of grape is it noted for?
a) Chardonnay
b) Pinot noir
c) Viognier

8. Oregon was one of the first states to decriminalize marijuana. When?
a) 1964
b) 1973
c) 1982

9. What is the state motto?
a) She Flies With Her Own Wings
b) We Only Advance Together
c) Revere The Green Gold

10. Which multinational company with annual revenue of $48 billion is headquartered in Beaverton?
a) Microsoft
b) Nike
c) Starbucks

11. Portland is home to Powell's, the world's largest independent what...?
a) Abattoir
b) Brewery
c) Bookstore

12. What is the Oregon state butterfly?
a) Oregon swallowtail
b) Monarch

13. The Simpsons creator, Matt Groening, is from Portland, and so many of the characters' names come from Portland streets. True or False?

14. On May 5, 1945, six civilians were killed near Bly, Oregon, by a Japanese Fu-Go balloon bomb. Launched from Japan and carried across the Pacific on the jet stream, what was the target?
a) Portland and Seattle industries
b) Random act of demoralizing terror
c) Northwest forests – intended to start fires

15. Crater Lake – Oregon's only national park – was created in a massive volcanic eruption between 6,000 and 8,000 years ago. How many species of fish live in the lake?
a) Two – kokanee salmon and rainbow trout
b) Seventeen

PENNSYLVANIA

The Keystone State is where the gears of an independent nation first turned, and Gettysburg, where the nation was saved

1. What is the state capital of Pennsylvania?
a) Harrisburg
b) Gettysburg
c) Pittsburgh

2. Philadelphia was the capital of the United States until what year?
a) 1799
b) 1807

3. What's odd about Betsy Ross's house in Philadelphia – the woman widely credited with sewing the first stars and stripes?
a) It's said to be haunted by her rival seamstress
b) Historians aren't sure if it was demolished or is the one next door, still standing

4. One of Pennsylvania's state animals (aka living insignia) is an Eastern Hellbender. What kind of animal is it?
a) Reptile

h) Mammal
c) Amphibian

5. Unsurprisingly – given it's a Quaker-founded state – there is a Bethlehem PA close to Nazareth PA. What is Bethlehem Pennsylvania famous for?
a) Steel
b) Aluminium
c) Truck engines

6. The Pittsburgh Steelers are the equal most successful NFL team, winning the Super Bowl six times. Who are they tied with?
a) Miami Dolphins
b) Philadelphia Eagles
c) New England Patriots

7. The world's largest clothespin is a 45-foot steel sculpture located in Philadelphia's Center Square Plaza. It and was designed by who?
a) Claes Oldenburg
b) Andy Warhol

8. Groundhog Day, now the subject of a movie and a musical, has been an annual weather prediction event in Punxsutawney since 1887. What is the name of the groundhog?
a) Bill
b) Ned
c) Phil

9. Pennsylvania has state parks that cover over 300,000 acres. How many parks are there?
a) 81
b) 124
c) 213

10. Which global megastar was born in Reading, Pennsylvania?
a) Beyonce Knowles
b) Billy Eilish
c) Taylor Swift

11. It's gone now, but one of the first large-scale baseball stadiums was built in Pittsburgh in 1909. What was it called?
a) Shibe Park
b) Forbes Field

12. The steps to the magnificent Philadelphia Museum of Art are featured in which iconic movie?
a) *The Philadelphia Story*
b) *Rocky*

13. Gettysburg is in Pennsylvania and Lincoln delivered his historic speech on November 19, 1863. How many words does it contain?
a) 146
b) 271
c) 1,776

14. There are 32 states with Amish communities, and one of the biggest is in which Pennsylvania county?
a) Bedford
b) Cumberland
c) Lancaster

15. The Amish population in the U.S. numbers over 390,000. What is the average family size for this industrious, self-sufficient community?
a) Five children
b) Six children
c) Seven children

RHODE ISLAND

The Ocean State makes the most of its limited seaboard and is known for its seafood, especially clam chowder and lobster rolls

1. What is the state capital of Rhode Island?
a) Pawtucket
b) Cranston
c) Providence

2. Rhode Island is easily the smallest state in the U.S. – you could fit Rhode Island into Alaska 425 times. But which has the greater population?
a) Rhode Island
b) Alaska

3. The state motto is very short. Like the state. What is it?
a) Faith
b) Hope
c) Charity

4. Rhode Island is known as 'The Ocean State', so on its state flag is...?
a) A sailor and a mermaid
b) A carrack (like the *Mayflower*)
c) An anchor

5. They were previously also known as 'John Macomber fowls'

and also 'Tripp fowls'. What are they?

6. Slater Mill in Pawtucket was the first water-powered cotton-spinning mill and is seen as the birthplace of the Industrial Revolution. Which inventor's work had Samuel Slater copied?
a) James Watt
b) Richard Arkwright

7. A now-defunct pro football team from Rhode Island won the 1928 NFL title. What were they called?
a) Providence Steamrollers
b) Newport Sailbaggers

8. What happened at the Newport Jazz Festival of 1965 that shocked the music world?
a) The Rolling Stones turned up and played a blues set
b) Bob Dylan plugged in an electric guitar
c) The Beatles played a Dixieland Jazz set

9. When admitted to the Union, the original name was 'State of Rhode Island and Providence Plantations'. When did they officially drop 'Providence Plantations'?
a) 1920
b) 2020

10. The first open golf tournament in the U.S. was held in 1895 at the Newport Golf Club. How many competitors took part?
a) 11
b) 55

11. Rhode Island outlawed alcohol in 1852 ... but retracted the law seven years later. In 1920 what did they do with the 18th Amendment (Prohibition)?
a) Continued it until 1946
b) Ignored it

12. The Vanderbilt family built a fabulous summer residence in Newport. What was it called?
a) The Breakers
b) Spyglass House
c) Camelot

13. Statistics show that there are more ... what ... per capita than any other state?
a) Libraries
b) Dunkin' Donuts
c) Escape Rooms

14. Newport is reputed to have the first gas-illuminated streets in America. When were the lamps first lit?
a) 1803
b) 1835

15. Jacob Bates was an English equestrian who took continental Europe by storm, riding four horses at once and firing guns from horseback. He toured New England in 1773 and inspired Newport resident Christopher Gardner who became the country's first circus performer. How was he billed?
a) 'The Original American Rider'
b) 'America's Jacob Bates'
c) 'The Celebrated Mr Gardner'

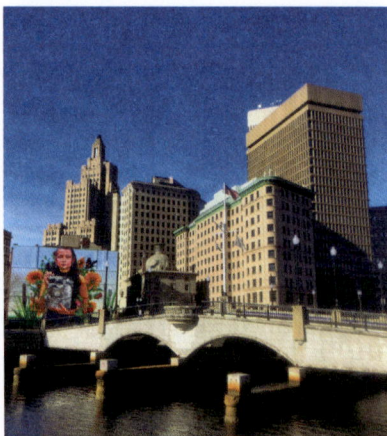

SOUTH CAROLINA

The Palmetto State is famous for its historic Charleston houses that have resisted city fires and hurricanes

1. What is the state capital of South Carolina?
a) Charleston
b) Greenville
c) Columbia

2. Settlers from which European nation explored the Savannah River before choosing Purrysburg, South Carolina?
a) Switzerland
b) Croatia
c) Denmark

3. Carolina was named in honor of which royal figure?
a) King Charles I of England (*Carolus* is Latin for Charles)
b) Queen Caroline of Brandenburg-Ansbach, wife of George II

4. What is the name of the state reptile?
a) Loggerhead sea turtle
b) Leatherback sea turtle
c) Olive Ridley sea turtle

5. The Gullah culture, found along the coast, preserves traditions from where?
a) Africa's 'rice coast'
b) Seminole tribal land

6. That crazy dance of the 1920s, the Charleston, was originated in Charleston, SC. Who was responsible?
a) The Jenkins Orphanage Band
b) Count Basie

7. South Carolina is known as the Palmetto State and has the sabal palmetto tree on its state flag. Which of these is *not* an alternative name?
a) Cabbage palm
b) Swamp cabbage
c) Carolina cabbage

8. Tourists go to Charleston for the old buildings and live oaks, but which is the most popular resort on the South Carolina coast, with 14m visitors?
a) Folly Beach
b) Myrtle Beach
c) Hilton Head Island

9. What happened to Charleston's Institute Hall (Secession Hall), where the secession vote was held?
a) It was torched by Union supporters after victory in 1865
b) It was consumed by flames in a citywide fire in 1861
c) It was demolished by order of President Andrew Johnson

10. What nationally important piece of equipment is built in North Charleston?
a) Falcon Heavy rocket
b) Boeing 787 Dreamliner
c) MQ-9 Reaper surveillance drone

11. What does the state produce more than any other in the U.S.?
a) Tires (Michelin and Bridgestone factories)
b) Cage and aviary birds
c) Baseballs and footballs (Rawlings and Wilson)

12. Since 1896, Clemson University Tigers' great rivals have been the University of South Carolina Gamecocks. The big match is known as...?
a) The Palmetto Bowl
b) The Secession Bowl

13. South Carolina has a Monkey Island (Morgan Island) which is uninhabited but home to over 3,000 free-roaming monkeys. How did they get there?
a) Released from a bankrupt traveling circus in 1930
b) Put there by the National Institute of Allergy and Infectious Diseases

14. The Firefly Distillery in Wadmalaw Island is known for making the first-ever...?
a) Sweet tea vodka
b) Palmetto liqor

15. What is the Carolina Reaper?
a) A very hot chilli pepper
b) A customized NASCAR Camaro
c) A Carolina corn-loving finch

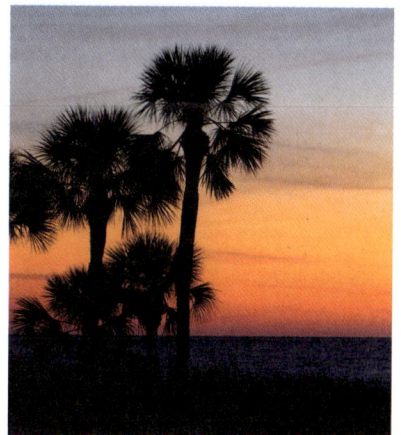

SOUTH DAKOTA

The Mount Rushmore State is also home to Deadwood with its five museums evoking the spirit of Gold Rush

1. What is the state capital of South Dakota?
a) Pierre
b) Sioux Falls
c) Aberdeen

2. The Black Hills (Black Elk Peak) are the highest mountains east of the Rockies, making them higher than any of the mountains of the Appalachians. True or False?

3. The Custer State Park Buffalo Roundup takes place every year around September. How many buffalo are rounded up?
a) Around 1300
b) 0

4. In Jackson County and Pennington County there is a National Historic Site commemorating what?
a) The ill-fated 7th Cavalry of George Armstrong Custer
b) Minuteman nuclear missile silos

5. The author of *Little House on the Prairie* lived in De Smet, SD. Who penned the great work?
a) Laura Ingalls Wilder
b) Louisa May Alcott

6. Since 2019 the language of the Great Sioux Nation, comprising three dialects, has become the official state indigenous language. These are Dakota, Lakota, and Nakota. True or False?

7. The Sioux had been granted the entire western half of present-day South Dakota (West River) in 1868 by the Treaty of Laramie. When gold was found in the Black Hills in 1874, who did they grant mining rights to?
a) Only J.P. Morgan's company
b) Nobody

8. The town of Deadwood grew up to cater for gold miners. Which well-known western figure was killed there during a poker game?
a) Wyatt Earp
b) Wild Bill Hickock
c) Doc Holliday

9. *The Deadwood Stage* is a song from the 1953 film *Calamity Jane*. Who sang it?
a) Ethel Merman
b) Doris Day
c) Gwen Verdon

10. The Jewel Cave National Monument looks after the second longest cave in the United States. How many miles of mapped passageways does it contain (not all open to the public)?
a) 137.4 miles
b) 220.1 miles

11. The Mammoth Site is a paleontological site near Hot Springs. It has one of the greatest concentrations of which ancient animal?
a) Saber-toothed tiger
b) Dire wolf
c) Mammoth

12. The giant Mount Rushmore sculpture in the Black Hills shows four presidents. When Barack Obama was asked about his inclusion, what was his response?
a) He would defer to Martin Luther King
b) He joked his ears were too large

13. The Sturgis Motorcycle Rally is an annual rally that started up in 1938 for Indian Motorcycle owners. Today anything goes and the rally attracts how many bikers?
a) 250,000
b) 500,000

14. Topographically South Dakota has many buttes. But which state has the biggest official buttes?
a) South Dakota
b) Idaho

15. The Badlands are home to big populations of prairie dogs, banded together underground in colonies, known as...?
a) Citadels
b) Towns
c) Bunkers

TENNESSEE

The Volunteer State has the mother church of country music, and the home of the blues in Nashville and Memphis

1. What is the state capital of Tennessee?
a) Nashville
b) Clarksville
c) Knoxville
d) Huntsville

2. Tennessee earned the nickname 'The Volunteer State' due to the large number of Tennesseans who volunteered for which war?
a) Revolutionary War
b) War of 1812 and the Mexican-American War
c) Civil War

3. According to the 2020 census, Tennessee's two biggest cities have populations of 633,000 and 689,000. Which is the biggest?
a) Memphis
b) Nashville

4. Tennessee is bordered by eight states: Kentucky, Virginia, North Carolina, Georgia, Alabama, Mississippi, Arkansas and...?

5. Elvis Presley's former home Graceland, in Memphis, is the second most visited house in the U.S. True or False?

6. Which famous brand of liqor is made in Lynchburg, Tennessee, ironically in a dry county?
a) Jim Beam
b) Jack Daniels

7. Another great Tennessee export, Dolly Parton, attended Sevier County High School and played which instrument in the marching band?
a) Glockenspiel
b) Drums
c) Trombone

8. Apart from the national park, Dollywood is Tennessee's most-visited tourist attraction. It started life in 1961 as the Rebel Railroad. It has grown and been renamed several times. Which of these is *not* a former name of the park?
a) Goldrush Junction
b) Silver Dollar City
c) Smoky Mountain Rails

9. There is another museum in Pigeon Forge with a half-scale model of which ship?
a) SS *America*
b) USS *Missouri*
c) RMS *Titanic*

10. Tennessee is famous for its 'Meat and Three' meals. What are they?
a) Meat dish with three sides
b) Meat dish with three potato dish sides
c) Three different meat dishes

11. Memphis is the birthplace of the 'Queen of Soul'. Who commands soul music?
a) Gladys Knight
b) Diana Ross
c) Aretha Franklin

12. MoonPies originated in Chattanooga, Tennessee, when a traveling salesman for a Chattanooga bakery was asked for a snack 'as big as the moon'.

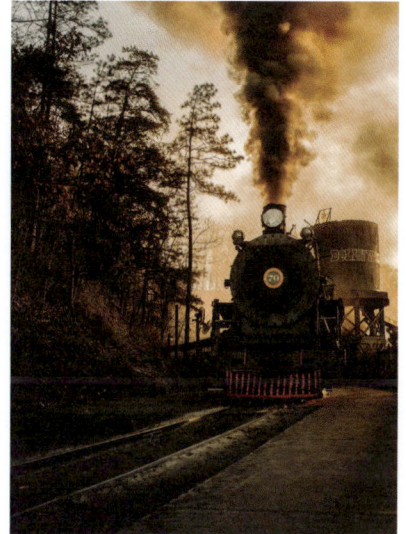

When were they first made?
a) 1917
b) 1957

13. Utah is not known for jazz and Memphis certainly has no grizzly bears. So where did NBA team the Memphis Grizzlies get their name in 2001?
a) Vancouver
b) Portland

14. Nashville has a full-scale replica of which wonder of the ancient world?
a) The Library at Pergamum
b) The Greek Parthenon
c) The Forum in Rome

15. The Sunsphere in Knoxville is a tower with a large globe on top that was built for the 1982 World Fair. Today it is a local landmark. What is its nickname?
a) The Lord's Golf Tee
b) The Lord's Bedside Lamp

TEXAS

The Lone Star State is a land of big skies, big cities, and the biggest of everything – whether its barbecues, rodeos or even bat colonies

1. What is the state capital of Texas?
a) Dallas
b) Houston
c) Austin

2. If Texas were a country – and it once was – where would it stand in the world by area?
a) 23rd biggest
b) 39th biggest
c) 57th biggest

3. Again, if Texas were a country, with its $2.4 trillion economy where would it stand in the world economies?
a) 7th largest economy
b) 9th biggest economy
c) 11th biggest economy

4. Which is closer to El Paso, Texas, as the crow flies – Los Angeles or Houston?

5. Texas has the biggest and best of lots of things, but California has 673 species compared to 664 for Texas. What kind of animal?
a) Reptile species
b) Bird species
c) Fish species

6. Texas is one of the states that make up Tornado Alley. What's the average number expected each year?
a) 43
b) 89

7. One of the nation's most loved drinks was created in Waco, Texas, in 1885. Which one?
a) 7-Up
b) Coca-Cola
c) Dr Pepper

8. The King Ranch has been in the same family since 1853. It is bigger than Rhode Island. True or False?

9. The state has had six different national flags flown over it: Spain, Mexico, the Republic of Texas, the United States, the Confederacy and which other nation?
a) England
b) France

10. Who started a major computer company while operating from an off-campus dormitory room at the University of Texas in Austin?
a) Michael Dell
b) Steve Jobs

11. The name 'Texas' comes from the Caddo Indian word 'taysha', which means what?
a) Friends/allies
b) Standing alone
c) Great gift

12. Which music/film festival takes over Austin each March?
a) ACL Austin City Limits
b) SXSW (South by Southwest)

13. The USS *Texas* is the last remaining battleship used in World War I and World War II. Where was it located for many decades?
a) San Jacinto Historic Site
b) Galveston Harbor
c) Beaumont Pier

14. The AT&T Stadium in Arlington is one of the biggest domed stadiums in the world. Who plays there?
a) Texas Rangers
b) Dallas Cowboys
c) Houston Texans

15. Which country legend was born in Abbott, Texas?
a) Willie Nelson
b) Johnny Cash
c) Emmylou Harris

UTAH

With stunning national parks along with the Great Salt Lake, the Beehive State is a place to get busy hiking and biking

1. What is the state capital of Utah?
a) Provo
b) Brigham City
c) Salt Lake City

2. What is the height of the lowest elevation in Utah, the Beaver Dam at the Arizona border?
a) 2,180 feet
b) 3,411 feet

3. Why is Utah nicknamed the Beehive State?
a) Because the Mormon Tabernacle resembles a bee skep
b) The state motto is 'Industry' and bees are industrious

4. Conservationists have warned that without drastic environmental action, the Great Salt Lake could dry up by which year?
a) 2030
b) 2050

5. Utah boasts spectacular natural features, none more so than the Arches National Park. How many natural sandstone arches does it contain?
a) 500

b) 1,000
c) 2,000

6. Utah is home to five stunning national parks: Arches, Bryce Canyon, Capitol Reef, Canyonlands and which other...?
a) Great Basin
b) Mesa Verde
c) Zion

7. Utah's natural beauty makes it a world-famous mountain biking destination, with trails centering on which town?
a) Boulder
b) Moab

8. Coral Pink Sand Dunes State Park was formed from the erosion of pink-colored Navajo Sandstone by strong winds. Which sport does the park help promote?
a) Kite sand surfing
b) Sandboarding

9. The Wasatch Range gets an average of 500 inches of snow per year. Utah has 15 ski resorts and one of the longest skiing seasons, giving it the nickname...?
a) The Greatest Snow on Earth
b) Resort of the Latter Day Ski Pass

10. The name 'Utah' comes from the Ute tribe, meaning...?
a) People of the mountains
b) People of the salt plains

11. Utah buys more of which food item per capita than any other state?
a) Slushies
b) Oats
c) Jell-O

12. Which national food chain opened its first out-of-state franchise in Salt Lake City?
a) McDonalds
b) White Castle
c) Kentucky Fried Chicken

13. What happened in 2016 that shocked/surprised Utah politicians
a) Utah no longer had the highest birth rate in the country
b) Brigham Young University revealed that 4% of students were not LDS members

14. The Bonneville Speed Flats, used for world record speed attempts, were once part of the Great Salt Lake. True or False?

15. There is an urban myth that landlocked Utah once voted to ban whaling. What was the kernel of truth to the rumor?
a) James Wickham planned to farm small whales in the Great Salt Lake
b) Utah-born Hiram Steel wanted to exploit a legal loophole and register his whaling ships in Utah

VERMONT

It's known for its ski resorts and some of New England's most spectacular landscapes in the fall

1. What is the state capital of Vermont?
a) Montpelier
b) Burlington
c) Windsor

2. When was Vermont admitted to the Union?
a) 1777
b) 1791

3. Which is Vermont's largest city?
a) Colchester
b) Rutland
c) Burlington

4. What is the highest peak in Vermont?
a) Mount Mansfield
b) Camel's Hump
c) Killington Peak

5. Where does Vermont rank in the most populated states in the U.S.?
a) 43rd
b) 49th

6. Lake Champlain, which Vermont shares with New York, is named after...
a) Theodore Champlain, politician
b) Samuel de Champlain, explorer
c) Eugene Champlain, fur trader

7. Which U.S. president was born in Plymouth Notch, Vermont?
a) William Taft
b) Grover Cleveland
c) Calvin Coolidge

8. What is the state's nickname?
a) The Canadian Frontier
b) The Green Mountain State
c) The Green Valley State

9. One of America's great industrialists was born in Rutland, Vermont, who was it?
a) Henry Ford
b) Cyrus McCormick
c) John Deere

10. Which famous British novelist spent his early married life in 'Bliss Cottage' near Brattleboro, Vermont?
a) Charles Dickens
b) Rudyard Kipling
c) Graham Greene

11. Which state is more northerly – Vermont or New Hampshire?

12. To the north, Vermont borders which Canadian state?
a) Ontario
b) Manitoba
c) Quebec

13. The official state bird of Vermont is...?
a) Brown thrasher
b) Hermit thrush
c) Mountain bluebird

14. The official state fish of Vermont is...?
a) Striped bass
b) Brook trout
c) Northern pike

15. The official tree of Vermont is...?
a) Sugar maple
b) Longleaf pine
c) Coastal redwood

VIRGINIA

The first English-speaking colony to be established in the New World and a fierce supporter of American democracy

1. What is the state capital of Virginia?
a) Richmond
b) Norfolk
c) Alexandria

2. When was Virginia admitted to the Union?
a) 1782
b) 1788

3. Which is the largest city in Virginia?
a) Arlington
b) Chesapeake
c) Virginia Beach

4. What is the highest peak in Virginia?
a) Bald Knob
b) Balsam Beartown Mountain
c) Mount Rogers

5. Where does Virginia rank in the most populated states in the U.S.?
a) 12th
b) 21st

6. In 1606, which English king issued a charter to the Virginia Company of London for a new colony?
a) James I
b) Elizabeth I
c) George I

7. Virginia is sometimes known as the 'Mother of Presidents'. How many U.S. presidents were Virginians?
a) 6
b) 8
c) 11

8. What slogan has been used on state 'Welcome' signs since 1969?
a) 'Virginia is for lovers'
b) 'Virginia – where it all started'
c) 'Virginia welcomes everyone from everywhere'

9. Which famous Virginian was born in Pope's Creek, Westmoreland County?
a) George Washington
b) Dave Grohl
c) James Madison

10. Virginia is the most populous U.S. state without what facility...?
a) A dedicated opera house
b) A major international airport
c) A major professional sports franchise

11. The Smithsonian's Steven F. Udvar-Hazy Center in Chantilly, Virginia, is the largest aerospace museum in America. True or False?

12. Virginia shares a border with how many other states?

13. The official state mammal of Virginia is ...?
a) Norfolk scuttling house mouse
b) Shenandoah bobcat
c) Virginia big-eared bat

14. The official state insect/ butterfly of Virginia is...?
a) Eastern tiger swallowtail
b) Pepper-spotted silverdrop
c) Zebra longwing

15. The official tree of Vermont is...?
a) Dogwood
b) Sitka spruce
c) Southern live oak

WASHINGTON

Home of America's global brands and a boater's paradise among the islands of Puget Sound

1. What is the state capital of Washington?
a) Tacoma
b) Olympia
c) Spokane

2. To reinforce the allegiance to the Washington family there is also a city named...?
a) Martha
b) Mount Vernon
c) Popes Creek

3. Washington was named by Congress during the creation of Washington Territory in 1853. What was the territory originally going to be called?
a) Tacoma
b) Olympia
c) Columbia

4. Seattle was renamed after Chief Seattle. What was it originally called?
a) Duwamps
b) Pugetville

5. Washington state has five major active volcanoes in the Cascade Range: Mount Baker, Glacier Peak, Mount Rainier, Mount Adams and which other?

6. Fire and ice ... Washington has the most glaciers in the Lower 48. How many?
a) 336
b) Over 3,000

7. Seattle is well known as home to Starbucks. When was the first branch opened?

a) 1962
b) 1971
c) 1978

8. Spokane hosts one of the world's largest specialist basketball tournaments known as Hoopfest. How is the game played at Hoopfest?
a) One on one
b) Two on two
c) Three on three

9. The Pacific Aero Products Company started up in Seattle in 1916. What did it later become?
a) McDonnell Douglas
b) Curtiss Aeroplane
c) Boeing

10. In 1889, the Great Seattle Fire destroyed 25 city blocks. What did the city decide to do?
a) Excavate the whole area and fill in parts of the shoreline
b) Build on top of the ruins and raise the street level 22 feet

11. The Yakima Valley is famous for producing a large majority of the nation's...?
a) Giant pumpkins
b) Hops
c) Cabernet sauvignon grapes

12. What are you likely to find lurking in the depths of Puget Sound?
a) The giant Pacific octopus
b) The Oregon spiny lobster
c) The Columbian weathervane scallop

13. Amazon, Costco and Microsoft all have bases in the Seattle Metropolitan Area. Maybe it's something to do with 'no state income tax'. Which is the largest employer?
a) Amazon
b) Costco
c) Microsoft

14. The Evergreen Point Floating Bridge which spans Lake Washington is the longest floating bridge in the world. How long is it?
a) 5,399 feet (1.02 miles)
b) 7,710 feet (1.46 miles)

15. The San Juan Islands in Puget Sound are a boater's paradise. What is the capital/main ferry port?
a) Friday Harbor
b) Sunday Harbor
c) Tuesday Harbor

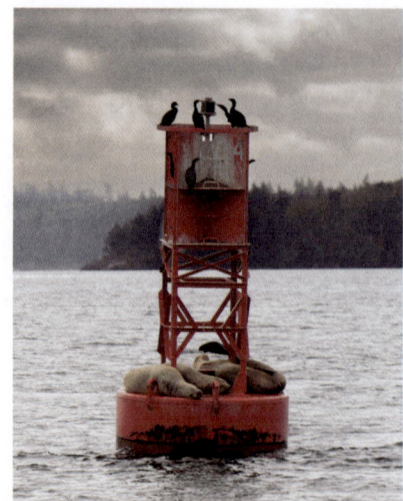

WEST VIRGINIA

Known for its breathtaking Appalachian landscapes – cascading rivers make it a dream destination for white-water rafting

1. What is the state capital of West Virginia?
a) Huntington
b) Morgantown
c) Charleston

2. The state capital may only have a population of 46,000, but they have a BIG capitol building standing 292 feet tall. Which is taller?
a) West Virginia Capitol
b) Washington, D.C. Capitol

3. What is the state motto?
a) Mountaineers Are Always Free
b) Follow Your Own Path

4. In 1861, residents of the western and northern counties of Virginia who resented the eastern Virginia planter elite seceded from the Confederacy. When were they admitted to the Union?
a) 1863
b) 1865

5. Until Union forces permanently reoccupied the town from July 8, 1864, the town at Harpers Ferry changed hands how many times in the Civil War?
a) Six
b) Fourteen

6. West Virginia is the third most forested state with 78.5% of the land under trees. Which state pips WV into second place with 81.9%?
a) New Hampshire
b) Vermont

7. Oak is an abundant tree in West Virginia forests – northern red oak is the most common, along with white oak and black oak. Which of these other oaks is *not* present?
a) Chestnut oak
b) Yellow oak
c) Live oak

8. West Virginia is the birthplace of which real-life character from the Tom Wolfe book on the early space program *The Right Stuff*?
a) Gus Grissom
b) Gordon Cooper
c) Chuck Yeager

9. *Take Me Home Country Roads* which contains the line 'Almost heaven, West Virginia,' is the state song written by Bill Danoff and Taffy Nivert. Danoff wanted to write about the country roads of Massachusetts, but didn't think the word Massachusetts was musical enough. True or False?

10. ...although John Denver seized hold of the song it was originally intended for which country performer?
a) Iris DeMent
b) Johnny Cash

11. The New River Gorge Bridge is one of the longest single-span arch bridges in the world. The bridge is so famous that 'Bridge Day' is celebrated every year. What happens?
a) A case of champagne is smashed against the brick piers
b) BASE jumpers are allowed to leap from the structure

12. The Greenbrier is a resort near White Sulphur Springs. It was the site of a large underground bunker to house Congress in the event of a nuclear strike during the Cold War. What was the bunker's name?
a) Project Greek Island
b) Project Ghost Town

13. The Lost World Caverns, outside Lewisburg, has a 500,000- year-old stalagmite called 'Warclub'. Bob Addis set the unofficial world record for Stalagmite Sitting by staying on top of it for how long?
a) 9 days
b)15 days
c) 31 days

14. Which is the biggest ski resort in West Virginia?
a) Snowshoe Mountain
b) Timberline Mountain

15. The town of Point Pleasant celebrates a phantom character known as...?
a) Flatwoods Monster
b) Mothman

WISCONSIN

Wisconsin is America's dairyland – famous for cheese, sausage, and Green Bay Packers with their Cheesehead hats

1. What is the state capital of Wisconsin?
a) Madison
b) Milwaukee
c) Kenosha

2. There are no hills or mountains in Wisconsin over 2,000 feet. True or False?

3. The state motto is a single word – which is...?
a) Outward
b) Forward
c) Upward

4. Wisconsin has an unusual state fish, the muskellunge. Often shortened to muskie or lunge, it's a species of large freshwater predatory fish. Which fish family is it part of?
a) Pike family
b) Catfish family

5. The state is known as 'America's Dairyland' and is the largest producer of cheese in the country. Monroe, Wisconsin, actually bills itself as what...?
a) 'The Cheddar Cheese Capital of the World'
b) 'The Swiss Cheese Capital of the World'

6. Over at Sheboygan on the western shore of Lake Michigan they like to lean into their German heritage, calling themselves...?
a) 'The Knackwurst Capital'
b) 'The Frankfurter Capital'
c) 'The Bratwurst Capital'

7. The state borders two Great Lakes: Lake Michigan and Lake Superior. Along the shores of Lake Michigan it has the world's largest freshwater what...?
a) Mussel beds
b) Sand dunes

8. Who owns NFL team the Green Bay Packers?
a) The City of Green Bay
b) The fans

9. Which major organization was founded in Ripon, Wisconsin, in 1854.
a) Dairy Farmers of Wisconsin
b) The Republican Party

10. Which Waukesha-born instrument inventor played a major role in the growth of rock music?
a) Robert Moog
b) Les Paul
c) Clarence Fender

11. Wisconsin consumes more of which alcoholic drink per capita than any other state?
a) Brandy
b) Bourbon
c) Bacardi

12. Over time, Milwaukee's position as the dominant producer of American beer has slipped. Of the 'big four' brewers: Miller, Schlitz, Pabst, and Blatz, which one is left?
a) Miller
b) Schlitz
c) Pabst

13. Milwaukee is famous for producing Harley-Davidson motorcycles. Two childhood friends started up the business in 1903. What were their first names?
a) William and James
b) James and Arthur
c) William and Arthur

14. Wisconsinites love a festival. There are festivals for cheese, cranberries, many Oktoberfests and a major air show at Oshkosh. What distinguishes the Oshkosh show?
a) It's for balloons
b) It's for single-person aircraft
c) It's for experimental aircraft

15. The Ringling Brothers from Wisconsin started off as a variety act, but in 1884 they expanded their act into a one-ring show and added what?
a) A horse and a bear
b) Clowns and a trapeze

WYOMING

Home to Yellowstone and the Grand Teton National Parks, the Equality State has also led the way in promoting women's rights

1. What is the state capital of Wyoming?
a) Casper
b) Laramie
c) Cheyenne

2. What is the name for someone who comes from Wyoming?
a) Wyomingian
b) Wyominger

3. It's the state with the fewest people (around 587,000 in 2025) ranking 50th in the states. It also has the lowest population density in the contiguous United States. True or False?

4. Wyoming's nickname is 'The Equality State' because it was the first state to grant women the right to vote. When?
a) 1869
b) 1894
c) 1914

5. Wyoming was the first state to allow women to serve on juries. It also elected America's first female governor, Nellie Tayloe Ross. When?
a) 1925
b) 1937
c) 1948

6. The Devils Tower National Monument was the first U.S. national monument, designated in 1906. It featured prominently in which movie?
a) *Close Encounters of the Third Kind*
b) *E.T.*
c) *Roswell*

7. What is the state flower?
a) Indian paintbrush
b) Dotted gayfeather
c) Prairie coneflower

8. The majority of Yellowstone National Park is in Wyoming and one of the most famous features is the Old Faithful geyser. How many geysers are active in Yellowstone?
a) 500
b) 1,000

9. There are six geysers which park rangers will give a predicted eruption time for. Not surprisingly Old Faithful has been the most reliable over the years. What time window do they typically give for a blast from the world's most famous geyser?
a) ± 3 minutes
b) ± 10 minutes

10. The magnificent Grand Teton mountain range was named by French explorers and fur traders. What does *téton* mean in French?
a) Head
b) Teat
c) Peak

11. Grand Teton is the highest mountain of the Tetons range soaring to 13,775 feet above the Teton Glacier and making it the highest peak in Wyoming. True or False?

12. In the late 1800s, the Johnson County War was a violent conflict between cattle barons and who?

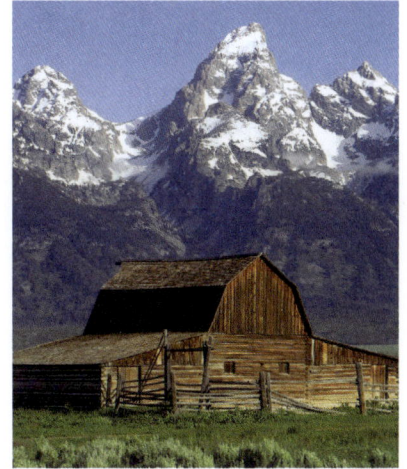

a) Arapaho and Cheyenne
b) Small ranchers
c) Gold prospectors

13. Jackson Hole in Wyoming is famous for...?
a) The location of the Wyoming-based Hole-in-the-Wall Gang
b) A cavern system with 126 miles of mapped pathways
c) A large ski resort

14. One of the nation's greatest painters was born in Cody. Who?
a) Mark Rothko
b) Edward Hopper
c) Jackson Pollock

15. Forget Sotheby's and Christie's, Jackson, Wyoming, holds one of the must-attend auctions on the calendar. What's up for sale?
a) Cowboy art
b) Elk antlers
c) Discarded ski equipment

TAR HEELS AND KNICKERBOCKERS

The official name of someone from South Carolina state is a South Carolinian, but there is also an unofficial demonym or nickname for those who call Charleston home. Some states have more than one official name – Michigan natives can be Michiganians or Michiganders but those born in Detroit also have a nickname drawn from the natural word. See if you can pair up the following nicknames with their correct states.

1. Arkie	**Indiana**	11. Cornhusker	**Rhode Island**
2. Nutmegger	**Georgia**	12. Tar Heel	**New Hampshire**
3. Muskrat	**Maine**	13. Swamp Yankee	**Hawaii**
4. Alligator	**Illinois**	14. Badger	**Wisconsin**
5. Flatlander	**Iowa**	15. Knickerbocker	**Kansas**
6. Hoosier	**Michigan**	16. Buckeye	**Nebraska**
7. Down Easter	**Arkansas**	17. Islander	**North Carolina**
8. Hawkeye	**Connecticut**	18. Grasshopper	**South Carolina**
9. Goober Grabber	**Delaware**	19. Granite Stater	**New York**
10. Wolverine	**Florida**	20. Sand Lapper	**Ohio**

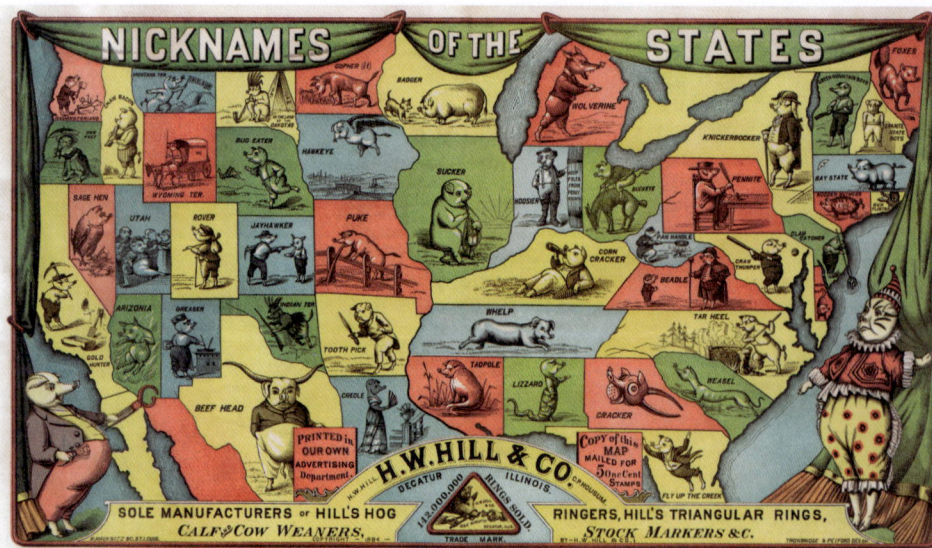

STATE NICKNAMES

The residents of the states have their nicknames, but states themselves have other names or short phrases by which they are known. More often than not they are put forward by a state committee and have a historical background, with many competing to be the 'Cradle of', the 'Birthplace of' or the 'Mother of' something or other. See if you can match the state to the correct epithet listed below.

1. Alaska **Dorothy's Home**

2. Colorado **Sunshine State**

3. Delaware **Lumber State**

4. Florida **The Birthplace of America's Music**

5. Hawaii **Casino State**

6. Illinois **Seward's Folly**

7. Kansas **Birthplace of Aviation**

8. Maine **Land of Lincoln**

9. Massachusetts **Big Bend State**

10. Mississippi **Inside the Beltway**

11. Nevada **The Switzerland of America**

12. New Jersey **Mother of Rivers**

13. Ohio **Codfish State**

14. Oregon **Pineapple State**

15. South Carolina **Beaver State**

16. South Dakota **Palmetto State**

17. Tennessee **The Cheese State**

18. Washington, D.C. **Coyote State**

19. West Virginia **Garden State**

20. Wisconsin **Corporate Capital**

ANSWERS

NATURE
Forests and Trees
1. c) Puerto Rico
2. b) Methuselah
3. a) Stuart Roosa
4. b) General Sherman
5. a) General Grant
6. b) Bristlecone pine
7. b) Yellowstone Timberland Reserve
8. a) Massachusetts governor
9. c) Live oaks
10. c) 380 feet
11. a) The Shaking Aspens
12. c) Gold was found
13. b) Mary Smith Peake
14. c) The Witness Tree Protection Program
15. d) All of them
16. b) 1912
17. c) 225 million
18. a) It owns itself
19. b) It was nursed back to health
20. c) Book-binding
21. a) Biltmore Forest School
22. b) *A River Runs Through It*
23. b) Vehicles and construction are allowed
24. b) Whiting Forest
25. c) Its bark is red and peeling
26. b) 1878
27. a) Mason Locke Weems
28. a) Treats mange
29. b) It emits chemicals
30. a) 33

Plants
1. b) Russia
2. Only found in the Americas
3. c) Maine
4. a) The Three Sisters
5. a) The seed bolls
6. b) The nettle
7. c) Deadly bouquet
8. c) Ten years
9. True
10. b) Once
11. c) Concord grape
12. c) Up to 200 gallons
13. b) Generates heat
14. a) Milkweed
15. a) An upside down carrot

Animals
1. b) Keratin
2. c) Brown bear has longer claws
3. a) Arizona
4. c) It only produces males
5. a) An insect
6. b) The brown recluse spider
7. True
8. b) Moose
9. b) Moose
10. c) Up to 35mph
11. b) Between 15 and 195
12. b) It stores fat
13. a) Bison
14. c) It burrows
15. a) Is not an antelope, but is American
16. b) The Rocky Mountains
17. b) He refused to shoot
18. c) Snails
19. a) Sparks from a campfire
20. b) A series of barks
21. c) It distributed lettuce
22. a) Northern cardinal
23. b) It means "white-headed"
24. a) Less than 100
25. c) A murmuration
26. b) Pacific salmon only spawn once
27. b) 5,600 miles
28. a) It can tolerate high salinity
29. a) Black, white and yellow bands
30. c) Up to 100 years
31. b) Frozen for eight months
32. c) 200mph
33. b) 25mph
34. c) The Edward Aquifer
35. b) Its puffin colony
36. a) 180 years
37. b) The Eastern Dobsonfly
38. a) 22
39. a) Honeybee
40. g) Wormguzzler

Islands
1. a) Both to the USA
2. c) 1864
3. b) 137
4. b) Whaling
5. c) The British Virgin Islands
6. a) Sea turtles
7. b) Shark attack numbers
8. b) American Samoa
9. a) Descendants of Tall Barny Beal
10. c) North Brother Island
11. a) William Kidd
12. b) Gannet
13. c) Three Mile Island
14. a) Black bears
15. c) 90 miles
16. a) 3,300 miles
17. b) The Pig War
18. a) Ellis Island
19. a) William Wrigley
20. a) Island of apples

Lakes
1. a) Michigan
2. b) It's a lake within a lake
3. c) 740 years
4. b) Lake Pontchartrain
5. a) 2028
6. a) Lake Ontario
7. a) Le lac Superieur
8. b) Both have freshwater seals

9. a) Iroquois
10. c) Five hundred billion gallons
11. c) Moose head outline
12. b) Broken ice sheets driven onshore
13. a) Osage
14. a) 1960
15. a) Crater Lake
16. False
17. a) Lake Victoria
18 c) 9 feet
19 b) Lake Powell
20. a) False. Lake Wobegon is fictional

River Deep
1. c) The Missouri
2. c) Colorado
3. a) Texas and New Mexico
4. c) The Niagara
5. b) The Yukon
6. b) 2
7. c) The Jefferson and Madison
8. a) The Colorado
9. b) Johnstown
10. c) France
11. a) The Columbia River
12. a) The Chattahoochee
13. a) Henderson Lake
14. b) Hawaii
15. c) Where it joins the Mississippi
16. b) Green Giant
17. c) The Allegheny and Monongahela Rivers
18. a) Harper's Ferry
19. b) Missouri
20. c) The Patapsco River

Mountain High
1. a) Mount Whitney
2. c) Colorado
3. a) Springer Mountain and Mount Katahdin
4. c) 2,200 miles
5. b) The Black Hills
6. a) Theodore Roosevelt

7. c) New Hampshire
8. c) It lost 1,314 feet
9. b) Crater Lake
10. a) Bitteroot Mountain
11. a) The sub-alpine zone
12. b) A fossilized coral reef
13. a) The Pacific Crest Trail
14. a) Mount Oxford
15. c) New Mexico
16. b) Puerto Rico
17. c) Made by bear claws
18. True
19. c) 4,629 miles
20. a) Florida

Weather
Rainy Cities:
1. Las Vegas, NV: 4.2
2. Albuquerque, NM: 9.5
3. Los Angeles, CA: 14.8
4. San Francisco, CA: 23.6
5. Minneapolis, MN: 30.6
6. Seattle, WA: 37.7
7. Washington, D.C.: 39.7
8. New York, NY: 49.9
9. Miami, FL: 61.9
10. New Orleans, LA: 62.7

Sunny Cities:
1. Las Vegas, NV: 3,825
2. San Diego, CA: 3,054
3. Dallas, TX: 2,850
4. Boston, MA: 2,634
5. Pittsburgh, PA: 2,021

Hurricanes:
1. Texas 64 hurricanes
2. Louisiana: 54 hurricanes
3. Alabama 24 hurricanes
4. Mississippi 19 hurricanes
5. Massachusetts 12 hurricanes

Tornadoes:
1. Illinois: 136
2. Alabama: 101
3. Texas: 89
4. Iowa: 73
5. Tennessee: 53

Foggy Days:
1. a) The windiest place
2. b) Sir Francis Drake
3. b) Karl
4. c) Cape Disappointment
5. a) Mistake Island
6. a) Convection fog
7. b) Carl Sandberg

ARTS
American Photographers
1. c) 70,000
2. c) John Lennon
3. a) Dorothea Lange
4. c) Life
5. c) 1908
6. b) Ansel Adams
7. a) Mimetic architecture
8. a) Robert Capa
9. c) Mathew Brady
10. c) *Detroit Then and Now*
11. c) Irving Penn
12. c) Patti Smith
13. c) One World Trade Center
14. a) *The Shining*
15. a) In Hitler's bathtub

Screen Test
1. *San Francisco*, 1936
2. *Escape From Los Angeles*, 1996
3 *Philadelphia*, 1993.
4. *Fargo*, 1996
5. *The Manhattan Project*, 1986
6. *Fear & Loathing in Las Vegas*, 1998
7. *Sleepless in Seattle*, 1993
8. *Dodge City*, 1939
9. *Escape From New York*, 1981
10. *Carson City*, 1952
11. *Beverly Hills Cop*, 1984
12 *Paris, Texas*, 1984.
13. *Bullets Over Broadway*, 1994
14. *Atlantic City*, 1980
15. *The Cincinnati Kid*, 1965
16. *Brooklyn*, 2015
17. *Things To Do In Denver When You're Dead*, 1995
18. *Gangs of New York* 2002

Writers and Places

1. b) Florida Keys
2. b) *Death of a Salesman*
3. c) Hannibal, Missouri
4. b) The House of Seven Gables
5. b) *The Whale*
6. c) Truman Capote
7. a) Cornish, New Hampshire
8. c) *Little Women* by Louisa May Alcott
9. a) A converted boathouse
10. b) Portland, Maine
11. a) Baltimore
12. b) Savannah

From L.A. to New York

1. *Boulder to Birmingham*
   – Emmylou Harris
2. *Going to California*
   – Led Zeppelin
3. *Sweet Home Alabama*
   – Lynyrd Skynyrd
4. *New York, New York*
   – Frank Sinatra
5. *Walking in Memphis* – Marc Cohn
6. *Midnight Train to Georgia*
   – Gladys Knight & The Pips
7. *The Lady Came from Baltimore* – Tim Hardin
8. *Jackson*
   – *Johnny Cash & June Carter*
9. *Philadelphia* – Bruce Springsteen
10. *California* – Phantom Planet
11. *From New York to L.A.*
    – Patsy Gallant
12. *Galveston* – Glen Campbell
13. *Banks of the Ohio*
    – Olivia Newton John
14. *Philadelphia Freedom*
    – Elton John
15. *Hollywood Nights* – Bob Seger
16. *Get out of Denver* – Bob Seger
17. *24 Hours from Tulsa*
    – Gene Pitney
18. *San Francisco* – Scott McKenzie
19. *California Dreamin'*
    – The Mamas and the Papas
20. *Rock Island Line*
    – Johnny Cash
21. *Kokomo* – Beach Boys
22. *Wichita Lineman*
    – Glen Campbell
23. *Indiana Wants Me*
    – R. Dean Taylor
24. *Last Train to Clarksville*
    – Monkees
25. *Ohio*
    – Crosby Stills Nash and Young
26. *Carolina in My Mind*
    – James Taylor
27. *Georgia on My Mind*
    – Ray Charles
28. *Massachusetts* – Bee Gees
29. *Woodstock* – Joni Mitchell
30. *This is Not America*
    – David Bowie

A Night at the... Musical

1. b) The Griffith Observatory
2. a) Angela Lansbury
3. c) Franki Valli and the Four Seasons
4. c) 1980
5. *Romeo and Juliet*
6. a) No
7. b) The 1903 St Louis World Fair
8. c) *Cell Block Tango*
9. b) Martin Scorsese
10. c) Ann-Margret

Live, On Stage!

1. b) 'The Dollywood Bowl'
2. b) The Troubador
3. b) JFK Stadium, Philadelphia
4. c) Griffith Park, Los Angeles
5. c) Taylor Swift
6. b) The Executioner
7. b) Dan Aykroyd
8. c) 150
9. c) The Fillmore
10. a) *U2 Live at Red Rocks*

On Location...

1. c) Calamity Jane
2. b) Scranton, Pennsylvania
3. a) 'Sonny' Crockett
4. c) Albuquerque
5. b) New money-laundering operation
6. c) Paddy's Pub
7. c) California
8. b) Atlantic City
9. b) Baltimore
10. b) Yes, Gotham Wisconsin

SPORT
Franchise-Go-Round

1. a) Ebbets Field
2. a) Needed new stadium
3. c) Milwaukee
4. b) Montreal Expos
5. a) Milwaukee Brewers
6. c) Kansas City
7. b) 1979
8. b) Minnesota
9. a) Vancouver
10. b) Fort Wayne
11. c) Buffalo Falcons
12. c) Kansas City
13. a) Charlotte Hornets
14. b) 2020
15. b) Overnight
16. a) SoFi Stadium
17. c) Baltimore Ravens
18. b) Tennessee Oilers then Titans
19. a) St Louis
20. b) Dallas

Par, Birdie, Eagle

1. a) Cypress Point
2. c) Too hot
3. a) Green Jacket
4. a) Ballesteros
5. False
6. b) 11th, 12th, 13th
7. b) Cell phones
8. a) Phil Mickelson
9. c) The Colosseum
10. b) Six years
11. a) Jack Nicklaus
12. a) 1979
13. a) Heatstroke Open
14. c) Pepper Spray
15. a) Shinnecock Hills, New York

16. c) Oakmont
17. c) Idaho
18. c) Justin Leonard
19. a) Seeds
20. b) Strip mine

Gridiron Greats

1. b) Sixth, 199th overall pick
2. c) He opted for a career as a foam rubber salesman
3. c) Alex Smith
4. b) Mr. Irrelevant
5. c) Oakland Raiders
6. b) A short-brimmed, gray fedora hat
7. c) Josh Allen
8. b) Defensive End
9. c) All-time rushing leader Walter Payton
10. a) Caleb Williams

We Are the Champions

1. False. She's won 4!
2. b) 'You cannot be serious!'
3. c) 8 seconds
4. c) Sonny Liston
5. a) Lotus
6. Michael Jordan
7. a) 2
8. b) Baywatch
9. c) 13 years
10. c) The King

Olympic Legends

1. b) Alpine skiing
2. a) Alpine skiing
3. c) Both 100m and 200m
4. c) Long jump
5. c) Both
6. c) 400m
7. a) He hit his head on the diving board and was concussed in the preliminaries
8. c) Seven
9. c) 23
10. b) 45 years
11. a) 4'8"
12. c) Salt Lake City, Utah

Maximum Revs

1. c) Caesar's Palace
2. a) Phill Hill
3. b) Ayrton Senna
4. c) Juan Pablo Montoya
5. c) Monaco
6. b) Corkscrew
7. May
8. c) Red, Italy chose red after 1907
9. b) Fake boats in a fake marina
10. b) Haas

College Football

1. Ohio State Buckeyes
2. Notre Dame Fighting Irish
3. Oregon Ducks
4. Texas Longhorns
5. Georgia Bulldogs
6. Arizona State Sun Devils
7. Boise State Broncos
8. Tennessee Volunteers
9. Indiana Hoosiers
10. Mississippi Rebels
11. Brigham Young (BYU) Cougars
12. Southern Methodist (SMU) Mustangs
13. Clemson Tigers
14. Michigan Wolverines
15. Iowa State Cyclones
16. Alabama Crimson Tide
17. Florida State Seminoles
18. Utah Utes
19. Oklahoma Sooners
20. South Carolina Gamecocks

Major League Soccer

1. Chicago Fire
2. Columbus Crew
3. Inter Miami
4. New England Revolution
5. Philadelphia Union
6. Colorado Rapids
7. Houston Dynamo
8. LA Galaxy
9. Portland Timbers
10. San Jose Earthquakes
11. Seattle Sounders
12. Sporting Kansas City

TRAVEL

Traveling Abroad ... at Home

1. Athens, Georgia
2. b) Kensington
3. a) New York
4. False. But the French *do* still use Pékin
5. a) Glasgow, PA
6. b) Lisbon, New York
7. c) South Carolina
8. a) The heroic stand against the mighty French empire
9. c) Prague
10. b) New city
11. a) Bethlehem PA
12. a) Nile Delta
13. b) Jericho, Vermont
14. False. It's the Trail Days Festival
15. b) 21,583,378
16. False
17. b) 144 miles
18. b) Florida
19. c) Rhode Island
20. c) An archaeology site

Premier Attractions

1. b) Roller coasters
2. a) Epcot, Florida
3. b) Griffith Jenkin Griffith
4. c) Alice Cooper
5. d) 'I Will Always Love You' Lurve Train
6. a) The Rocket Garden
7. a) Las Vegas railroad station
8. True
9. a) Lewis & Clark, Buffalo Bill and Chief Crazy Horse
10. c) The Ghost Town

New York, New York

1. b) Frédéric Auguste Bartholdi
2. b) Jacqueline Kennedy Onassis
3. b) Five cents
4. c) 10
5. b) The Crossroads of the World

6. c) 8 million
7. c) Hudson Yards
8. c) $75,000
9. c) 500 seats
10. a) The Rose Main Reading Room

Road America
1. a) Kansas
2. a) Claremore
3. a) Hackberry General Store
4. c) Seligman
5. True
6. b) 1932
7. c) 469 miles
8. b) Grandfather Mountain
9. c) 10
10. b) The Loneliest Road in America
11. a) The Overseas Highway
12. a) 5 months
13. b) U.S. Route 101
14. b) Shenandoah National Park
15. a) Nashville
16. a) Journey Through Time Scenic Byway
17. b) The Continental Divide
18. a) Ontario
19. b) 400
20. c) 90.5mph

National Parks
1. Great Smoky Mountains National Park (Tennessee & North Carolina)
2. Grand Canyon National Park (Arizona)
3. Zion National Park (Utah)
4. Yellowstone National Park (Wyoming, Montana & Idaho)
5. Rocky Mountain National Park (Colorado)
6. Acadia National Park (Maine)
7. Grand Teton National Park (Wyoming)
8. Joshua Tree National Park (California)
9. Olympic National Park (Washington)
10. Glacier National Park (Montana)
11. Cuyahoga Valley National Park (Ohio)
12. Hot Springs National Park (Arkansas)
13. Gateway Arch National Park (Missouri)
14. New River Gorge National Park (West Virginia)
15. Shenandoah National Park (Virginia)
16. Death Valley National Park (California & Nevada)
17. Badlands National Park (South Dakota)
18. Gates of the Arctic National Park (Alaska)
19. Crater Lake National Park (Oregon)
20. Carlsbad Caverns National Park (New Mexico)

Hotels, Motels, Holiday Inns...
1. c) Oscar Wilde, who said on his Parisian hotel deathbed. 'Either that wallpaper goes or I do.'
2. a) The Peabody Ducks
3. The Oscar statuette
4. c) John Lennon
5. c) Janis Joplin
6. c) Dorothy Parker
7. b) The International Monetary Fund (IMF)
8. a) Nathaniel Hawthorne
9. c) The Waldorf Astoria
10. b) 288
11. b) Harry S. Truman
12. False. It wasn't open for guests
13. b) *The Shining*
14. c) Hotel del Coronado, San Diego, California
15. a) The Dunes
16. b) The Venetian
17. a) MGM Grand
18. e) DoubleTree
19. a) Tybee Island
20. b) Beverly Hills Hotel

ARCHITECTURE
American Architects
1. c) William Thornton
2. Central Park
3. c) The Flatiron Building
4. a) William LeBaron Jenney
5. a) Carson Pirie Scott store
6. c) She thought FLW was dead
7. b) Dulles, Washington, D.C.
8. a) I.M. Pei
9. a) Stone
10. a) 100 feet taller

American Houses
1. b) Hopi
2. b) Dallas
3. Adobe
4. b) Salt box houses
5. a) Nebraska
6. b) 1820
7. Brownstone
8. a) Chicago
9. c) Tudor Revival
10. a) Plantation style
11. a) Cedar
12. b) The Hindi word 'bangla'

The Bridge
1. Austin
2. a) Chesapeake Bay Bridge
3. b) His home was demolished
4. True
5. a) Black and yellow stripes
6. c) It's still not high enough
7. c) The Florida Keys
8. b) The Silver Bridge
9. c) Oakland Bay Bridge, California
10. c) The Eads Bridge

A Bridge Over...
1. George Washington Bridge (NY) – Hudson River
2. Manhattan Bridge (NY) – East River

3. Tacoma Narrows Bridge (WA) – Puget Sound
4. Arthur Ravenel Jr. Bridge (SC) – Cooper River
5. Rainbow Bridge (NY) – Niagara River
6. Glen Canyon Bridge (AZ) – Colorado River
7. Longfellow Bridge (MA) – Charles River
8. Fremont Bridge (OR) – Willamette River
9. Benjamin Franklin Bridge (PA/NJ) – Delaware River
10. Perrine Bridge (ID) – Snake River
11. London Bridge (AZ) – Lake Havasu
12. John A. Roebling Suspension Bridge (KY/OH) – Ohio River

Great Lost Buildings
1. c) Madison Square Garden
2. b) 2021
3. b) 1965
4. False
5. b) He was killed
6. b) An oil well gusher
7. b) The Empire State Building
8. c) Ballys
9. a) The parking garage was demolished
10. a) Madison Square Garden

The Old College Test
1. c) 640
2. a) A forgery discovered
3. b) Montana
4. a) Syracuse
5. b) Old Queens
6. b) 1897
7. a) Sir Christopher Wren
8. b) Alexander Hamilton and John Jay
9. c) Venice
10. c) Agricultural and Mechanical

Sports Stadiums
1. c) Fenway Park, Boston
2. a) $2 billion
3. Astroturf
4. No, it was one block over
5. a) The United Center
6. c) 11
7. c) Tampa Bay Rays
8. Lambeau Field (from 1957) The bears only moved to Soldier Field in 1971
9. a) Oriole Park
10. a) Chase Field 1998

Station to Station
1. a) Alvarado Hotel
2. b) Chicago
3. b) Cincinnati Museum Center
4. a) Baltimore and Ohio Railroad
5. b) Ford
6. b) 21.6 million
7. c) NFL Draft
8. b) New Orleans
9. True
10. a) Pacific Surfliner

Higher and Higher
1. e) Massachusetts
2. a) The Empire State Building
3. b) Charles Lindbergh
4. b) Freedom Tower
5. a) 1972
6. c) Marina City
7. c) 7th
8. c) 200mph
9. c) A revolving restaurant
10. c) 1,700,000

Theaters and Picture Palaces
1. b) Moorish Palace
2. c) Judy Garland
3. a) Edison's Vitascope
4. c) Foxville
5. a) The Mayan
6. c) Memphis
7. b) 1950
8. a) The Tiller Girls
9. c) Madison Square Gardens Inc.
10. c) *Star Wars*

TRANSPORT
On The Road...
1. c) 10,402,000
2. b) The Roadster
3. a) Cyberbeast
4. b) 85mph
5. a) Toyota Camry
6. a) 1948
7. True
8. c) 230mph
9. c) The Cannonball Run
10. a) $3,490
11. b) 2004
12. c) 1 million
13. b) Ford GT40
14. b) Humvee
15. a) 1963
16. b) 1959
17. a) American Indian tribe
18. b) Clipper
19. a) Armor-plated glass shattered
20. b) Black Rock Desert

Amazing Aviators
1. a) Bell X-1
2. c) Boeing B-17 Flying Fortress
3. b) He fathered seven German children
4. b) New Guinea
5. b) Behind Allied lines in China
6. b) Thrown from the cockpit
7. a) The London Science Museum
8. a) Discovery
9. b) $200 check
10. a) He had lost sight

Motorcyles
1. c) Milwaukee
2. b) 1953
3. c) Avenue Glide
4. c) 20%
5. c) 1932-1973
6. a) 1957
7. c) Nicky Hayden
8. Evel Knievel
9. b) Porsche

10. b) LiveWire

Trainspotting
1. The Best Friend of Charleston
2. b) Buster Keaton
3. a) Jupiter
4. a) The beaver tail observation car
5. c) 1983
6. c) First
7. a) Too much wheelslip
8. a) The 'engine that helped kill steam'
9. c) 1993
10. b) 150mph

Air Travel
1. b) $5
2. b) 23 Passengers and 39 crew
3. b) Crop dusting
4. a) Clipper
5. b) December 2022
6. c) 3,500 miles
7. a) Aspen-Pitkin County Airport, Colorado
8. a) Hartsfield Jackson Atlanta International Airport
9. a) Boeing 707
10. a) Boston to Honolulu

Departures and Arrivals
1. b) BHM
2. c) LIT
3. a) LGB
4. b) OAK
5 c) DEN
6. c) TUS
7. a) DAB
8. c) ORD
9. c) GRR
10. b) SFO
11. a) MCO
12. b) LGA
13. b) RDU
14. c) FAR
15. c) DFW
16. a) SLC
17. b) IAH
18. a) MEM
19. a) IAD
20. a) ANC
21. a) Montgomery, AL
22. b) St. Petersburg, FL
23. a) Fresno, CA
24. a) Pueblo, CO
25. a) Fayetteville, NC
26. b) Dayton, OH
27. b) Corpus Christie, TX
28. a) Casper, WY
29. b) Seattle, WA
30. a) Endeavour, FL

The Final Frontier
1. a) Redstone
2. a) He bought the farm
3. c) Gus Grissom
4. a) Alan Shepard
5. a) John Glenn
6. b) Apollo 8
7. b) Almost. He meant to say 'for a man'
8. c) Twenty-five seconds
9. b) The Sea of Tranquility
10. c) Apollo 15
11. b) 1972
12. b) 325 million
13. c) 2314
14. a) John Young
15. b) 135
16. b) Curiosity Rover
17. b) Ingenuity
18. a) NASA chief from 1961 to 1968
19. c) Texas
20. a) Artemis

HISTORY
Early Settlers
1. a) Great Britain
2. c) Modern-day Montana
3. b) Roanoke
4. c) Gold
5. b) Williamsburg
6. a) The Delaware
7. b) Peter Stuyvesant
8. a) The *Speedwell*
9. c) 1880
10. a) Fort Ross

Revolutionaries
1. a) 1689
2. b) Mohawk people
3. b) New York
4. b) Pennsylvania State House
5. c) A signature
6. George Washington
7. c) Revere, Dawes, Prescott and Bissell
8. c) George Washington's aide-de-camp
9. a) Brandywine
10. b) France
11. a) Washington Old Hall
12. True (though Martha did)
13. b) *The Rules of Civility*
14. c) Barbados
15. a) He killed a diplomat
16. c) Two horses and six bullets
17. b) He bought luxury goods
18. a) John Adams
19. d) All of them
20. c) He built a distillery

The War of 1812
1. a) Tecumseh
2. b) It press-ganged American sailors
3. a) It's the narrowest majority
4. b) Three weeks
5. a) 1775
6. b) Threatened to secede
7. a) The burning of York
8. b) The Defence of Fort McHenry
9. b) No change at all

Taking Mexico
1. a) America
2. c) Florida
3. c) They declared the Republic of Texas
4. b) 257
5. b) William B. Travis
6. c) In a ditch
7. b) Alta California and Nuevo Mexico

8. c) It bought another piece of Mexico
9. b) The younger brother of the Austrian Emperor

Native American History
1. b) They walked
2. c) Watson Brake
3. a) Cahokia
4. c) 80-95%
5. b) The government confiscated the land
6. c) The Battle of Little Bighorn
7. a) Guaranteed citizenship
8. c) The one who yawns
9. b) The Hard Rock Café
10. c) They joined the Marines

Journeys West
1. b) The Corps of Discovery
2. c) The Oregon Trail
3. a) John Jacob Astor
4. c) The Trail of Tears
5 b) Brigham Young
6. b) Sutter's Mill
7. b) Donner-Reed
8. c) 50,000
9. c) Twelve hours
10. b) Abandoned in 1904

Civil War
1. c) South Carolina
2. b) A small stream
3. b) Two ironclad warships
4. c) Europe found cheaper cotton
5. a) 2%
6. a) Worst riots in history
7. c) 22, 727
8. a) James bros. were members
9. a) 1863
10. a) 'I beg to present'
11. b) Blockade runners
12. a) Deadline
13. a) Secretary of War
14. a) He was a powder monkey
15. b) Prisoners of War
16. a) It was composed of Black Americans

17. c) He was allowed to keep his sword and horse
18. c) Brigadier General Stand Watie
19. b) Liverpool, England
20. c) Ku Klux Klan

City Founders and Tycoons
1. c) Colorado (Kit Carson Peak)
2. c) General Francis Nash
3. b) Stonewall
4. c) The city street grid
5. a) Helena in Arkansas
6. b) 'My visits receive little affection'
7. c) Savannah (Georgia)
8. a) Astoria
9. a) Louisburg
10. b) He died in the Gold Rush
11. c) Exporting opium to China
12. c) John D. Rockefeller
13. b) Robber baron
14. c) 90%
15. c) 2,509
16. b) Thomas Edison
17. b) Silver
18. b) Maximum tax-deductible amount
19. c) The Desert Inn
20. c) Daniel K. Ludwig

Great Fires and Other Disasters
1. a) Twice
2. c) Peshtigo, Wisconsin
3. b) A spark from two millstones
4. a) With dynamite
5. d) All of them
6. a) One Pole and four Italians
7. a) Western Electric in Cicero
8. c) One of its engines fell off
9. a) 240 miles
10. b) Hurricane Maria
11. b) A thick syrup
12. b) It was packed with paroled prisoners-of-war
13. c) 17,400
14. c) 80%
15. c) Washington

World Fairs
1. a) The Crystal Palace
2. b) Philadelphia
3. b) Centennial Monorail
4. b) Art by Native Americans
5. a) San Francisco
6. b) San Diego
7. c) World War II
8. b) Tennis and Baseball
9. c) $57
10. a) Seymour D. Fair

Lawless America
1. b) Tax evasion
2. c) The Untouchables
3. c) The Hole-in-the-Wall Gang
4. False. A journalist made it up
5. a) *War is Hell*
6. b) Henry McCarty
7. a) The Simbionese Liberation Army
8. c) John Gotti
9. c) Rose of Cimarron
10. c) Unresolved

Monuments
1 c) In the 1830s
2 b) A broken shackle and chains
3 a) The Crazy Horse Memorial
4 c) 'I have a dream'
5 a) It struck the arch
6 b) Frederick Douglass
7 b) The Eiffel Tower
8 a) The project ran out of funds
9 b) Iwo Jima
10 c) John F. Kennedy
11. c) World War I
12. a) USS *Arizona*
13. b) 58,000
14. a) 1950-1953
15. c) Sky and Earth
16. b) To sculpt them as full figures
17. b) Annapolis, Maryland
18. c) Franklin D. Roosevelt
19. True
20. e) Pulaski Expressway

Civil Rights History
1. c) Women to get the vote
2. a) She boarded 'the white people's car'
3. b) Blackface stage routine
4. c) Native Americans
5. a) His daughter had to travel far to school
6. c) Bus boycott
7. b) MLK
8. a) Expansion into Cambodia
9. b) 2015
10. a) Utah

American Museums
1. a) A fossilized skeleton
2. b) Recycled drinks cans
3. b) 1847
4. a) Annie Moore from Ireland
5. b) Emanuel Leutze
6. c) Paul Allen
7. a) New Orleans, Louisiana
8. b) The Children's Museum of Indianapolis
9. c) Lennon wrote *Imagine* on it
10. a) It's housed in the USS *Midway*

History of Tech
1. b) 1963
2. a) 1975
3. True
4. b) Creeper
5. b) Ray Tomlinson
6. a) IBM Simon
7. b) SixDegrees.com
8. a) Mosaic (1993)
9. c) Hedy Lamarr
10. a) 2020

Buying America
1. c) $15m
2. b) British and Dutch banks
3. b) He needed the troops to invade Britain
4. a) The Danish Virgin Island
5. c) Water Island
6. b) CZ

7. c) Zonians
8. b) Puerto Rico
9. c) $4,085
10. a) Costly defeat by the British

Inventions
1. c) Their three-axis control system
2. b) Alternating Current AC
3. a) Manually-operated traffic signal arms
4. a) Dr. Jonas Salk
5. a) $2
6. b) A lithographing and publishing company
7. a) Earl Tupper
8. b) Kevlar
9. c) Little Boy
10. b) Liquid fueled rocket
11. b) Jane Austen
12. a) China
13. a) Belgium
14. b) The Dutch
15. b) Mexican vaqueros
16. a) Nimes in France
17. b) A Canadian
18. c) Rugby School
19. a) Belgium
20. b) Whitechapel, London

ACROSS THE 50 STATES
American Capitals of the World
1. Roswell, New Mexico
2. Boring, Oregon
3. Punxsutawney, Pennsylvania
4. Weed, California
5. Westminster (Dog Show)
6. Pinehurst, North Carolina (U.S. Open)
7. Beeville, Texas
8. San Antonio, Texas
9. Niagara Falls, New York
10. Bandera, Texas
11. Perry, Georgia
12. Chattanooga, Tennessee
13. Hershey, Pennsylvania
14. Omaha, Nebraska

15. Newport, Rhode Island
16. Lafayette, Louisiana
17. Greenfield, California
18. New Orleans, Louisiana
19. North Pole, Alaska
20. Cuba, Missouri
21. a) The Sideshow Capital of the World
22. c) Ducks
23. a) The Goat Racing Capital of the World
24. b) Fudgies
25. a) There is a large retailer of unclaimed baggage
26. a) Bend, Oregon
27. b) Rounded pebbles of obsidian, a volcanic glass
28. False, the tradition goes back to the 1800s
29. a) Le Havre, France
30. b) Trout Fishing Capital of the World
31. a) Dried cow dung
32. b) No, there's one in Texas
33. a) World's largest mailbox
34. a) 64
35. True
36. b) *The Simpsons*
37. b) 500,000
38. a) Annual watermelon festival
39. a) License plates with red and green chillis
40. a) Chicago, Illinois

Alabama
1. c) Montgomery
2. b) 1819
3. a) Hunstville
4. True
5. a) 24th
6. c) Vulcan
7. c) Christmas Day
8. c) 154
9. a) Talladega Speedway
10. a) Cleveland Avenue
11. c) Deaf and blind
12. a) Saturn V
13. a) Red-bellied turtle

14. c) Britain
15. b) Snails

Alaska
1. c) Juneau
2. b) 1959
3. c) Anchorage
4. a) Denali
5. a) 48th
6. a) $7.2m
7. c) -80F
8. b) Valdez
9. b) Dog mushing
10. b) Balto
11. b) *Dances with Wolves*
12. a) Dawson City
13. a) Kodiak archipelago
14. a) Moose
15. c) Sitka Spruce

Arizona
1. b) Phoenix
2. b) 1912
3. c) Allendale
4. True
5. b) 14th
6. b) Utah
7. c) Prescott
8. b) Copper
9. a) Pluto
10. c) Wyatt Earp and Doc Holiday
11. c) Navajonia
12. a) Biosphere 2
13. a) Apache trout
14. b) Arizona tree frog
15. b) Tower Bridge

Arkansas
1. c) Little Rock
2. b) 1836
3. c) Arkopolis
4. True
5. a) Mount Magazine
6. b) Squirrels
7. a) Walmart
8. c) Hope
9. c) Rice
10. a) 'Wooo Pig Sooie'

11. a) Duck calling
12. Tennessee
13. b) Aluminium
14. Crater of Diamonds
15. a) Mockingbird

California
1. c) Sacramento
2. a) 1850
3. c) Miners
4. b) Mount Whitney
5. a) 1st
6. c) Good herbs
7. b) The Pallisades Fire
8. c) Hollywoodland
9. True
10. a) San Bernardino
11. b) 1937
12. b) RMS *Queen Mary*
13. a) Grizzly bear
14. b) Route 66
15. b) Balboa Park

Colorado
1. c) Denver
2. b) 1876
3. b) 3,317 ft
4. b) Fourteeners
5. False
6. a) Marijuana
7. c) Vail
8. b) The Cheeseburger
9. a) International Hillclimb
10. a) Henry Deutschendorf Jr.
11. a) 1906
12. b) Film festival
13. c) Adolph Coors
14. a) Rocky Mountain bighorn sheep
15. c) Greenback cutthroat trout

Connecticut
1. a) Hartford
2. b) 1636
3. b) Long Island
4. b) Massachusetts
5. a) 29th
6. a) In the Charter Oak
7. b) Samuel Colt

8. b) 50
9. b) The Polaroid camera
10. c) Riverboat pilot
11. True
12. b) ESPN
13. b) 12 mph
14. c) The Bulldogs
15. c) American robin

Delaware
1. a) Dover
2. a) First State
3. b) Henry VIII
4. False
5. Rhode Island, Delaware, Connecticut, New Jersey
6. c) No sales tax
7. Joe Biden
8. a) Peach
9. c) DuPont
10. c) Heimlich maneuver
11. c) Horseshoe crabs
12. True
13. c) Dover Speedway
14. a) Delaware blue hen
15. b) Hurl the farthest

Florida
1. a) Tallahassee
2. a) 1845
3. b) Jacksonville
4. True
5. a) 3rd
6. c) Hurricanes
7. True
8. c) Miami Beach
9. b) Feast of flowers
10. a) Golf courses
11. b) Yes
12. b) 1971
13. a) Von Braun
14. c) Manatee is not a reptile
15. a) Cape Sable

Georgia
1. b) Atlanta
2. b) 13th
3. a) Savannah

4. b) George II
5. c) *Georgia on My Mind*
6. c) Coca Cola
7. a) REM
8. c) Elton John
9. b) Bobby Jones
10. b) 1996
11. c) Savannah
12. a) Johnny Mercer
13. a) Sherman
14. Martin Luther King Jr.
15. a) Southern live oak

Hawaii
1. c) James Cook
2. b) The Sandwich islands
3. a) Shield volcano
4. a) 1898
5. b) 1959
6. False
7. a) Yamamoto
8. b) Snake
9. c) Surfing
10. Barack Obama
11. a) Billboards
12. Whaling
13. True
14. a) Big Island
15. b) Valley Isle

Idaho
1. a) Boise
2. b) 1890
3. c) National Forestry Service
4. True
5. b) Potatoes
6. Huckleberry
7. b) Aaron Paul
8. c) Nuclear
9. c) 3,100 miles
10. b) Hot springs
11. True
12. Wyoming
13. b) Floating green
14. c) 72
15. c) Hemingway

Illinois
1. c) Springfield
2. b) 1818
3. a) Mormons
4. c) Mother Road
5. c) Sears Tower
6. b) Ronald Reagan
7. True
8. c) Football stadium
9. c) 'Bugs' Moran
10. a) Cow
11. a) Bigger, 1,188 acres
12. Michigan
13. b) Superman
14. c) Deep dish
15. b) Oak Park

Indiana
1. a) Indianapolis
2. c) Indianapolis
3. a) Hoosier Hill
4. b) 45 miles
5. b) Electric streetlights
6. Girls
7. c) Jackson Five
8. b) The Brickyard
9. a) Helium balloons
10. b) Santa Claus
11. b) Steel
12. a) Tulip tree
13. b) Johnny Appleseed
14. a) 24
15. a) Firefly Capital

Iowa
1. b) Des Moines
2. a) 1846
3. a) The monks
4. c) 7 to 1
5. a) Dyersville
6. a) Ron de Santis
7. a) John Deere
8. a) Pony Express
9. a) Bread slicer
10. a) Grant Wood
11. c) Germany
12. b) 2228
13. b) Gala

14. South Dakota
15. a) Butter

Kansas
1. b) Topeka
2. b)1861
3. b) Geographical center
4. False. Sunflower River is in Mississippi
5. b) Pizza Hut
6. a) White Castle
7. a) Arrowhead
8. b) Amelia Earhart
9. a) El Capitan
10. b) Film reels
11. b) Buster Keaton
12. a) Monument Rocks
13. a) Dalton gang
14. c) Toto
15 .a) Ornate box turtle

Kentucky
1. b) Frankfort
2. a) 1792
3. b) Clogging
4. b) 95%
5. b) Harland
6. c) 1963
7. c) 426
8. a) Churchill Downs
9. a) A moonbow
10. b) The U.S. Mint Police
11. a) Dueling
12. a) NCAA basketball
13. Missouri
14. c) Abraham Lincoln
15. c) Chevrolet Corvette

Louisiana
1. b) Baton Rouge
2. b) 1812
3. b) Louis XIV of France
4. a) A year
5. True
6. a) Ten-dollar note
7. False. It was third largest by population
8. a) Zydeco

9. b) Louisiana
10. c) Crawfish
11. b) Tabasco
12. a) 535 feet
13. a) Crappie
14. a) *A Streetcar Named Desire*
15. a) He fell off a horse

Maine
1. c) Augusta
2. c) Portland
3. b) 23rd
4. c) Whoopie pie
5. b) The gentle giant
6. c) Quadruple
7. b) 90%
8. b) Mount Cadillac
9. b) Biggest tidal range
10. c) Wooden sail craft
11. d) *The Green Mile*
12. b) Blueberries
13. b) Kennebunkport
14. b) The Pine Tree State
15. c) Moose

Maryland
1. c) Annapolis
2. a) Baltimore checkerspot
3. b) Fort McHenry
4. c) Edgar Allan Poe
5. a) Frederick Douglass
6. c) Babe Ruth
7. c) Jousting
8. True
9. c) The U.S. Naval Academy
10. d) Blue crabs
11. b) 1827
12. b) Samuel Morse
13. b) Battle of Sharpsburg
14. b) Space research/ instruments
15. c) China

Massachusetts
1. a) Boston
2. c) Massachusetteer
3. c) Philadelphia
4. a) John Adams, future 2nd President

5. False
6. c) 1620
7. b) To train clergymen
8. b) Netball
9. b) 1876
10. b) Subway line
11. b) Dunkin' Donuts
12. b) The Berkshires
13. c) Massachusetts
14. a) 1897
15. c) John F. Kennedy

Michigan
1. b) Lansing
2. a) If you seek a pleasant peninsula...
3. a) Wild rice
4. c) Ontario
5. a) 120 lighthouses
6. a) The Mighty Mac
7. b) Floating zip code
8. a) Kellogg's
9. b) Yoopers
10. b) Fishtown
11. b) Coral
12. b) Mayor of Hell
13. b) Assign telephone numbers
14. b) Superior
15. b) Ernest Hemingway

Minnesota
1. a) Saint Paul
2. b) 1858
3. b) Minneapolis
4. a) Gopher State
5. a) Common loon duck
6. b) Fishing houses
7. c) Boats
8. c) Prince
9. a) A wedding chapel
10. c) Metropolitan Stadium
11. a) Skyway for pedestrians
12. b) Gray wolf
13. a) The Spam Museum
14. a) Greyhound Bus
15. b) 6,700 miles

Mississippi
1. a) Jackson
2. b) 1870
3. b) The Hospitality State
4. a) Li'l Miss
5. b) Farmed
6. b) Churches
7. c) Elvis Presley
8. b) Racoons
9. b) One day after Gettysburg
10. b) Cotton
11. c) 1966
12. b) 2005
13. b) Jim Henson
14. c) 50th
15. b) Darth Vader in *Star Wars*

Missouri
1. a) Jefferson City
2. b) Kansas City
3. a) Let the good of the people be the supreme law
4. c) Anheuser-Busch
5. c) Missouri Rhineland
6. a) 18 months
7. a) Robert Ford
8. b) *Huckleberry Finn*
9. b) 6,000
10. a) The Missouri Dragon
11. a) The doctor's horse
12. a) Laughing waters
13. b) Wooden prosthetic leg
14. c) Rome
15. True

Montana
1. b) Helena
2. b) 1889
3. c) Shoshone
4. a) Idaho
5. b) 1,804 feet
6. a) Italy
7. a) Mammals
8. b) Around 2,000 (they don't stick to state boundaries!)
9. a) Lakota Sioux, Northern Cheyenne, Arapaho
10. c) Bicycles

ANSWERS

11. b) Wyoming
12. b) Dinosaur fossils
13. a) 4%
14. c) Copper
15. True

Nebraska
1. b) Lincoln
2. b) Flat water
3. a) Lancaster
4. b) Toadstool Geologic Park
5. b) South Korea
6. b) Chimney Rock
7. b) North Dakota
8. a) Carhenge
9. b) Cabbage/Sauerkraut
10. a) Sand Hills
11. c) Bruce Springsteen
12. b) Kool-Aid
13. a) Water reserves
14. b) Buffalo grass
15. True

Nevada
1. c) Carson City
2. a) United Kingdom
3. b) 85%
4. c) 314
5. a) Petroglyphs
6. a) Drilling for a well
7. b) Horses
8. b) Over 80 years
9. b) Burning Man
10. b) Silver
11. b) Area 51
12. b) Paradise
13. c) 928
14. c) Luxor
15. b) Betty Willis

New Hampshire
1. b) Concord
2. b) 18
3. b) 231 mph
4. a) Connecticut
5. b) Mandatory auto insurance
6. b) No
7. a) Live fast, die young

8. b) 'Go west, young man'
9. a) Educate Native Americans
10. Hampshire
11. b) Alan Shepard
12. a) Christa McAuliffe
13. b) Adam Sandler
14. b) Same-sex civil unions
15. b) Giant single pumpkins

New Jersey
1. b) Trenton
2. c) Newark
3. c) 3
4. False. It's No.1
5. a) Massachusetts
6. a) Princeton
7. a) The Knickerbockers
8. b) Menlo Park
9. b) Horses
10. c) A sandy spit
11. a) Pump your own Gas
12. b) Campbell's
13. c) Saltwater taffy
14. b) Removed for the winter
15. a) Lucy the elephant

New Mexico
1. a) Santa Fe
2. b) 2,845 feet
3. a) It's the oldest
4. True
5. a) State bird: Roadrunner
6. a) The Trinity Site
7. b) PhDs
8. a) Harmony and balance
9. b) 1950
10. b) Hot air balloons
11. a) 'Red or Green?' – it's the chilli state
12. a) The first spaceport
13. b) A crashed army spy balloon
14. a) Truth or Consequences
15. a) The Big Room

New York
1. c) Albany
2. False. It's in New Jersey
3. b) Cave exploring

4. Kodak
5. c) Baseball
6. c) Jell-O
7. a) Vermont
8. a) Anchor Bar, Buffalo
9. True
10. a) The Strong Museum
11. c) Latter Day Saints
12. a) The 'pilot's house'
13. b) 'The Grand Canyon...'
14. a) Watkins Glen
15. True

North Carolina
1. a) Raleigh
2. b) 'Most military friendly state'
3. b) Too large to administer
4. b) 17lbs (today $714,000)
5. c) Fort Liberty
6. a) The Outer Banks
7. b) Krispy Kreme
8. a) Texas Pete Hot Sauce
9. a) George Washington Vanderbilt II
10. b) Four
11. c) Michael Jordan
12. c) The Research Triangle
13. b) James Taylor
14. b) Road signs started disappearing
15. a) Muscadine

North Dakota
1. a) Bismarck
2. b) 1887
3. a) Shuffled the papers
4. b) No major tourist attraction
5. b) 144 miles
6. a) National Wildlife Refuges
7. b) Half the size
8. b) 200
9. c) Theodore Roosevelt
10. a) Flax
11. b) Salem Sue
12. a) Strength from the soil
13. b) Oktoberfest
14. b) Frances McDormand
15. True

Ohio
1. c) Columbus
2. b) Columbus
3. a) Non-rectangular flag
4. a) 220 miles
5. c) Great river
6. b) 1,549 feet
7. True. Pollution on surface
8. b) LeBron James
9. c) The Dawg Pound
10. c) Pro Football
11. a) The Cincinnati Red Stockings
12. c) Alan Freed
13. c) Amusement park
14. True. Now on sale.
15. b) 1969

Oklahoma
1. c) Oklahoma City
2. c) Indian Territory
3. a) Cherokee
4. a) Seminole
5. b) Camels
6. a) Scissor-tailed flycatcher
7. a) Four
8. c) Seattle SuperSonics
9. b) Shopping trolley
10. b) Meteorology
11. c) The Oil Capital
12. b) Route 66
13. b) 62
14. c) Oklahoma!
15. b) Will Rogers

Oregon
1. c) Salem
2. b) Different designs
3. c) Mount Hood
4. a) A fungus
5. c) Beaches made public land
6. a) Lumber
7. b) Pinot noir
8. b) 1973
9. a) She Flies With Her Own Wings
10. b) Nike
11. c) Bookstore
12. a) Oregon swallowtail
13. True

14. c) Forest fires
15. a) Two – both introduced

Pennsylvania
1. a) Harrisburg
2. a) 1799
3. b) House next door...
4. c) Amphibian
5. a) Steel
6. c) New England Patriots
7. a) Claes Oldenburg
8. c) Phil
9. b) 124
10. c) Taylor Swift
11. b) Forbes Field
12. b) *Rocky*
13. b) 271
14. c) Lancaster
15. c) Seven

Rhode Island
1. c) Providence
2. a) Rhode Island
3. b) Hope
4. c) An anchor
5. Rhode Island Reds/Chickens
6. b) Richard Arkwright
7. a) Providence Steamrollers
8. b) Bob Dylan went electric
9. b) 2020
10. a) 11
11. b) Ignored it
12. a) The Breakers
13. b) Dunkin' Donuts
14. a) 1803
15. a) 'The Original American Rider'

South Carolina
1. c) Columbia
2. a) Switzerland
3. a) King Charles I
4. a) Loggerhead sea turtle
5. a) Africa's 'rice coast'
6. a) The Jenkins Orphanage Band
7. c) Carolina cabbage
8. b) Myrtle Beach
9. b) Citywide fire in 1861
10. b) Boeing 787 Dreamliner

11. a) Tires
12. a) The Palmetto Bowl
13. b) National Institute
14. a) Sweet tea vodka
15. a) A very hot chilli pepper

South Dakota
1. a) Pierre
2. True
3. b) 0, they're all bison
4. b) Minuteman
5. a) Laura Ingalls Wilder
6. True
7. b) Nobody
8. b) Wild Bill Hickock
9. b) Doris Day
10. b) 220.1 miles
11. c) Mammoth
12. b) Ears too large
13. b) 500,000
14. b) Idaho has Big Southern Butte
15. b) Towns

Tennessee
1. a) Nashville
2. b) War of 1812
3. b) Nashville
4. Missouri
5. True
6. b) Jack Daniels
7. b) Drums
8. c) Smoky Mountain Rails
9. c) RMS *Titanic*
10. a) Meat dish with three sides
11. c) Aretha Franklin
12. a) 1917
13. a) Vancouver
14. b) The Greek Parthenon
15. a) The Lord's Golf Tee

Texas
1. c) Austin
2. b) 39th biggest
3. b) 9th biggest economy
4. Los Angeles
5. b) Bird species
6. b) 89
7. c) Dr Pepper

8. True
9. b) France
10. a) Michael Dell
11. a) Friends/allies
12. b) SXSW (South by Southwest)
13. a) San Jacinto Historic Site

Utah
1. c) Salt Lake City
2. a) 2,180 feet
3. b) Bees are industrious
4. a) 2030
5. c) 2,000
6. c) Zion
7. b) Moab
8. b) Sandboarding
9. a) The Greatest Snow on Earth
10. a) People of the mountains
11. c) Jell-O
12. c) Kentucky Fried Chicken
13. a) Birth rate slipped
14. True
15. a) Whale farming

Vermont
1. a) Montpelier
2. b) 1791
3. c) Burlington
4. a) Mount Mansfield
5. b) 49th
6. b) Samuel de Champlain
7. c) Calvin Coolidge
8. b) The Green Mountain State
9. c) John Deere
10. b) Rudyard Kipling
11. New Hampshire
12. c) Quebec
13. b) Hermit thrush
14. b) Brook trout
15. a) Sugar maple

Virginia
1. a) Richmond
2. b) 1788
3. c) Virginia Beach
4. c) Mount Rogers
5. a) 12th
6. a) James I

7. b) 8
8. a) 'Virginia is for Lovers'
9. a) George Washington
10. c) Sports franchise
11. True
12. Five: Maryland, West Virginia, Kentucky, Tennessee, North Carolina
13. c) Big-eared bat
14. a) Eastern tiger swallowtail
15. a) Dogwood

Washington State
1. b) Olympia
2. b) Mount Vernon
3. c) Columbia
4. a) Duwamps
5. Mount St Helens
6. b) Over 3,000
7. b) 1971
8. c) Three on three
9. c) Boeing
10. b) Build on top
11. b) Hops
12. a) Pacific octopus
13. a) Amazon
14. b) 7,710 feet
15. a) Friday Harbor

West Virginia
1. c) Charleston
2. a) West Virginia Capitol
3. a) Mountaineers Are Always Free
4. a) 1863
5. b) Fourteen
6. a) New Hampshire
7. c) Live oak
8. c) Chuck Yeager
9. True
10. b) Johnny Cash
11. b) BASE jumpers
12. a) Project Greek Island
13. b) Fifteen days
14. a) Snowshoe Mountain
15. b) Mothman

Wisconsin
1. a) Madison

2. True
3. b) Forward
4. a) Pike family
5. b) 'Swiss Cheese'
6. c) 'Bratwurst'
7. b) Sand dunes
8. b) The fans
9. b) The Republican Party
10. b) Les Paul
11. a) Brandy
12. a) Miller
13. c) William H. and Arthur D.
14. c) Experimental aircraft
15. a) Ringling bought Barnum

Wyoming
1. c) Cheyenne
2. a) Wyomingian
3. True
4. a) 1869
5. a) 1925
6. a) *Close Encounters of the Third Kind*
7. a) Indian paintbrush
8. a) 500
9. b) ± 10 minutes
10. b) Teat
11. False. It's Gannett Peak
12. b) Small ranchers
13. c) A large ski resort
14. c) Jackson Pollock
15. b) Elk antlers

Tar Heels and Knickerbockers
1. Arkie: Arkansas
2. Nutmegger: Connecticut
3. Muskrat: Delaware
4. Alligator: Florida
5. Flatlander: Illinois
6. Hoosier: Indiana
7. Down Easter: Maine
8. Hawkeye: Iowa
9. Goober Grabber: Georgia
10. Wolverine: Michigan
11. Cornhusker: Nebraska
12. Tar Heel: North Carolina
13. Swamp Yankee: Rhode Island
14. Badger: Wisconsin

15. Knickerbocker: New York
16. Buckeye: Ohio
17. Islander: Hawaii
18. Grasshopper: Kansas
19. Granite Stater: New Hampshire
20. Sand Lapper: South Carolina

State Nicknames

1. Alaska: Seward's Folly
2. Colorado: Mother of Rivers
3. Delaware: Corporate Capital
4. Florida: Sunshine State
5. Hawaii: Pineapple State
6. Illinois: Land of Lincoln
7. Kansas: Dorothy's Home
8. Maine: Lumber State
9. Massachusetts: Codfish State
10. Mississippi: The Birthplace of America's Music
11. Nevada: Casino State
12. New Jersey: Garden State
13. Ohio: Birthplace of Aviation
14. Oregon: Beaver State
15. South Carolina: Palmetto State
16. South Dakota: Coyote State
17. Tennessee: Big Bend State
18. Washington, DC: Inside the Beltway
19. West Virginia: The Switzerland of America
20. Wisconsin: The Cheese State

PICTURE CREDITS

Introduction
Julien di Majo

NATURE
Zdenek Machacek/Unsplash
Trees
Anagha Varrier/Unsplash
Venki Allu/Unsplash
Holly Landkammer/Unsplash
Mark Tegethoff/Unsplash
Joshua Woroniecki/Unsplash
Animals
Michael Jerrard/Unsplash
Pete Nuij/Unsplash
Liz Guertin/Unsplash
Ingo Doerrie/Unsplash
Dan Pancamo/Unsplash
Suzanne D. Williams/Unsplash
Jose F. Sosa/Unsplash
Plants
Dulcey Lima/Unsplash
Library of Congress
Mary Hammel/Unsplash
Islands
Andrew Wolff/Unsplash
Zoshua Colah/Unsplash
Ethan Dow/Unsplash
Lakes
Charlie Wollborg/Unsplash
Isobel Slater/Unsplash
Rivers
Island Group Studios/Unsplash
Vidar Nnordli Mathisen/Unsplash
Mountains
Peter Luo/Unsplash
Gary Cole/Unsplash
Weather
Andre Benz/Unsplash
Russ Martin/Unsplash
Isso69-E/Unsplash
Nikolas Noonan/Unsplash
Riley/Unsplash

ARTS
The Bay Peak/Unsplash
Photographers
Carol M. Highsmith, LOC
Marc Silber of www.silberstudios.com
Dorothea Lange, LOC
Margaret Bourke White, LOC
Lewis Wickes Hine, LOC
Ansel Adams, LOC
John Margolies, LOC
Mathew Brady, LOC
Karl Mondon
Jack Delano, LOC
Evan Joseph
U.S. Army
Diane Arbus, Wikimedia
Writers and Places
Andreas Lamecker
Eric Koch, Dutch National Archives
Detroit Publishing, LOC
Arthur C. Haskell, LOC
Shirley Smith, Lippincott
Lotte Jacobi
Bernard Gotfryd, LOC
Detroit Publishing, LOC
LA to New York
Entertainment International
Live, On Stage
Corkythehornetfan
Nils Huenerfuerst/Unsplash
Ryan Loughlin/Unsplash
On Location
Were in the Rockies.com
Lucas Pelucas/Unsplash
Jayden Herr

SPORT
Peter Nygaard
Franchise Go Round
Sean Pierce/Unsplash
Mick Haupt/Unsplash
Leo Visions/Unsplash
Kj1595
Golf
Bain News Service LOC
Barratt Hayes, Flickr
Coeur d'Alene Golf Club
Wolf Creek Golf Course
Ryder Cup Tartan
Gary Lisbon
NFL
Brendan Beale/Unsplash
Fredrick Lee/Unsplash
Myron Mott/Unsplash
NFL
Champs
Ira Rosenberg, LOC
Peter Nygaard
Keith Allison, Flickr
Desmond Farley, Flickr
Olympians
Library of Congress (3)
Agência Brasil Fotografias
Maximum Revs
Peter Nygaard
Library of Congress
College Football/MLS
Steve Dimatteo/Unsplash
We The Creators/Unsplash
Tareq Ismail/Unsplash

TRAVEL
Laila Skalsky/Unsplash
Traveling Abroad
Lydia Matza/Unsplash
Library of Congress
Joe Sonderman Postcard Collection
Paola Andrea/Unsplash
Premier Attractions
Jorge Martinez/Unsplash
Venti Views/Unsplash
Gabe/Unsplash
Wes Mcfee/Unsplash
Mike Strachwsky/Unsplash
Sung Shin/Unsplash
Frank Hopkinson
Dennis Guten/Unsplash
New York
Richard Iwak/Unsplash
Harry Gillen/Unsplash
Partha Hnarasimhan/Unsplash
Demure Storyteller/Unsplash
Andre Benz/Unsplash
Simon Bak/Unsplash
Clay Banks/Unsplash
Sole D. Alessandro/Unsplash
Sudan Ouyang/Unsplash
Clay Banks/Unsplash
Road America
Frank Hopkinson
National 66 Convention
Mana5280/Unsplash
Esperanza Doronila/Unsplash
National Park Service
Bruno Bergher/Unsplash
Pahcal123
Brett Melit/Unsplash
Nathaniel Redmon/Unsplash
National Parks
R.D. Mcclenagan/Unsplash
Karan Chawla/Unsplash
Laura Nyhuis/Unsplash
Jairph/Unsplash
Explore With Joshua/Unsplash

Jachan Devol/Unsplash
Jason Runnells/Unsplash
Samantha Beaty/Unsplash
Library of Congress
Nick Rickert/Unsplash
Gary Yost/Unsplash
Valerie Little/Unsplash
Hotels, Motels...
Library of Congress
Iain Feeney/Unsplash
Maria Kliepikova/Unsplash
Library of Congress
Eden, Janine, Jim NYC
Tony Hisgett
Ben Kelsey/Unsplash
David Vives/Unsplash
Julian Paefgen/Unsplash
Gavin Wilson/Unsplash

ARCHITECTURE
Venti Views/Unsplash
Architects
Nicholas Ceglia/Unsplash
Carol M. Highsmith, LOC
HABS, LOC
Carol M. Highsmith, LOC
Percival Kestreltail
American Houses
Carol M. Highsmith, LOC (3)
Library of Congress
Finton Gray, Flickr
Frank Hopkinson
Steve Strang/Unsplash
Andy Henderson/Unsplash
Austin Walker/Unsplash
The Bridge
Dan Pancamo/Unsplash
Clay Banks/Unsplash
Maarten van den Heuvel/
    Unsplash
Frank Hopkinson
Mitchell Schultheis
A Bridge Over
Josh Miller/Unsplash
Eugeniu Baidiuc/Unsplash
Nathan-shintas/Unsplash
Manish Tulaskar/Unsplash
Sahaj Bedi/Unsplash
Parkerjh/Quadcopter
David Nieto/Unsplash
Lost Buildings
Library of Congress
Old College Test
Daderot
Joss Broward/Unsplash
Darshan Patel/Unsplash
Steven Cordes/Unsplash
Zeete
Jimmy Woo/Unsplash
Miguel Yerena
Ajay Suresh, NY
Tristan Harward
Sports Stadiums
Bobak Ha'Eri
Library of Congress

Carol M. Highsmith, LOC
Ty Downs/Unsplash
Library of Congress
Station to Station
Velvet
M
VeggieGarden
Coreyfein01
Meric Dagli/Unsplash
Dough4872
Tristan Loper
Higher and Higher
Frank Hopkinson
Carol M. Highsmith, LOC
Library of Congress
Ravi Patel/Unsplash
James Ohlerking/Unsplash
Toni Pomar/Unsplash
Timo Wagner/Unsplash
Andrea Leopardi/Unsplash
Theaters
Carol M. Highsmith, LOC
Ajay Suresh
Josh Hammond/Unsplash
Library of Congress
Joshua J. Cotten/Unsplash
Calstanhope
Sebastien Cordat/Unsplash
Library of Congress
Carol M. Highsmith, LOC

TRANSPORT
Colin Lloyd/Unsplash
On The Road
Maxim
Caleb White/Unsplash
Chevrolet.com
Greg Gjerdingen
Sokol Eugeniu/Unsplash
Josh Collesano/Unsplash
Aviators
U.S. Air Force (2)
Harris & Ewing, LOC
Library of Congress
National Air and Space
    Museum
Motorcycles
Harley-Davidson/Unsplash
Arthur Edelmans/Unsplash
Indian Motorcycles
Harley Davidson/Unsplash
Trains
Library of Congress
Milwaukee Road
Sam Churchill
Jack Delano, LOC (2)
Morven
Air Travel
Library of Congress (2)
Trac Vu/Unsplash
Justin Hu/Unsplash
Miguel Angel/Unsplash
Final Frontier
NASA
Frank Hopkinson

NASA
Bill Jelen/Unsplash

HISTORY
Levi Jones/Unsplash
Early Settlers
Carol M. Highsmith, LOC (2)
Anthony Dewitt/Unsplash
Revolutionaries/1812/
Mexico/Native American
History
Library of Congress
Gabriel Tovar/Unsplash
Journeys West
Jon Tyson/Unsplash
Simon Hurry/Unsplash
Carol M. Highsmith, LOC
Library of Congress
Civil War
Library of Congress
City Founders & Tycoons
Katy-Anne/Unsplash
Pieter van de Sande/
    Unsplash
Library of Congress
Great Fires
Library of Congress (2)
U.S. Coast Guard
World Fairs/Lawless America
Library of Congress (3)
Monuments
Frank Hopkinson (2)
Brittney Butler/Unsplash
Rafik Wahba/Unsplash
Aiden Montoya/Unsplash
Frank Hopkinson (2)
Civil Rights
Jennifer Bonauer/Unsplash
Unseen-Histories/
    Unsplash(3)
Annie Spratt/Unsplash
American Museums
Hester Qiang/Unsplash
Heyminhy/Unsplash
Bernd Dittrich/Unsplash
Finn/Unsplash
Dsdugan
Tech/Buying/Inventions
Gibblesmash/Unsplash
Rikin Katyal/Unsplash
Library of Congress
Kobby Mendez/Unsplash
Jimi A/Unsplash
Joe Richmond/Unsplash

ACROSS THE 50 STATES
Pierre Jeanneret/Unsplash
World Capitals
Mathew Browne/Unsplash
Madison Kaminski/Unsplash
Claud Richmond/Unsplash
Pawan Thapa/Unsplash
Sartre Liu/Unsplash
Library of Congress (2)
Barbara Burgess/Unsplash

50 States
David Lundgren/Unsplash
Sandra Seitamaa/Unsplash
Kaileen Fitzpatrick/Unsplash
Joshua J. Cotton//Unsplash
TWA, LOC
Thomas Morse/Unsplash
Rusty Watson/Unsplash
Michael Pierce/Unsplash
Avalon
Venti Views/Unsplash
Braden Jarvis/Unsplash
Porter Raab/Unsplash
Stephan Cassara/Unsplash
Carol M. Highsmith, LOC
Christopher-Osten/Unsplash
Seraph1888
Daniel Norris/Unsplash
Chelsea Audibert/Unsplash
Bee Felten Leidel/Unsplash
Brendan Beale/Unsplash
Hazal Ozturk/Unsplash
Brad Switzer/Unsplash
Weston M./Unsplash
Justin Wilkens/Unsplash
Library of Congress
Pradeep Nayak/Unsplash
Andy Staver/Unsplash
Brady Stoeltzing/Unsplash
Clay Banks/Unsplash
Santeri Liukkonen/Unsplash
Evan Wise/Unsplash
Evan Clark/Unsplash
Kyle Calhoun/Unsplash
Rich Martello/Unsplash
Longaberger
Raychel Sanner/Unsplash
Elijah Austin/Unsplash
Clark Young/Unsplash
Tom Henell/Unsplash
Drew Beamer/Unsplash
Josh Miller/Unsplash
Adam Kring/Unsplash
Bailey Alexander/Unsplash
Eelco Bohtlingk/Unsplash
Greg Sellentin/Unsplash
Steve Wrzeszczynski/
    Unsplash
Library of Congress
Jon Sullivan/PD Photo
Tar Heels
Library of Congress

COVER
Wes McFee/Unsplash
Annie Spratt/Unsplash
Gemini Books Group
Chad H/Flikr
Carol Highsmith
Robert Linsdell
FreePik
Noah James
Library of Congress
U.S. National Archives